T0271224

Conversations with Steve Erickson

Literary Conversations Series
Monika Gehlawat
General Editor

Conversations with Steve Erickson

Edited by Matthew Luter and Mike Miley

University Press of Mississippi / Jackson

Books by Steve Erickson
Days Between Stations. New York: Poseidon Press, 1985.
Rubicon Beach. New York: Poseidon Press, 1986.
Tours of the Black Clock. New York: Poseidon Press, 1989.
Leap Year. New York: Poseidon Press, 1989.
Arc d'X. New York: Poseidon Press, 1993.
Amnesiascope. New York: Henry Holt, 1996.
American Nomad. New York: Henry Holt, 1997.
The Sea Came in at Midnight. New York: William Morrow, 1999.
Our Ecstatic Days. New York: Simon & Schuster, 2005.
Zeroville. New York: Europa, 2007.
These Dreams of You. New York: Europa, 2012.
Shadowbahn. New York: Blue Rider Press, 2017.

The University Press of Mississippi is the scholarly publishing agency of
the Mississippi Institutions of Higher Learning: Alcorn State University,
Delta State University, Jackson State University, Mississippi State University,
Mississippi University for Women, Mississippi Valley State University,
University of Mississippi, and University of Southern Mississippi.

www.upress.state.ms.us

The University Press of Mississippi is a member
of the Association of University Presses.

Library of Congress Control Number: 2021938297
Hardback ISBN 978-1-4968-3387-7
Trade paperback ISBN 978-1-4968-3388-4
Epub single ISBN 978-1-4968-3389-1
Epub institutional ISBN 978-1-4968-3390-7
PDF single ISBN 978-1-4968-3391-4
PDF institutional ISBN 978-1-4968-3392-1

British Library Cataloging-in-Publication Data available

Contents

Introduction

Steve Erickson's work values the under-heralded and the unexpectedly, unexplainably intense. Much like his novels, Erickson himself exists on the periphery of our perception, a shadow figure lurking on the margins and threatening to break through but never fully emerging. Despite receiving prestigious honors such as a Guggenheim grant, a Lannan Lifetime Achievement Award, and the Academy of Arts and Letters Award in Literature—not to mention acclaim from the likes of Thomas Pynchon, David Foster Wallace, Jonathan Lethem, Dana Spiotta, and Haruki Murakami—Erickson has remained a subterranean literary figure, receiving effusive praise from his fans, befuddled or cautious assessments from major reviewers, and limited scholarly attention. Erickson's obscurity comes in part from the difficulty of categorizing his work neatly within current trends in fiction, and in part from the wide variety of concerns that populate his writing: literature, music, film, politics, history, time, and the multifaceted city of Los Angeles. His unique, dream-fueled blend of European modernism, American pulp, and paranoid late-century metafiction makes him simultaneously essential to an appreciation of the last forty years of American fiction and difficult to classify within that same realm. He is at once thoroughly of his time and distinctly outside it.

"These are movies that make no sense at all—and we understand them completely." In defining what he calls "the Cinema of Hysteria," the film critic who narrates *Amnesiascope*—Erickson's most autobiographical novel—may as well be summarizing Erickson's own aesthetic. The critic's commitment to hysterical film in what seems a hysterical age emphasizes how Erickson's own work operates more through the logic of lucid dreams than linear causes and rational effects. "In an age riddled with uncertainty," the narrator continues, "the undercurrent of the age pulls us to an irrational truth, for which only an irrational cinema is sufficient." Similarly, while Erickson's work does not offer art as an easy solution to all that ails a soul or a nation, it does posit that fiction is necessary to an understanding of our shared, chaotic present—and vice versa.

In the interviews collected in *Conversations with Steve Erickson*, this author makes ever clearer how his aesthetic and political visions are inextricable from each other, even as they may appear at first glance surreal or, yes, even hysterical. Erickson's political concerns are on full display and hard-hitting from the very first conversation, with several interviews allowing Erickson to sound more like a political commentator than an allegedly postmodern novelist. And while these two roles may be viewed as mutually exclusive by many in the culture, Erickson demonstrates how necessary they are to each other. Erickson wrote in a 1993 autobiographical essay that "over all [his] novels hovers the ghost of America," and in these wide-ranging yet consistent conversations we see someone committed to diagnosing the contemporary American condition, only to discover that America's triumphs and failures have been consistent since its inception. As Erickson told Alec Baldwin in 2017, "We've always been these twin Americas, the one that made a promise and the one that broke the promise the moment it was made. And we've never really reconciled the two."

Erickson's characters mirror those prides and shames in their own lives and experiences. And as Erickson elaborates on them in these interviews, he reveals himself—as unfairly under-heralded as some creators within his pantheon of hysterical cinema—to have been remarkably consistent and prescient in his concerns. Like many of his characters, the Erickson of these interviews imagined a future that we currently inhabit. Erickson's breadth of interests and expertise might make it difficult for critics to pin him down, but this considerable range also demonstrates what makes him uniquely equipped to determine the root causes of America's current moment. In reading his interviews from the 1980s and 1990s, we recognize our present moment—and we realize that Erickson described this present America twenty, even thirty years ago.

The seriousness of these concerns need not preclude playfulness and innovation in form, however. Erickson discusses repeatedly his conviction that it is counterproductive to label narratively innovative work as "experimental" or to draw sharp lines between reality and fantasy within a literary world—and most intriguingly, he applies this standard equally to his novels and his nonfiction. "Reviewers have referred to my fiction as being 'cinematic,'" Erickson tells Larry McCaffery and Takayuki Tatsumi, "but the truth is my work doesn't take place so much in the camera's eye as in the mind's eye, or maybe the mind's version of the camera's eye, and in the last days of the twentieth century, distinctions between the artifice of the media and the artifice of the mind become more difficult to make." This is evident in Michael Silverblatt's references to the surprising appearances of Al and Tipper Gore in *Leap Year*—Erickson's commentary on the 1988 presidential election—as well as the casualness with which Erickson describes how he came to imagine the return of the Twin Towers in the Badlands in his most recent novel, *Shadowbahn*. Like Erickson's work, the sources of these interviews cross boundaries between genres, cultures, and hierarchies. Publications such as *Contemporary Literature* interview Erickson, but so do science fiction magazines, alt-weeklies, literary blogs, and even a Chuck Palahniuk fansite, providing scholars and fans with a strong sense of the various constituencies to which Erickson's work appeals.

Erickson's repeated references to dream logic, along with a stated desire to tap into the subconscious, point to a consistent rejection of the limitations of traditional realism. They also underline a recurrent point in how Erickson discusses his writing process: his decision to eschew outlines or planning as he composes, instead letting surprising discoveries guide plots, characters, and images. Additionally, in some of these interviews—especially those that originally appeared in sci-fi periodicals—Erickson cautiously embraces the idea that science fiction might be a useful category in which to place his work. Elsewhere, however, he discusses reference points that may be more unexpected. He mentions William Faulkner and Gabriel García Márquez repeatedly as influences who helped him see how fiction might approach time in nonlinear fashions. The formative experiences of hearing Bob Dylan's *Highway 61 Revisited* and *Blonde on Blonde* and seeing Stanley Kubrick's *2001: A Space Odyssey* led him to experimentation with surrealist imagery. And just as revealing is Erickson's reaction to those labels he chooses not to embrace: when asked if he should be thought of as a "postmodern" writer, he questions how useful such a label is at all, electing to align himself more closely with the Brontës than with the ironic likes of Thomas Pynchon. In conversation with Andrew Hedgecock, Erickson suggests, "I think sometimes there's more psychic truth in melodrama than 'high' culture wants to acknowledge."

Taken together, this wide variety of claimed influences points to yet another way in which his aesthetic feels so present: Erickson—a cultural omnivore who is equally at home talking about rock 'n' roll, art film, pulp novels, and European modernism—depicts worlds in which these high-art and pop-culture signifiers collide to the point that any distinctions between them begin to fade away, just as those distinctions have blurred ever more increasingly in recent decades. "But there's never been any conscious, conceptual intent to blend anything," Erickson insists to Hedgecock, as "it came to me naturally."

With the exception of his debut novel, *Days Between Stations*—which does get some retrospective discussion—all of Erickson's eleven other books receive substantial attention within this volume. The frequency and prominence of these interviews match the arc of Erickson's career: brief and specialized as his work attracts a small but devoted audience in the 1980s and '90s, only to escalate significantly in 2007 when *Zeroville*'s comparative accessibility and industry appeal allow Erickson to break through to more traditional outlets. As a result, the remarkable consistency of Erickson's vision over time comes into clear focus through these interviews, revealing a startling continuity across his career while capturing the new threads that appear in his later fiction as they emerge in his thought. His suggestion that his body of work might be understood ultimately as one large novel, written over a few decades, rings true as he draws direct connections from book to book. Every subsequent book, he explains, attempts to complete or revisit something that the previous book left unfinished. Indeed, as longtime Erickson readers, we have noticed that each Erickson book one reads (or rereads) sheds new light on the rest of the Erickson shelf. One can perceive glimmers of his most recent novels, *These Dreams of You* and *Shadowbahn*, as early as 1987, while other interviews show an Erickson keenly aware that he has come to the end of a phase in his work. More than one interview ends with Erickson admitting he has no idea what to write next, only to be followed by another that reveals he has written a work that both derives and departs from its predecessor. Every work, it seems, is, as he tells McCaffery and Tatsumi, "either the end of something or the beginning, or both." As rumors simmer that *Shadowbahn* may be Erickson's last novel, the time is right for a collection such as this one that can begin the work of centralizing his vast but scattered presence in the cultural landscape. We hope this collection will enable scholars to assess the clarity, scope, and prescience of his vision and his resonance throughout American culture.

But for all of his power as a cultural commentator, Erickson deserves to be thought of first as a notable narrative stylist and radically inventive novelist: he creates lyrical, hallucinatory tales of a world that is always already on the edge—of centuries, of millennia, of apocalypse, of sanity—and exposes the obsessive madness at the heart of American fiction.

We hope these interviews will similarly deepen readers' understanding of how Erickson's books work—and why this utterly singular writer deserves greater attention. We would not have been able to assemble this collection without the generosity of many people, and we are grateful especially to Katie Keene and Mary Heath for their fantastic editorial advice and support,

Susan Henderson for her early and vital guidance, Michael Silverblatt for his kind and gracious ear, the staff of the Monroe Library at Loyola University New Orleans for interlibrary loan assistance, and Julianna Holley, for pushing "send."

Additional thanks are due to Steve Erickson, for help in contacting some interviewers and for his kind support of this project.

ML
MM

Chronology

1950	Born April 20 in Granada Hills, California.
1972	Graduates from UCLA with a degree in film studies.
1973	Earns master's in journalism from UCLA. Publishes first piece in the Calendar section of the *Los Angeles Times*.
1975	Hired as a staff writer for *Westways* magazine.
Early 1980s	Writes the "Guerrilla Pop" column for the *Los Angeles Reader*.
1985	*Days Between Stations* published.
1986	*Rubicon Beach* published. Marries singer and writer Astrid Ryterband.
1987	Receives National Endowment for the Arts award. The *New York Times Book Review* selects *Rubicon Beach* as one of its Notable Books of the Year.
1989	*Tours of the Black Clock* and *Leap Year* published. Becomes arts and film editor for *LA Weekly*. The *New York Times Book Review* selects *Tours of the Black Clock* as one of its Notable Books of the Year, and the *Village Voice* selects *Tours of the Black Clock* as one of the Best Books of the Year. Marriage to Ryterband ends.
1992	"The End of Cynicism" published in the *New York Times*.
1993	*Arc d'X* published. Covers the first Clinton inauguration for *LA Weekly*. Autobiographical essay with a mathematical formula for its title published in *Science Fiction Eye*, issue 12. The *New York Times Book Review* selects *Arc d'X* as one of its Notable Books of the Year, and *Entertainment Weekly* includes it in its list of the Best Fiction of the Year. Quits writing for *LA Weekly*.
1995	"American Weimar" published in January 8 *Los Angeles Times Sunday Magazine*. The political reporting that will become *American Nomad* begins appearing in *Rolling Stone* in December.
1996	More political reporting that will become part of *American*

Nomad appears in *Rolling Stone* in January and March. *Amnesiascope* published.

1997   *American Nomad* published. Tribute to Henry Miller, "Exhibitionist of the Soul," published in *Conjunctions*. The British Fantasy Society nominates *Amnesiascope* for Best Novel. *Spin* hires Erickson as its film critic. Marries artist and filmmaker Lori Precious. Son Miles is born.

1999   *The Sea Came in at Midnight* published. The British Fantasy Society nominates *The Sea Came in at Midnight* for Best Novel. *Uncut* names *The Sea Came in at Midnight* as one of the Best Books of the Year.

2000   Joins faculty of the California Institute of the Arts. Profile of Neil Young, "Neil Young on a Good Day," published in the *New York Times Sunday Magazine*. Major political essay "The New Sanctimony" published in *Salon*.

2001   Awarded a MacDowell fellowship. Becomes film critic for *Los Angeles* magazine.

2002   Awarded another MacDowell fellowship.

2004   Publishes first issue of national literary journal *Black Clock* as founding editor.

2005   *Our Ecstatic Days* published. The *Los Angeles Times Book Review* and *Uncut* name *Our Ecstatic Days* as one of the Best Books of the Year.

2006   Writes the introduction to Zak Smith's *Pictures Showing What Happens on Each Page of Thomas Pynchon's Novel "Gravity's Rainbow."*

2007   *Zeroville* published. Awarded a Guggenheim fellowship. The *Los Angeles Times Book Review*, *Newsweek*, and the *Washington Post Book World* name *Zeroville* as one of the Best Books of the Year. Daughter Silanchi is adopted at age two from Ethiopia.

2010   Receives American Academy of Letters Award in Arts and Literature.

2011   Contributes annotations to *The Exegesis of Philip K. Dick*, edited by Pamela Jackson and Jonathan Lethem.

2012   *These Dreams of You* published. The *Los Angeles Times* names *These Dreams of You* as one of the Best Books of the Year.

2013   Cowrites the twenty-one-minute short film *Curse of the Sunset Starlet*, directed by Lori Precious, which plays several film festivals in 2013 and 2014.

2014   Receives Lannan Lifetime Achievement Award. Joins faculty at University of California–Riverside as distinguished professor. Principal photography begins on James Franco's film adaptation of *Zeroville*, starring Franco, Seth Rogen, Jacki Weaver, and Megan Fox.

2016   *Black Clock* closes after publishing final issue, no. 21.

2017   *Shadowbahn* published. *Bookworm* and the *Los Angeles Times* name *Shadowbahn* one of the Best Books of the Year.

2018   BBC 4 broadcasts radio adaptation of *Shadowbahn*.

2019   Release of James Franco's film adaptation of *Zeroville*.

Conversations with
Steve Erickson

Phantasmal America

Michael Ventura / 1986

From *LA Weekly* (August 29–September 4, 1986). Reprinted by permission.

"The best compliment I've gotten on *Rubicon Beach* is from [*LA Style* editor] Bob LaBrasca, who said, 'I've read ten pages of this book and I can't find my own bathroom.'"

Steve Erickson delivers the line with as close as he gets to glee. His second novel, *Rubicon Beach*, is being shipped to bookstores as we speak; his first, *Days Between Stations*, will soon be in paperback as part of the prestigious Vintage Contemporaries series. Both books carry a heady quote from Thomas Pynchon hailing Erickson's "rare and luminous gift." Meanwhile, Erickson, 35 and newly married, does some freelance journalism and mans a cash register nights in a comic-book store in Hollywood.

Why would an author not want his readers to easily find their bathrooms? I didn't want to ask the question at the time, but if I had it wouldn't have been flip, because a character in *Rubicon Beach* suddenly does become lost in his own house. He can't find his study, bathroom, bedroom, or front door. It looks to him like even the windows are in different places. He keeps hiring contractors to work at putting things right. His wife, who isn't lost in the house, is terrified as she sees him demand that rooms and windows be drastically rearranged in patterns that make no sense to her. Her husband is trying to take his inner journey as far as he can, and that can be damned inconvenient. Earlier in the novel another character thinks, "By the plain form of my delirium I will blast the obstruction of every form around me into something barely called shadow." Sometimes that's how meaning is discovered. Sometimes that's what passion demands. Sometimes you have to be willing to go that far, and farther.

Which is what *Rubicon Beach* is all about: how much we've lost, and how far we may have to go to get it back. And this is quite a "we." On one level Erickson's "we" is men and women in all our convoluted efforts to

3

simultaneously find and escape each other. But his "we" also speaks of Americans as Americans, citizens of a country defined, as Erickson told me, "not by a common territory or a common language or common customs or common religion, but an idea, a dream." Hence it is easier for us to lose our country.

Erickson's style echoes the approach of a character in Norman Mailer's story "The Man Who Studied Yoga": "He does not want to write a realistic novel because reality is no longer realistic." A literary descendant of Faulkner, Henry Miller, and Philip K. Dick, rather than of Hemingway and the literalists who followed him, Erickson tells a story by re-creating the essence of the world rather than describing its surfaces. *Rubicon Beach*, in its first part, gives us a Los Angeles in which a wide river passes through downtown, a Los Angeles of deserted buildings and noisy waterfront bars where a few remaining citizens travel by boat on canals, and where Hancock Park is an island populated by whores. This Los Angeles is an annex of America Two, where people who remember America One are arrested as subversives.

But this isn't the future. In part 2 we see that the Los Angeles of part 1 exists just under the surface of the present, in our nightmares and in our mistakes. It is an LA and an America that are already quite alive, in inner life rather than daily life.

Then, in part 3, this is all taken frighteningly further. In elegant, intricate plot twists the characters realize that they have come together under the auspices of "a dream that destroys what is not fulfilled."

What an idea. What a force loose in the world. I have never seen it expressed with such precision. To have a dream—as individuals, as lovers, or as a country—is to subject yourself to the law that your very dream will reach out to destroy you if you fail its demands. Erickson is saying that this is a plight not only of America today, but of the twentieth century itself. Our society is being demolished from within by the force of the dreams it has betrayed.

Obviously Steve Erickson is playing for much higher stakes than, say, a Jay McInerney, an Ann Beattie, or a T. C. Boyle—as one would expect of a man who has exhorted his fellow writers like this: "We have to write every word as though it is the first or last ever written."

Here, in *Rubicon Beach*, is a musical prose of utter clarity that can weld the abstract and the concrete, the daily and the surreal, into a seamless whole. Here is a mind that can both conceive visions and follow them way over any edge. Here, I mean, is a writer—a man whose words reach for you where you live and whose meanings look back at you from your mirror, whether you like it or not.

So, yes, while reading *Rubicon Beach* you may not be able to find your bathroom or your front door as easily as you're used to. But you may find that by inducing this confusion Erickson has enabled you to see several worlds at once: and that this act of vision will bring you closer to the quick of your dreams.

Which is the most an artist can do: put you in proper danger. The rest is up to you.

Ventura: You once wrote in a "Guerrilla Pop" column about how in our century it is both terrifying and releasing that all things, even the end of the world, have become possible. You ended it with this remarkable sentence: "On this beach, we stay alive by the mutuality of our nightmares." I think that could be a plot summary of *Rubicon Beach*. So let's frame that as a question: Do you think so?

Erickson: Why don't you elaborate before I elaborate?

Ventura: *Rubicon Beach* is divided into three parts concentrating on three different characters, and each of them dreams of the others. The connection between them—

Erickson:—is their nightmares. Right. It's true. But I wonder if they survive by that.

Ventura: Well, it depends on what you call survival. I've resurrected an old word: *square*. My kid asked about the behavior of certain people who will go unnamed in this interview, and I said, "Man, they're just squares. You can't expect too much of squares. The worst punishment for being a square is that you're a square—a person who can't get beyond those four points." Well, in a square sense your characters may not survive, but—

Erickson:—they find meaning. In their lives and in the things that are important to them.

Ventura: That's why I consider *Rubicon Beach* such a moral book— each of the characters makes a decision to stay conscious through the pain. Nobody decides to numb out.

Erickson: I think that's true of both the novels. They're about people trying to resurrect their passion in this scheme where things are crumbling, and falling apart. I have a good friend who once wrote me this tortured letter about whatever love affair he was going through at the time, and I wrote back and said, "You've got to remember, Fred, that a lot of people go through their lives never feeling anything at all." And that's what these books are about. It's easy to go numb. It's the easiest thing in the world. And these are characters who will not go numb. They'll slap themselves silly to get the feeling back. To keep the blood going. To keep even the worst nightmares alive—because at least that's a dream. It may be a bad dream but it's a dream, and it's better than no dream.

Ventura: Your setting for this issue, this struggle, is Los Angeles. Other than the fact that you've lived here most of your life, is there a reason for that?

Erickson: I think most Los Angeles novels have been written as an aberration of America—have seen Los Angeles as this little port of weirdness in America, not connected with the rest. That is not what I wanted to do. I wanted to write a Los Angeles novel which was by definition an American novel, that is, Los Angeles as the furthest psychological and geological extension of America—America as far as it goes before it comes to the point of no return.

Ventura: You once wrote in a column, "Los Angeles does not exist in time. Los Angeles is a vapor-trail of yet-to-be-lived memories that glides by as you're hurtling down the years . . ."

Erickson: It sounds good. I don't know what the fuck it means. But certainly in the novel I took Los Angeles out of time. I wanted to create a free-floating Los Angeles that was rootless in time, where the past and the future are all kind of the same thing. The assumption of everyone who reads part 1 of *Rubicon Beach* is that it's a future Los Angeles, but, as you find out in part 2, that's not necessarily the case at all. Part 1 shows a different Los Angeles in a different time, rather than a future time. I'm trying to get at a sense of Los Angeles being an existential blank, a psychological white wall, a geographical neuter.

Ventura: How would you say the "existential blank" that is, perhaps, the background or backdrop of the Los Angeles sensibility differs from the New York or East Coast sensibility?

Erickson: I don't know what the East Coast sensibility is, exactly, except I know it has a pretty narrow idea of what the West Coast is about. That's why they loved Bret Ellis's book [*Less Than Zero*], because it confirmed everything they just know Los Angeles is about.

Ventura: They're not wrong, but it only applies to a tiny segment.

Erickson: A segment, exactly. My own feeling is—and I've made this point to New Yorkers who are a little disgruntled to hear it—that I think Los Angeles, of all the major cities in this country, has the most creative possibilities. That isn't to say the possibilities are being fulfilled. But it has the most creative possibilities because Los Angeles is a blank slate on which you can write basically what you want to. That's what attracts a lot of people here. And it's also why so many people come here wind up so lost. Because if you live in New York you may not know who you are but you know you're a New Yorker. You don't have that here. If you come expecting the city is going to give you some kind of identity, you're going to wind up one of those crazy people walking Hollywood Boulevard. It's a great town for self-invention, but the problem with self-invention is you've got to know what you're inventing. You've got to come here with some sense of self in order to reinvent it.

Ventura: How did growing up in this "existential blank" influence your writing?

Erickson: I grew up in the San Fernando Valley basically before it was the San Fernando Valley, when it was virtually rural. We were in Encino and we were moving north across the Valley just about three steps ahead of the telephone lines. I'd be going to school one year—going from my house to school and walking through an orchard of lemon trees lined by eucalyptus, and there'd be horses and dogs and stuff. And a year later the landscape was different. I mean, completely different. Absolutely transformed, going from the same point A to the same point B—instead of orchards there were malls, theaters, McDonald's. And when I was ten years old I thought, "Well, this is the way reality is. Things change just like that." Then later I read Faulkner, who basically blows away the world between exterior landscape and interior landscape; blows away the world between literal time and figurative time, metaphorical time—the way, for instance, in *The Sound and the Fury*, you've got Benjy, who will be five years old at the beginning of a sentence and he's thirty-two by the time you get to the end of the sentence. Faulkner crystallized for me the kind of reality I'd basically grown up in. And I realized that this was the way I had always wanted to tell a story.

Ventura: Both *Rubicon Beach* and *Days Between Stations* postulate the end of America.

Erickson: *Rubicon Beach* assumes that America ended a while ago. That may or may not be true. I'm still not clear whether Ronald Reagan is the end of an old America or the beginning of a new America. I would rather believe the former, because it would mean there's still a chance for the new America. But I have a funny feeling that may not be the case. There are just too many scary things going on right now. We've got an attorney general who says the states are not obligated to enforce the Bill of Rights. This is an America that's been losing its identity for at least twenty years. A pivotal day in *Rubicon Beach*, the coordinate that all three parts fall on, is the sixth of June, 1968, when Robert Kennedy died. And I chose that day not because I'm especially convinced that Kennedy was a great man or would have been a great leader. I chose it because probably that's the point at which America turned away from the possibilities of redemption.

Ventura: Redemption?

Erickson: The failure involves not how pure or impure America is. Nobody is pure. There's a litany of American sins, beginning with what America did to the Indians, followed by what America did to the Blacks, but I don't think the measure of a great country is how pure it is. I think it's in whether or not it confronts the way it has sinned, if you will; and then in the ways it finds redemption. There was a period between November of 1963 and June of 1968 where I think America looked for redemption, or it looked for the means by which it could redeem itself. Then the wind really went out of the country's sails. I think what has happened is one kind of dream got displaced with another. The hard dream got displaced with the easier dream. Reagan's great insidious success is that he has persuaded people to redefine the dream, at least for the time being—yet still keep calling it the American Dream. When Reagan had his debate with Carter he said, "Are you better off now than you were four years ago?" which is the sentence people latch on to; but the follow-up sentence was to the effect of, "Can you still go into the stores and buy what you used to buy?" There it was, the essence of being an American as summed up by Reagan: Can you still buy what you used to buy? The real insidious thing is that the current conviction seems to be that being an American should be easy. It shouldn't involve risks. It should be a society, a place, an experience in which success is somehow guaranteed to you and you don't have to make the hard choices that I think were meant to be made on an almost daily basis. I think the guys who invented this country saw it as a long and hard road, and one that was never going to be easy if, as was the ideal of this country, you were going to keep a lot of different interests free and in balance. People on all sides of the issues are latching on to simplifications. In order to protect ourselves from Ed Meese censoring what we read, people are beginning to argue that pornography cannot corrupt somebody. I think that is a dangerous point to make. Because I believe in a culture that has consequences. If my book can make somebody better off you have to accept the consequences of the fact that maybe pornography can make somebody worse, and that those are consequences we live with. Or else we can live in Russia, where they write social realism, quote, unquote, and produce a culture that is basically innocuous. But for all the things that are wrong with America, there is a vibrancy about the culture here, a dynamic quality that you just don't see in the rest of the Western world, because we've got a culture of consequence, a culture that involves risks on both the part of the artist and the audience. What somebody like Meese wants is a culture of no consequence. The guys in this administration, when talking about economics, talk about freedom to fail, one of the basic tenets of capitalism—you have to have that risk, that's what makes capitalism a vibrant economic system. But culturally they don't want it. So I guess I'm writing about the ways the American idea has failed. And the ways in which it's been brought to failure by the people who give it the cheapest kind of talk.

Ventura: Let's back up a little. Define what you mean by the "hard dream."

Erickson: The most radical thing about America was not democracy, because that's not really a radical idea; it was the idea that they would establish in the second sentence of the Declaration of Independence, and later in the Bill of Rights, the idea that there are moments when the state must subvert its will to accommodate the freedom of one citizen. That is probably the hardest part of it, especially when you've got a democratic system constantly reinforcing the idea of majority rule. The idea, especially, is that that right—the right of individual free speech, for instance—is not a right given to the citizen by the state; it's a right that a citizen has by virtue of being a person. That is what the second sentence of the Declaration says: God gave you certain inalienable rights; the state cannot take them away. The state doesn't give you the right to free speech: you've got that right; you were born with that right. The only thing the state can do is not take it away.

Ventura: But in *Rubicon Beach* you handle all this metaphorically—almost allegorically. Your characters are threatened by the state not for their exercise of free speech but for their search for a private, inner identity. When your character Catherine appears in Los Angeles, you write, "The town was terrorized by her. America was terrorized by her, by the mere fact of her being."

Erickson: They're terrorized by the idealism of her self-knowledge, the free self-knowledge of her own identity that she has brought with her from the jungle where she was born. She is sort of a last American.

Ventura: Never more so than when she says, "Not another moment will I be the sacrifice by which America pretends that its dreams have never changed." But it interests me that neither Catherine and Cale of *Rubicon Beach*, nor Michel and Lauren of *Days Between Stations*, ever try to change the world they're in.

Erickson: Cale doesn't really try to change the world, but he does try to change his own life.

Ventura: They all try to change their own lives, in some way, but your concept of change is always private. Nobody in these novels thinks they could effect a wider change.

Erickson: No. They're all loners. And I'm a loner.

Ventura: At the same time, you're writing novels.

Erickson: Which is a loner's work. That's the paradox. A loner who goes a singular individual path which is going to then be received by a lot of people and maybe change them, hopefully. But that brings up a point I want to make. I'm not a radical. I wasn't raised a left-wing radical. I've always basically accepted the system. I come to this as somebody who considers himself a basically conservative person. But I think America is not the kind of dream you turn away from without the knife coming down, as it does in *Rubicon Beach*. Because both in terms of the psyche of America and in terms of the institutional liberties of America, I don't think America will be able to live with itself having betrayed the dream from which it was born.

Steve Erickson by James Mx Lane

James Mx Lane / 1987

This interview, "Steve Erickson by James Mx Lane," was commissioned by and first published in *BOMB*, no. 20 (Summer 1987). © *BOMB* magazine, New Art Publications, and its contributors. All rights reserved. The *BOMB* Digital Archive can be viewed at www.bombmagazine.org.

I was born in America. It was somewhere inland. At the junction of two dirt roads about 300 yards from my house was a black telephone in a yellow booth; sometimes walking by you could hear it ringing. Sometimes walking by you'd answer, but no one ever spoke; there'd either be the buzz of disconnection or no sound at all. By the time I was 18 I thought I had outgrown the sound of telephone calls that weren't for me.
—from *Rubicon Beach* by Steve Erickson

There has been no middle ground with the reception of Steve Erickson's *Days Between Stations* and *Rubicon Beach*. The usual silence that greets an unestablished writer has been broken by a faction of readers who regard him as one of the most brilliant of contemporary American novelists.

Erickson, a Los Angeles native, treats his city not as a cloud-cuckooland, not as a sunny, upwind version of New York City, but as, in his surreal vision, the meta-town toward which the culture is marching.

The critics struggle to categorize his work. The truth may be that Steve Erickson, delivering prose with the force of the assault on Pearl Harbor, cannot be labeled at this time. His influences may be impossible to decipher. His work may require a category all its own.

At Charmers Market in Venice, California, Steve Erickson spoke about his fiction.

James Mx Lane: You've mentioned that you're not real happy with some of the labels that reviewers have been throwing at you . . . that you are writing in the Pynchon vein, or the Márquez, or the Serling.

Steve Erickson: I think that no writer is ever enthusiastic about being compared to other writers, but it's a natural process that reviewers go through, both for themselves and for their readers. So it's not that I'm unhappy about it. I just think that any writer shies away from it, and probably those writers are genuinely surprised by it. When I think of writers who have had an impact on me, I come up with people that never get named. Faulkner, Henry Miller, the Brontës, Stendhal, Paul Bowles, Philip K. Dick, Raymond Chandler. I would have to include in that group Márquez, who is one writer that has been cited, and you've probably got to include in that group Pynchon, simply because Pynchon is a little like Joyce. His influence is so pervasive these days that you can't help but be influenced by him.

MX: Raymond Chandler. Let me get back to him. He's often cited as a novelist of Los Angeles, a place you focus on intensely. Do you consider Los Angeles your territory? Is that a product of your living here, or is that something you try to work with consciously?

SE: The novel that I'm thinking about next, as it is forming in my mind, will have nothing to do with Los Angeles at all. I'm from Los Angeles; I've spent enough time away from it that I think I have a vague, intuitive sense of what it is. Which is probably as concrete a sense as one can get of Los Angeles. It's very much a city that exists in people's heads. It's so geographically amorphous. Certainly with *Rubicon Beach* the intention was to write a novel which was in a strong sense about Los Angeles as an extension of America. I've got to add that Los Angeles is presented in most literature as an aberration. My view was of a Los Angeles that was America taken to its furthest, and at the same time most logical and perverse extreme.

MX: The point was raised that *Rubicon Beach* was weak as political satire, or as a political novel.

SE: I think I know what Paul Auster meant in the *Times* when he said that he found the political subtext . . . I think he said "vague and unpersuasive," and I want to be careful that this doesn't come across as an objection to that opinion, which is a valid one. In my own mind, it was never calculated; it was never contrived in a way that Auster may have felt. I had this political subtext in mind from the start: it was an important part of the book. Whether I should have brought it out more directly is another question. I think I manifested it as much as I intended to. Or would have wanted to.

MX: You have been referred to as "a novelist for the 1980s." Do you consider yourself as such?

SE: I guess I'm turning out to be a novelist of the eighties. I tried to be a novelist of the seventies. This may be a time that responds to something

I'm doing. I'm a guy who grew up on movies and rock 'n' roll and books, and all of these things had an equal impact on me. Fusion has to take place in terms of the alchemy of your own creativity, and your own head, and to use a grand term, your own vision. And maybe that's what's happened [in the eighties]. It's the result of a lot of people growing up with all these influences and finding that those influences have consciously produced something that has not been seen before.

MX: Your work has been described as cinematic.

SE: I got my BA in cinema. It would probably be disingenuous of me to deny the influence. I have to say that . . .

MX: Are you inclined to deny it?

SE: Yeah. Well, again I would say that I'm not unhappy about it, because I can see why people feel that way. My own reaction is that the work is visual, but not necessarily cinematic, and that there's a distinction to be made between the two. There are a lot of ways in both these books that the internal drama, the drama that's going on inside of these people, is finding some kind of external representation. Michael Ventura I think made a really valid distinction when he reviewed both of these books for the [LA] *Weekly*, when he said that both these books don't take place in the camera's eye, but in the mind's eye. There's a difference in that the audience, or the reader, brings to the visual sense of the book a lot of his own visual sense. I think that if these books somehow got translated into a celluloid representation they would be a lot more literal than the final effect of the books when they're read. I guess I feel that books may capture a cinematic sense, but I'm not sure if they are really cinematic in terms of their form, or even in terms of the visual language.

MX: Your writing tends to be intensely focused. Are you a very structured writer?

SE: No, I let it incubate in my head for a long time. I kind of wait until I build up a good head of psychic scenes before I start writing. And in both of these books I did remarkably little rewriting, and also I wrote them in basically chronological order. I did write patches and go back, but especially *Rubicon Beach* there were two short, short sections in the middle of the book that I ended up reversing, and except for that I wrote it page 1 to page 300 sequentially.

MX: With *Rubicon Beach*, were you trying to write a three-hundred-page novel that has to be read as a single moment in time?

SE: I think that's the ideal. I'd like to write big books that masquerade as little books. As opposed to a lot of books that are little books masquerading as big books.

MX: Name a book in that context.

SE: No, I've gotten into trouble on this in the past. I know I presume a lot of readers. I'm not trying to come up with revolutionary forms. In fact, I'm very conscious of trying to write a book that's going to sweep the reader along, that's going to pull the reader along, that's going to make the reader exchange his reality for the book's. Because I think that's the ultimate triumph of art. The audience wants to exchange his or her reality for the reality of the artist's, and the measure of a good book is how long that exchange goes on, how long after a reader leaves the book does he take that bit of reality with him. I would like to write very readable books. I'm not looking to lay *Finnegans Wake* on the reader.

MX: Do you feel that *Days Between Stations*, your first novel, was successful in those terms?

SE: It was a successful first novel in that it got good reviews, and in that it got picked up by a popular and currently prestigious paperback line [Vintage Contemporaries]. It didn't sell worth shit.

MX: *Rubicon Beach* was your second novel. You sustain a very intensive mood throughout it. Is this something that, in the planning stages, you say, "This is what I want throughout," or . . . ?

SE: You know, these books sort of present themselves. They're there and they say to you: Write me. In *Rubicon Beach* I chose to write in a more direct prose than in *Days Between Stations*. And in shorter segments. I knew that the book was thematically and conceptually "out there," and there are going to be readers who go, "What is this book doing, and where is this book taking me?" And I wanted to seduce the reader. I wanted to make it easy for the reader to be pulled in.

MX: Yet, in *Rubicon Beach*, characters pop up whom nobody can exactly place; events are replayed over and over again, never exactly as before; people seem to forget why they've arrived at the places they find themselves in. Is the lack of stability, or memory, something that disturbs you?

SE: I think this is a time that demands that everything have an immediate value. That bothers me. I hope it bothers most thinking people. The attention span is short. Things have to prove themselves now, and next year it's "What have you done lately?" We live in a "What have you done lately?" culture. And yet I guess to a certain extent, having acknowledged that and distrusting that, I also find myself tactically recognizing that and working with it. Going back to what you said about the entire book striving to have the power of a single moment, as though it could be read in a single moment: that's a reinforcement, I think, of the immediacy principle that seems to beat work.

MX: Even more so in Los Angeles.

SE: Definitely. Especially here because we're so fucking passive. I live in a section of town which is old Los Angeles. That means that the buildings were built in the 1930s. There is no past. History is a blank slate. The upside of that is that you can basically write on the slate what you choose. The downside is that you better damn well know who you are here, because if you don't you'll end up one of the crazy people wandering Hollywood Boulevard, or you'll wind up somebody sitting in a hot tub in Pacific Palisades. All the people who come here, and I made the point in *Rubicon Beach*, who come here hating the city and what it stands for: four months later they confirm every stereotype you've ever seen or heard about Los Angeles, because they came here looking for Los Angeles to tell them who they were.

MX: Is this something you're going to pick up in your next book?

SE: I don't know. I think I stated that as directly as I want to state it for awhile. The whole middle section of *Rubicon Beach*, where the poet becomes a screenwriter, is about that.

MX: Is America "back and standing tall again?"

SE: No, I think America's gone. It's gone. It's not the same place. I say that as someone who was raised by his parents as a conservative Republican, who still thinks that the original idea of America is pretty mind-boggling— in the sense of a place where there are times that the will of the state must subvert its will to the will of a single citizen. There are certain inalienable rights that 220 million Americans voting tomorrow couldn't vote away from you. That I think is still a pretty amazing idea, but that America's gone. I think the new America is hostile to the idea that there are certain things about individual rights that are so valued that they take precedence over the will of the state. I think that we have a president and an attorney general who talk about freedom and getting the government off people's backs, but they wouldn't think twice about trying to tell you what you can read, whether the CIA can read your mail, or listen to your telephone, or what kind of lifestyle you should adhere to. I don't think the government would think twice about that. I think that Ronald Reagan and Ed Meese are hostile to the basic principles of the Bill of Rights.

MX: That may not make it into the interview. You'll get on one of those lists.

SE: I don't care about that. That you can put in, and I'd just as soon you did. My concern about this interview, and we never touched on this, is that I'm not especially enamored with what passes today for current American fiction, and I've made that fairly plain in interviews, and it tends to come off as though I'm saying that I'm the one person who can write something good, which is ridiculous and not what I'm saying at all. What I'm most critical of . . . my agent is going to kill me . . .

MX: We can strike this.

SE: Well, no . . . you can say this . . . as long as I don't get into specific names. What is most bothersome is that American fiction today seems to have accepted its own inconsequentiality. And I would only hasten to add that that doesn't mean that there aren't some good people writing some good things. I think Don DeLillo, Louise Erdrich, William Kennedy, Rob Lowenson, Henry Bean: those people are writing good books, and more people I'm not thinking of. And a lot of people working in genre fiction. I think that over the last thirty years a lot of genre fiction has been some of the most interesting and disturbing American fiction. Jim Thompson. Do you know Jim Thompson?

MX: No, I don't.

SE: He's going through a renaissance right now. He was a hard-boiled writer of the 1950s. Books with titles like *The Killer Inside Me* and *Savage Night* and *Wild Town*. I think he's being rediscovered as a major American writer. Of course, the French had to make the discovery first. But America's finding out about him. His books have just been reissued by a small press called Black Lizard Press. If Celine had been an American pulp writer, he would've been Jim Thompson. Philip K. Dick is an important American writer, but he's so out there, so off the wall that even the science fiction community took awhile to accept him. Now he's lionized because he's dead. Guys like Márquez and Milan Kundera and V. S. Naipaul . . . if there are giants these days, these guys are the closest thing to it. Probably because they're just far enough beyond the boundary of the technological world that they haven't been rendered numb by it.

MX: Escaping the numbness. Is that part of being a writer? An alienated youth?

SE: I kind of think and hope that a new generation of Americans is shaking the numbness off. We didn't live through the trauma of the bomb. The bomb was something that was there from the day that we were born. And I think that that's where the numbness came from. The trauma.

Both of these books are books about people trying to shake themselves out of a numbness. They're slapping themselves silly trying to get the blood going again.

MX: Is that why you write? To get the blood going again?

SE: Probably.

An Interview with Steve Erickson

Michael Silverblatt / 1993

From *Bookworm*, KCRW-FM (June 21, 1993). Copyright © 1993 by KCRW-FM.
Reprinted by permission.

Michael Silverblatt: Hi, this is Michael Silverblatt, and welcome to
Bookworm. Today my guest is Steve Erickson, the author of *Arc d'X*. It's
published by Poseidon Press, and he's the author as well of *Leap Year,
Tours of the Black Clock, Rubicon Beach*, and *Days Between Stations*, as
well as being the film critic for the *LA Weekly*. Well, I thought I'd begin by
asking, each of these last three books has been presided over by a tutelary
political figure—Jefferson here in *Arc d'X*, Hitler in *Tours of the Black Clock*,
the presidential campaign—and it makes for a very unusual mix because,
to some extent, these are experimental novels, and you always end up
associating these things with art for art's sake, and yet they have, it seems,
icons that they begin with. Could you talk a bit about that?

Steve Erickson: Well, I think my books have grown progressively political from the first one. In *Days Between Stations*, if there's any politics at
all, it's removed by metaphysics gone crazy in the world, and social anarchy is expressed in that way. And in *Rubicon Beach*, although he doesn't
have the presence that Hitler does in *Tours* or that Jefferson does in this
book, Robert Kennedy and his assassination is an event that casts a shadow
across what's going on in the rest of the book. I think that it's probably
typical, in some way I can't explain, of my view of politics in fiction, that
Hitler, for instance, is never named in *Tours of the Black Clock*—and Jefferson is referred to as Thomas in *Arc d'X*—because I wanted to make
these men *my* characters, and because I didn't want them to necessarily be confused for the real people. I wanted them to be part of the world
of the book that I was creating. The chaos of their humanity is the cata-
lyst for the chaos of each respective book. They were both people who
changed the world, one for the better and one obviously for the worse.

I wanted to take apart the machinery of their iconography and see what happened.

MS: You know, some years ago, probably around twenty now, Rudolph Wurlitzer said something that intrigued me: he said that, in comparison to East Coast experimental fiction, which he said was about structures breaking down, the West Coast is used to the idea of entropy. Entropy is old news—we're interested in taking that trash and building new shapes from it. The end has already occurred and we're reinventing the future. And I thought that that was appropriate for this book. It's sort of as if the shapes of the past are joined by the shape of the future. This is the X of *Arc d'X*. It's the meeting point of different worldviews, time processes. I wondered if you could speak a little bit about the kind of novel you find yourself writing.

SE: Well, I think that, to a certain degree, that sense of entropy that you talk about is what brought a lot of people this far west to begin with. It seems a natural part of my fiction—to the extent that I've never really sat back and figured it out and calculated it—but being in this place at this particular time, being as far as America can go geographically and psychologically, and as far as this particular millennium can go temporally, these books are a kind of natural expression of that. They take on an entropy of their own. I really sat down with this novel intending to write a pretty straightforward novel. By the time I had written seventy-five pages of it, I knew it wasn't going to be a very straightforward novel, so I followed that. But I'm not especially calculated about these things.

MS: Well, what, for instance, is your idea of a straightforward novel? What would an example of such a novel be?

SE: I don't know, *The Sun Also Rises* is a pretty straightforward novel, I think. It starts at one point and goes to another and follows the trajectory of people moving in a straight line from one place to another and one time to another. I'm speaking structurally as much as anything else, as well as thematically. I think in my case the structure and the theme are both out-growths of each other.

MS: I guess I'm asking: Was your desire to do something more straightforward a personal desire or a response to editorial suggestion or a wondering, if you went in that direction, would you find the audience that has otherwise perhaps eluded you?

SE: I think it was mostly the first. It was not at all a response to editorial suggestion. Simon & Schuster and Poseidon Press have been very good at letting me write the novels that I want to, and I don't think I've ever been especially mindful of the audience that the book is going to attract. I'd like to attract a huge audience, but realistically, I want to do it on my terms, and I know what the likelihood of that is with a book like this. But I was attracted by the idea of imposing on myself the discipline of a straightforward linear novel to see if I could do it, you know? And I'm still not sure I can, because it starts off fairly routine enough, as you've mentioned, and then it sort of loops off into the stratosphere or something.

MS: Well, it's very exciting. The other thing I noticed about your work—you know, many people use outrageous and bizarre humor to effect the dislocations in their books. I think, for many people, *Gravity's Rainbow*, for instance, starts with the English candy drill. That's where their minds say, "Oh, I like this book." Your work is not particularly known for its humor, and I wonder if you could describe—it *is* apocalyptic. It is, to my mind, very tense. And sinister, I guess, is a way I'd describe it. But can you give me some other bearing grounds? It's very odd for a writer to describe his own work, but how do you think of it?

SE: Well, I guess I'm the only person who thinks my books are actually kind of funny, but to be more precise about it, I'm not an ironic writer. I think that, without getting into specific examples, I think that irony in North American fiction over the last thirty years has pretty much reached endgame. It's about exhausted itself. We now write fiction in which we're so afraid of being sentimental that we risk no emotion or passion. And in that sense, I think I'm a pretty old-fashioned writer, really. My sensibility is, I don't know—compared to Thomas Pynchon, I'm basically a sentimental slob, you know? My concerns are very old-fashioned, traditional concerns of love and identity and sex and obsession and memory and history, and my take on them is not especially ironic, which I think is the way American fiction came to grips with the abyss, you know? Writers stared into it after 1945 and felt compelled to make fun of it. That was the way of American fiction to deal with that, I think. I'd just as soon jump in.

MS: Yes, the avoidance of the abyss. I think that once, with the example of Céline, it was thought that a certain amount of heartlessness and irony and terrorism would bring the writer into the abyss, but it turns out to have been, would you say, a delaying tactic?

SE: I think the abyss changed. I mean, I think it shifted, and our understanding of its nature was transformed. The abyss that Céline had looked into was World War I. The abyss we looked into was Hiroshima. I think that as the abyss grows wider or deeper or darker, the point of literature becomes more elusive. I've said this before, but in my more rational, lucid moments, I know that I'm obsolete. I know that I am involved in an obsolete art that becomes more and more marginalized, and yet it's my talent and temperament to do this, I think.

MS: Is your knowledge of its obsolescence what leads you to take risks? Because it seems to me, for instance, in *Leap Year*, the book goes along with, to my mind, more than usual energy, and there's a kind of ecstasy in that book that's more tempered I think elsewhere in the novels. And then suddenly, I believe, Tipper Gore appears and performs sex acts with the (so far) realistic hero, and Al comes out of the closet and they begin a fight, and there's a genuine sense that something truly bizarre, something unpermitted, has happened with the texture of the book. And you start to say, "Aha! It's not really a journal. What in the world is this thing?" which is, I think, the question one asks of a Steve Erickson novel, just the first question. There will come a point for a reader where what they've been reading gives way to something else, and it's in that suture point that you begin to examine: What is this thing? What joins these modes? Does obsolescence help you free yourself? Because this doesn't seem to me to be the old phrase "tap dancing at the abyss." It does seem to like to take the leap.

SE: Well, I think that there's a peculiar tension that I pursue between being mindful of the abyss and forgetting about it, because if I believe as I'm writing the book that what I'm doing is futile, then it has no passion. It becomes impossible to invest passion in it. I think that the paradox is one of leaping into an abyss that the other side of your mind is pretending isn't there.

MS: If you think about Faulkner, who is a writer who I think is one that you have affection and esteem for—if you think about Faulkner, the works that influence him insofar as one can reconstruct: He loves Romantic poetry, he loves imagist decadent French poetry—but they're fairly high-culture models. I noticed when I was writing down the kind of modes that go into your book, *Arc d'X*—the current book by Steve Erickson, my guest—begins with not even a pastiche but I think a full-hearted attempt to write historical fiction. This could be a chapter from a different period's *Gone with the Wind*. It seems like a romance, it begins in a funeral chamber, and it proceeds to the beginning of an illicit passion. It switches its tone and takes on serious noir, a kind of—I don't even know how to describe these sentences—but they're subject-verb-object, fairly direct, tough-guy sentences. And then veers again into a kind of pornographic genre, but they all seem to be stylizations. They don't seem to be the equipment of what was, even for experimental writers, the essence of fiction. Any comment?

SE: I think that from my perspective, for starters, the historical part of the book: if you go back and look at it, there's already some strange things going on there in terms of the relationship, for instance, between Thomas and a slave who was burned when he was five years old. I would hope the novel does not read to somebody like an ongoing series of stylistic experiments, because I didn't write it like that at all. I read a lot of history and I read crime fiction and I read some of the nineteenth-century Romantic fiction that we've talked about. And I also grew up in a time—I came of age in a time when the significance of fiction was shoved out of the limelight by movies and rock 'n' roll, both of which had a huge impact on me. So all of these things have sort of woven into one, and I gather that this is what's called postmodern, although I've never had a clue what that really means. But it is not for me an experiment or an examination of the uses of artifice. That's something I don't care about. These are all things that kind of naturally, for me, wind their way into the world of the novel, and I can only hope that for the reader it works like that as well.

MS: Yes. What I do find interesting is that, as I say, the work doesn't seem to be pastiche in the way that an experiment in modes would, but rather—I guess the best way to describe it would be this: I was talking to Maurice Sendak, who wanted, he said, to illustrate Melville's *Pierre*—kind of a dangerous enterprise. He said that what he thought *Pierre* was like was that if you had a dial that could deform prose, that Melville turns the dial during that book, sometimes to shriek level, sometimes to a mutter, sometimes to unintelligibility, and that the way perhaps to illustrate *Pierre* would be to use one picture—

SE: That's great.

MS:—and colorize it in different ways, deform it, make it hysterical, make it factual, make it, you know, metaphysical. And *that* more seems to be your mode here, that some kind of pressurizing of event is forcing the emotional torque in a new direction. But stylization is necessary to it: What if we take the story of black-and-white passion and place it in a police state? And now sexualize the police state? And now . . . that kind of thing. It's a very strange and exciting experience to read it.

SE: And I don't think I've understood it ever so well until right now. I couldn't comment, I couldn't elaborate on what you've just said. I think you've said it. If I were better at defining and explaining my own work, that's probably something pretty close to what I'd say.

MS: Well, thank you. Now tell me, does that make the work harder?

SE: For whom?

MS: If you were able to describe it, would that make it harder for you to write it?

SE: Yeah, maybe. Without wanting to sound too mystic about it, I think I'm a pretty instinctive writer. The subconscious is important in the creative process of writing these books, and I'm wary of figuring it out, you know? I'm not even sure I'm really smart enough to understand it, truthfully. I'm not sure that my literary intelligence quite keeps apace with my instincts.

MS: One of the things I noticed when I was reading the book, I frequently had to take long walks. I was very excited but very disturbed, because it seemed like a book that was challenging my ability to master it. It's a kind of exciting thing. I read so much that not to know what would be on the next page and sometimes not to know how to describe what happened on the page before was a very kind of elating and disturbing thing.

SE: People must wonder what the hell we're talking about right now.

MS: Well, you know, but, I think that they—

SE: They must be asking themselves, "What kind of book is this?"

MS: Well, I think that the idea, in fact, of anything is to describe the experience as well as possible, however odd that might be. I like that feeling, in fact. I often think about this radio show the way we're describing this book, as something someone tumbles into and is processed by, and whatever they've retrieved from it, well, very well. It was there. Nothing? Good. Sometimes there's nothing.

SE: Right. Right.

MS and SE: [*laughter*]

MS: But I found myself thinking that the experience I was having in reading the book was like the experience of dream. I'm able in a dream in a single night to dream the same character first as a man, then as a woman, first in the eighteenth century and then now. Why, I kept asking myself, was it so hard for me to make those rapid transformations in the course of a novel? I'm used to reading, I'm said to be a pretty good reader, and I thought maybe it had to do with the fact that reading is so linear—left, right, left, right, the eyes going up and down the page—and that this process—

SE: And the pages are sequential and you go from beginning to end.

MS:—and that the action, the texture of what you do is in contradiction to the reading process. It wouldn't be to the film process. The camera has become Möbius, you know, capable of all sorts of exfoliations. But reading itself is sort of a reminder of the tension between logic and the novel you, Steve Erickson, have written.

SE: My novels have been described as dreamlike, and probably the best compliment I ever got from somebody was they said they were driving along and they suddenly remembered a dream they had had, and then they realized it wasn't a dream, it was my novel. I never remember my dreams, but the vague sense I have of them is that all the transitions fall out of the bottom. There are no transitions in dreams. Place and time is jammed up together and there are no juxtapositions really. Or none of the boundaries of juxtapositions. That seems to come naturally to me when I'm writing.

MS: Thank you. I've been talking to Steve Erickson, the author, most recently, of *Arc d'X*, from Poseidon Books. Thank you for joining me.

SE: Thank you.

History Changes Itself: An Interview with Steve Erickson

Yoshiaki Koshikawa / 1993

From *The Study of Current English* (July 1993): 1–38. Reprinted with permission.

Los Angeles as Dream Factory

Yoshiaki Koshikawa: First I want to talk about the themes of your fiction. You deal with many characters who are in some way related to the film industry. Michel Sarre, the protagonist of *Days Between Stations*, has an uncle who is also a Hollywood producer, and Michel eventually makes a film of his own. His quest for himself involves the quest for the history of Hollywood starting from the age of D. W. Griffith. And we have another example in *Rubicon Beach*. Part 2 of that novel deals mainly with Llewellyn Edgar, a failed poet who is also a screenwriter in Hollywood. Hollywood has a double meaning in American history. It is a symbol of the American Dream—you can be a big shot and live in Beverly Hills if you are very lucky— but it has also a negative aspect seen in the age of the red purge, McCarthy's witch hunting of the 1950s. And there's Catherine in *Rubicon Beach*, and she thinks Hollywood is America. She finds Hollywood representative of the United States.

As a writer of fiction, what do you think of Hollywood and its film industry?

Steve Erickson: Well, I grew up here. And I also grew up at a time when movies had supplanted, to a large extent, the cultural center of America. And all the duality that you are talking about was something that was subconsciously at work when I wrote the novel. But as I think will become clear in the course of this interview, I tend to be a pretty instinctive writer. Sometimes we do things that we don't provide an analysis for until later on. That's exactly the way that I write. I hadn't, especially in the case of *Days*

Between Stations, set out to write a book about Hollywood. I basically set out to write a love story. And it was a very modest ambition; the film stuff came into it later on. In the case of *Days Between Stations*, it's as much a European film theme as it is a Hollywood one. And that reflected my own background because I started out a film student at UCLA. I was not a literature student. I had even toyed with the idea of making movies. And I decided that my temperament and my talent lay elsewhere.

In the case of *Rubicon Beach*, I intended to write not a Hollywood novel but a Los Angeles novel. That's a fine distinction but an important one. I wrote about Hollywood in terms of Los Angeles, rather than Los Angeles in terms of Hollywood. It's a novel in which all of the myth-making and the legend-making displaces the reality of the people who live here, and particularly the people who come here from somewhere else, which is true of most people who live in Los Angeles. They come here for the specific reason of displacing their reality with the one that Los Angeles allows them to invent.

Catherine—which is not her name, of course—comes out of the jungle, where her self-consciousness is so undeveloped that she doesn't even recognize her own face when she sees it reflected in the water. And when she gets here, her own beauty winds up driving her mad. That seemed to me a pretty good metaphor for what I wanted to say about Los Angeles.

YK: In *Days Between Stations*, Lauren also wanders into the streets of Los Angeles. The city is just like a black hole, you know? Everyone falls into this vacant spot.

SE: And the first time she comes to Los Angeles in the beginning of the book, what happens to her is something that she can't remember later on. She has to come back here to find that memory manifested for her in the form of Michel, who also can barely remember. People not understanding the meaning of their own memories is one of the important themes of that book.

YK: Though I've been to Los Angeles once before, I've never been to the San Fernando Valley. And you wrote about your boyhood there in *Leap Year*. Can you tell me about that?

SE: Well, as I wrote *Leap Year*, the important thing about the Valley for me was that the San Fernando Valley typified Los Angeles and it typified the fifties and it typified the way both those things could change overnight, and the way reality could change overnight. I was a kid, and when I was less than five years old, we lived in one part of the Valley where they had barely laid telephone lines, and you had to go down to the corner to make a phone call. We moved to another part of the Valley in which one month there was nothing there and the next month there was a neighborhood, there were houses, and the next month after that there were lawns and there was ivy, and the next month after that there were swimming pools, and ten years later it was all gone again because they put through a freeway. And I just took it as a matter of course that all of your reference points could be established and eliminated within the course of a childhood. And that's what I grew up with. I grew up walking to school one year through an orchard, and the next year there would be a bunch of tract homes there, and the next year there would be a supermarket complex there. And the landscape changed like this [*snaps fingers*], constantly. Because I grew up with that, I had no way of knowing that that was extraordinary. That that was unusual or a little bit strange. And the big cultural shock for me was when I was twenty years old, and the first time I ever left Los Angeles to go to Paris, where things haven't changed for hundreds of years, you know? I saw buildings that had been there since the 1400s. And that was kind of stunning. And I had to leave Los Angeles and come back to realize what a really strange place Los Angeles is.

YK: So familiar things might disappear by next year.

SE: Right. It's possible. I mean, things never stayed around long enough to get familiar, you know?

YK: I see [*laughs*]. Because you Americans, generally speaking, put stress on new things.

SE: Right.

YK: And you're always thinking new things are best.

SE: And Los Angeles is the ultimate expression of that idea. Los Angeles is not just up-to-the-hour new, it's up-to-the-minute new. And in Los Angeles, if you drive by a building that was built in the 1930s, you're driving by history. That's history for Los Angeles.

YK: But—I think you love this city a lot. You write about Los Angeles and you live in Los Angeles. Since you came back—I don't know when, but— have you ever gone somewhere else?

SE: Well, I wrote about Los Angeles after I came back, and I'm fascinated with Los Angeles. I can't say that I love Los Angeles, and I sort of distrust anybody that says they either love or hate Los Angeles, because it's like loving or hating a blank slate, and it depends what you want to write on the blank slate. Los Angeles is a relatively livable city if you know who you are and what you want to do. It imposes no civic identity of its own. It's not like New York or Paris, where you may not know who you are, but you know you are a New Yorker, or you know you are a Parisian. Here if you don't know who you are, you end up walking up and down Hollywood Boulevard talking to yourself. And that's why there are so many genuinely crazy people here, because Los Angeles is this dream factory. They come here looking for Los Angeles to help them define themselves, and LA ain't gonna do it. It's just not going to do it. So I'm back here. From a political standpoint it would be much more to my advantage to live in New York, but it's not who I am. I'm not a New Yorker, and I like the way Los Angeles cuts me loose, you know?

The "Other World" of Film

YK: As you mentioned, you studied film and wanted to be a director or screenwriter. Which films have influenced you? Which films do you like a lot? And if you were a film director, which films would you want to make?

SE: *Vertigo*, by Hitchcock, with James Stewart and Kim Novak. It's basically an obsessive, surreal love story. And *The Third Man*, the Carol Reed/Orson Welles film. It's hard for me to know which films have influenced me, but I know the films that I've liked, the films I can watch again and again: *Out of the Past* by Jacques Tourneur, *My Darling Clementine* by John Ford, *Last Tango in Paris* by Bernardo Bertolucci, and *Once Upon a Time in the West* by Sergio Leone.

YK: How about Japanese films? How about Kurosawa?

SE: I saw *Seven Samurai* about twenty years ago. There's a scene toward the end of the film where Mifune is standing on this knoll. And I think he's got all the swords and it's raining. The rain is pouring down and he's pulling out one sword after another as the warriors charge him. That kind of dreamlike quality is what made an impression on me. And it's not totally unlike the nightmare quality you see in some of Hitchcock's best films or even in some of Leone's best films. It's not exactly surreal. I don't really think of myself as a surrealist. But there is something about the light that is a little bit otherworldly. I think that's the attraction of films for me in general, and it's just one of the important things in my first two novels.

YK: Do you have some images of film stars in mind when you create fictional characters?

SE: No. I see the characters in much more personal terms. They don't resemble particular actors. I would have a hard time casting films of my book because I don't think I could find anybody. I can't find anybody that looks like Catherine, for example.

YK: How about Nastassja Kinski taking a role? The reason I ask is that when I was reading your fiction, I thought of Nastassja Kinski in that role.

SE: Which role?

YK: Catherine's. She comes from the jungle, and she reminds me of Kinski in *Cat People* by Paul Schrader.

SE: She's not dark enough, though. I can almost see Nastassja Kinski playing Dania in *Tours of the Black Clock*. The dancer. But I'm not sure she's dark enough to play Catherine.

YK: Anyway, I think your imagination is much richer, and that many of your imagined characters are more complex, more ambivalent, than any individual actor or actress on the screen.

Imagination and Invention

YK: American people have been shown in Westerns a stereotyped image of the Native American in Hollywood films. But it seems to me that you're trying to demystify, to deconstruct, that kind of image or myth. How did the old Westerns influence your idea of Native Americans?

SE: Well, I think that most people have come to understand that the image of the Native Americans as presented in American movies is a pretty distorted one. I don't presume to write realistically about Native Americans. That would be arrogance on my part. But I think that there is an elemental purity about the image of American Indians that I embrace in my fiction, not so much in historical terms but in metaphorical terms. In the case of *Tours of the Black Clock*, you've got a major character who is, in fact, part Indian.

YK: Banning Jainlight?

SE: Right. And that presents a conflict in images, which says more about his own psyche than it does about Native Americans.

YK: Did you see the film *One Flew Over the Cuckoo's Nest* with Chief Bromden as an Indian? That guy reminds me of Banning Jainlight.

SE: Well, of course, he's big, which Banning Jainlight is as well.

YK: Not only big, but powerful and violent, you know? The violence may be bad, but it could be good, just like the Hitler you presented in *Tours of the Black Clock*.

SE: I meant to present Hitler in human terms, almost in pathetic terms, because morally it's too easy to dismiss him as an aberration. The horror of

Hitler is that his monstrousness was human, not something utterly freakish. If you read the history of the Third Reich you find yourself shaking your head over and over that people could have pursued those nightmares with such abandon. At one point near the end of *Tours*, Banning says to Hitler, "You must have sat in the Chancellery racking your brains at night, trying to figure out just how evil you could be. You couldn't have been born with such abysmal visions."

YK: I understand that Native Americans make up what you call a "minority group" or "displaced persons" like Blacks, Asians, Jews, whomever.

SE: Well, this is especially true because they were here first. They were the first Americans, so they are the ultimate displaced Americans.

YK: It seems like both Hitler and Banning Jainlight are charismatic characters. Characters with superpower, you know? Both are violent and have obsessions. It doesn't matter whether one is a political dictator or not, whether one comes from a minority group or not.

SE: Right.

YK: You're not just a local LA writer. The places you write about in *Tours of the Black Clock* are not limited to LA. You also cover New York City, Chicago, and some cities in Europe. Last night I was thinking, Why haven't you written about Asia? It crossed my mind that maybe you have. You wrote about Asia through Davenhall. Is that right?

SE: Right. And also there are Asian aspects in the very beginning of *Rubicon Beach*, where Los Angeles has been submerged beneath the water. But it's a culture I don't know a lot about. I constantly worry about my presumptuousness in writing about something that I don't know a lot about. In *Arc d'X*, the new novel that I've just published, the principal character is a Black woman. I wind up dealing with that too in a metaphorical way, from what is inescapably a white perspective. I don't know how Black people might feel about that. I guess I'll find out.

YK: I think it's challenging.

SE: On the one hand, you want to be careful and sensitive, but on the other hand, you don't want to be too careful, because the whole idea of writing a novel is to take risks and to push yourself as far as you can go. So we'll just have to see what people's reactions are.

YK: When you write about a woman, it's also easy to make a mistake because you are a man.

SE: That's what I'm saying. Exactly. You can wind up feeling so constrained by all the things you don't know that you just write novels about a bunch of white guys, and that is not interesting. For me, in each novel there is a female character that is really the key of the entire novel, the crux of the novel. Take Lauren or Catherine or the girl in *Tours of the Black Clock*, whom we see principally as a fantasy figure. Then when we see her, the girl, she's really not very much like the fantasy figure at all. The fantasy girl that Banning Jainlight is writing about is a beautiful girl, and when we finally meet her she's not especially beautiful. Part of the point of the book is that Banning Jainlight has basically reinvented a woman and it changes history.

Rewriting American History in *Arc d'X*

YK: In *Arc d'X* as well as *Leap Year* you dealt with Thomas Jefferson's ambivalence, the ambivalence of American "white" democracy. It seems to me that you're involved in rewriting American history from the viewpoint of the displaced Black woman. Maybe in your view Sally Hemings changed the whole course of American history.

SE: John Locke, whom Jefferson considered one of the three greatest men that ever lived, once wrote of the right to life, liberty, and property. But when Jefferson wrote in the Declaration of Independence of the inalienable rights given to men by God, he replaced "property" with the "pursuit of happiness." The country born of that pursuit broke loose of history. In *Arc d'X*, Thomas's own happiness is embodied by his property—the fourteen-year-old slave girl he owns, who one afternoon finds herself free of the bonds of his ownership and must choose either to return to her country as his property or leave everything behind in freedom, including her family and home. Sally makes a decision that changes the nature of freedom for her country and history. She becomes the first modern American, changing the outcome of not just one revolution but two, and the man who inspired both is consumed by the dark expression of his own idealism.

YK: Other writers have also treated Jefferson's ambivalence: there is, for example, William Wells Brown's *Clotel; or, The President's Daughter*, Robert Penn Warren's *Brother to Dragons*, etc. Did you refer to any other historical books when you wrote about Jefferson and Hemings in *Leap Year* and *Arc d'X*?

SE: I haven't read either Brown or Warren. My references were Jefferson's own writing and historical texts by Henry Adams, Fawn Brodie, and others. I took the basic facts and then invented from there.

Shadow Presidents

YK: I'd like to ask you a question about American presidents. In *Leap Year* you wrote about the 1988 presidential campaign. Robert Coover once wrote a book called *The Cat in the Hat for President: A Political Fable* (1968). It's a parody of a children's book.

SE: Right. It was a Dr. Seuss book.

YK: In that book, Coover described the presidential campaign in a very comic way. His idea that all big events—from presidential campaign to the Olympic Games—are showbiz, where everybody enjoys themselves and gets crazy, you know? Like a carnival. How do you think about campaigns in general and about the one you had last year? Do you see such a comical aspect in the campaign?

SE: Well, I've always been fascinated with presidential campaigns, in part for the theater. I mean, it's a theater of power. But there are ways in which the presidential elections in this country become more and more disheartening, become more and more depressing.

YK: Because of?

SE: Because of the process itself and because the problems in this country are so profound and involved. They involve choices that the public doesn't want to make. And for all the rage that I think the American public currently feels toward American politicians, toward the American political process, the hard truth is that the American public has nobody to blame but itself. It does not reward truth-tellers. It doesn't like truth-tellers. Candidates who try to tell the truth lose. And if I had known at the outset of 1988 what a truly dismal and disheartening experience the presidential campaign of that year was going to be, I would never have written *Leap Year*. I would never have signed the contract to write the book. And that's one of the reasons that it turned out to be such a short book, because it was a depressing book to write. It was a depressing experience to watch the campaign. And the only good thing about it was the trip around the country I took. I wound up writing as much about that as about the politics.

YK: I read in a Japanese book that, since the Reagan age, politicians have used the media to create good images, not showing the content of what they say, but what they look like. And today, handlers control everything in the campaign, like the director of a film. In a sense, handlers are more important than the president. The president listens to their words.

SE: Well, I mean, Ronald Reagan in particular, but George Bush as well, raised that situation to its highest, or perhaps I should say lowest, level.

The country is basically run by people who decide what is going to get the president on the evening news in the most advantageous sixty seconds possible.

YK: And that's why handlers are important.

SE: And if the handlers decide that George Bush go to a flag factory, then that's what he does. That's what the entire 1988 campaign was waged on, you know, who liked the flag more, who was more "American." And it was disgusting. It was truly disgusting.

YK: It's kind of fake, you know?

SE: It's completely fake. It's completely synthetic. Ronald Reagan . . . you've got to say on Ronald Reagan's behalf that at least Ronald Reagan had some things he believed in. George Bush has nothing he believes in. George Bush believes in his own political ambitions. And now the country is paying for that. The people ultimately are going to have to take control or lose control completely. The public is held captive by these people. It allows itself to be held captive because people are too lazy to read a newspaper or read a magazine or think about things or turn off the football game and watch a news show, and yet every November, every four years, they get angry because they don't have a better choice. And they have to take responsibility for the fact that they allowed the truth to be taken away from them.

YK: How about Bill Clinton? Some people say Bill Clinton thought much of the importance of the media, and took advantage of media news and TV debates. Some say Bill Clinton, for that matter, resembles Ronald Reagan. What do you think about him as a president?

SE: There is a sense among many people in America now that Bill Clinton is the Last-Chance President. There's a sense that he represents the last chance to make things right.

YK: Why haven't you had a female president so far? You haven't had a Black, Jewish, Asian, or Hispanic president either.

SE: Because this is a country that for two hundred years has been run by white men. It wasn't until seventy or eighty years ago that women could even vote. It wasn't until much more recently that Black people could vote without being obstructed or harassed. In 1983, when Congress passed an extension of the Voting Rights Act, which assured people the right to vote without being harassed, Ronald Reagan almost vetoed it. So I think that a "minority" president will come, but I don't know how soon. I mean it's very striking that of the last four presidents, in a lot of ways, their wives were more impressive. Barbara Bush is, in a lot of ways, a more impressive person than George Bush. Nancy Reagan was, whatever else was true of her, a more formidable person than Ronald Reagan. Rosalynn Carter was, in a lot of ways, a stronger person than Jimmy Carter, and the same was true of Betty and Gerald Ford.

YK: So we have a shadow president?

SE: Yeah, right, exactly. And if you look at Bill Clinton. His wife is a very powerful woman.

Backward/Forward

YK: Well, let's change the topic and talk about the form of your fiction. You don't write short stories. You've written only novels. I wonder why you don't write short stories.

SE: I don't know. I just tend to think in novel terms. The stories I tend to think of are novel-length stories, and as you know, they tend to involve a number of characters, and they also include smaller stories that kind of shoot off here and there. I just don't think in the concise terms of a short story writer. I really think it's harder to write a great short story than a great novel. I think this is so in general, because a really good novel can have flaws or problems, and if there are other things about it that are strong, it will overcome those flaws. A really great short story can't have any flaws. It doesn't have the space or the luxury to have flaws, and so I have a lot of respect for somebody like Flannery O'Connor, who was both a short story writer and a novelist. I think her short stories are her best work, because she wrote these little gems that are perfect.

YK: When you didn't write short stories in the 1980s, the wind might have been against you, because the minimalist writers flourished in that decade. However, we are now in the nineties, so I think it's your age.

SE: Well, maybe. But in the final analysis, I can't worry about that. You know, I write the things that I write, and my time is going to come or not.

YK: I read an *LA Times* interview a couple of years ago, in which I learned that your first five novels were rejected. This came into my mind: If the 1980s had not been an age of short stories, you might have debuted earlier than 1985. Did you really throw a couple of unpublished novels into the garbage?

SE: Actually, I've destroyed virtually all of my unpublished novels.

YK: You mean you physically destroyed them? Why did you do that?

SE: Because I don't want to fall over dead some day and have somebody go into my garage and dig up the stuff and publish it, which is what you see happened to other writers. When I got my first novel published, I had the option of going back and trying to publish my earlier novels. I decided I didn't want to go back, I wanted to go forward. I decided the next novel was going to be better than those novels.

YK: I think you are serious, honest, and courageous.

SE: Well, thanks.

YK: You're really a brave writer. You put many hours, much energy into those works. You can't throw that away easily. You have some affection for the material you wrote. I don't know many writers who can do that.

SE: Well, I can't say that it was easy for me, but I made a decision and I did it. I think that nothing is lost. I think there are themes or ideas or images or characters from all of those unpublished novels that occasionally pop up in a new novel. That stuff was all like a laboratory; it's where I did all of my experiments. And I just decided that from the standpoint of my development as a novelist, it was important for me to go forward and not backward.

YK: Did you make that decision after you published *Leap Year*?

SE: No. I decided this after I sold *Days Between Stations*.

YK: Oh, that early! I admire you. Wow! But didn't you think you could consciously use the unpublished materials later?

SE: No. I knew that whatever stuff was in those first novels that was redeemable or worth saving would manifest itself again in some hopefully better version.

YK: But is it not possible that the agent or editors didn't appreciate the quality of the unpublished novels? Someone might think they're good enough to publish.

SE: Yeah, they might. And a few of them might have been good enough to publish. But none of them was going to be as good as the next book that I wrote. That was the attitude I had to take.

YK: So you thought those manuscripts were not as good as *Days Between Stations*.

SE: But more importantly, I decided they were not as good as the next novel, which was *Rubicon Beach*—that the novel that I had in my head was going to be better than those.

YK: I see. As a matter of fact, we've now got a very experimental new work of fiction from you. But if we can forget about *Arc d'X*, *Rubicon Beach* is the most risk-taking and experimental work in the sense that you didn't trust the conventional cause-and-effect scenario. You drive the reader through to the end of the fiction through the power of your narration. The narration depends on the subconscious images and obsessions of the main characters. And of course, you know, this is also true of your other novels.

But it crossed my mind when I read the *LA Times* interview, that *Rubicon Beach* might have been written before *Days Between Stations*. One of the reasons I thought this is that you published *Rubicon Beach* so quickly after *Days Between Stations*.
SE: That's because it took me a long time to sell *Days Between Stations*. *Days Between Stations* was turned down by four agents and twelve publishers. By the time it was published I was already well into *Rubicon Beach*. So I wrote *Rubicon Beach* after *Days Between Stations*. They've been published in chronological order, the four books.

Faulkner, Miller, Soseki, Dylan

YK: Now that you are already established as a writer, it doesn't matter what difficulties you got through to get your first work published. But my question is: When you decided to be a writer, did you have a role model, or an author you admired? Do you like William Faulkner?
SE: Yeah. The two American writers who influenced me the most were Faulkner and Henry Miller.
YK: Faulkner and Henry Miller.
SE: Right. Faulkner because from him I learned about fiction that ticks to the chronology of an inner clock: the clock of memory rather than the clock of physical time. And from Faulkner I also learned about the way the barrier between the internal and external worlds can collapse. I also learned things about structure from Faulkner. His structures are radical. And when I was going to the university I would take some literature courses along with the film courses that I took. The professors would always say, "William Faulkner, he was a wonderful writer but he didn't know how to structure his books." And it was clear to me that his structures were the most revolutionary things about his books. So, *Light in August, The Sound and the Fury, Go Down, Moses*, those were very important books. And then from Henry Miller, I learned about how you become naked as an artist.
YK: You reveal yourself.
SE: Exactly. And how you strip away artifice, or how you use artifice in confessional terms. And *Tropic of Cancer, Black Spring, The Cosmological Eye*, those were very important books for me.
YK: It reminds me of many Japanese writers: you reveal your soul, your naked shame to the reader. It seems a bit naïve, but it's definitely a writer's honesty.

SE: [*Showing a book*] You probably know this book.

YK: *Kokoro*, Soseki. Yeah. This is one of the books I had in mind.

SE: This book had a big, big impact on me. I think this is a great book. There is an emotional and psychological exactitude, even in translation, about it that I've never seen in Western fiction. The way he can get that intangible, inexplicable feeling precisely. And a lot of the French existentialists later on tried to do same thing, but they didn't do it like *Kokoro*. This is a great novel.

YK: I think this is in the mainstream of Japanese literature. The self-confession.

SE: Right. Well, I don't know a lot about Japanese fiction. So it might be that in Japan this is very conventional. But in the West it's not. In the West this is revolutionary. And I read this book in the summer of 1975, and the novel that I read right before it was *Wuthering Heights* by Emily Brontë. The two back to back made a big impact, a big impact.

YK: Even Genichiro Takahashi, who is called the first postmodern Japanese writer, also puts some self-confession in his novels, just as you did in *Leap Year*. I think we have that tradition.

SE: Well, *Arc d'X* is certainly the most personal and confessional novel that I've written, on the one hand. And on the other, it takes all the time-space paradoxes a step further than the other books.

YK: The reason I said you might be a bit naïve is that you can still lie in your novels. You can confess a big lie when you honestly try to reveal yourself. It's a matter of writing, isn't it?

SE: In *Arc d'X*, there's a character that sometimes speaks in the first person about what he is doing. And then there is another character that comes in about three-quarters of the way through the book. He's a minor character, but his name's Erickson, which is obviously mine, and parallels what the main character has been talking about in the first person. So the line between artifice and confession and the exchange between the two gets blurred.

I've got one more thing to add. The third writer that I have to add to Faulkner and Miller, who had a big impact on me, is Bob Dylan, who I think may be the most influential contemporary American writer of the last twenty-five years. And particularly in the vacuum of contemporary American fiction, for a lot of us, Dylan was writing the great American novels. *Blonde on Blonde* was a great American novel.

But I think that with Dylan the music was important. I think the sound of Dylan's best records, which is a sort of wild, almost surreal honky-tonk sound, was as much a part of what he was writing as the words. And I think the words got a lot of attention, but the sound of his records is as much a part of that language. And the sound of his voice.

YK: So as a singer, he influenced you?

SE: Well, Dylan as a musician in general, as an artist in general, where the poetry and the musicianship and the vocals are all part of the same, all part of the art. But hearing *Highway 61 Revisited* was a really liberating moment for me because it was one of those moments that freed my mind in terms of what art could be.

Writing from the Head and Heart

YK: Last spring I went over to Morocco to see Paul Bowles. He uses kif to get high, to relax in the evening. There are many artists and writers, like William Burroughs for example, who have used drugs to get what they want in their works. Do you use drugs to get some inspiration for your writings?

SE: No. I've never taken drugs at all. Never. I think I've smoked marijuana twice. But that's the extent of my drug history. I've never taken hallucinogens. I've never taken LSD. I've never taken speed. I have actually tried to write when I drink. Actually, it's very easy to understand why writers become alcoholics. Because sitting down to that typewriter or that computer is really difficult. And it's a lot easier if you've got a scotch sitting next to you. But fortunately after a drink or two I lose my edge. I'm not sharp and I lose my focus and I lose my intensity. So I'm completely sober when I write. Completely sober, completely straight.

YK: I read a book about American writers and alcohol. Faulkner, I think he didn't drink while he was writing.

SE: Really?

YK: They said he always drank, so that the image was spread, that he was a drunk. But he never did. Faulkner was a strict disciplinarian. He never drank while he was writing. But after six or seven hours of writing, he started drinking.

SE: Right. Well, that I have done occasionally. I've had periods of my life where I drank a little more, or where I drank a little less. As I get older, it's harder for me to drink, because I don't recover as well. I write on a daily basis, and I can't afford to be hungover when I wake up, because I generally write either late at night or in the morning. My best time is in the morning, when I get up.

YK: After you get up.

SE: I get up, I put on a pot of tea, I come here, and I sit down. I don't read the paper. I don't listen to music or the radio. I start working. Because if I don't, I wind up procrastinating the entire day, you know?

YK: So how many hours a day do you work?

SE: It varies. When I'm really into a book, I might write three or four hours in the morning, take off the rest of the day, then at night write a couple more hours. But I'm exhausted. If I write four to six hours a day, my brain is just fried.

YK: Because you're using a computer?

SE: Yeah. But I mean it was also true before. *Arc d'X* is the first book I've written on a computer. All other books I wrote on a typewriter.

YK: Really? I thought you used a computer from the beginning, from *Days Between Stations.* So in *Days Between Stations, Rubicon Beach, Tours of the Black Clock,* and *Leap Year,* you typed all those manuscripts and rewrote them?

SE: Right.

YK: Oh, that's beyond my imagination! But how do you rewrite your manuscript?

SE: I usually rewrite as I'm going along. I start on page 1 and write through to the end.

YK: So when you finish a part, a fragment of a novel—

SE: I go back and rewrite that.

YK: Rewrite the first part?

SE: Yes.

YK: Well, when you finish rewriting the first part you go onto another part?

SE: Right. So by the time I get to the end, it's essentially done. When I get to the end, I will go back over it one more time. I have been rewriting as I go along. Every thirty pages or so I go back and I rewrite what I've done before I go on to the next part, because when I go on to that next part I want to be very clear in my head about where I've just come from.

YK: That's exactly the opposite of what I heard about Mark Leyner. He just writes some fragments, puts them away in a box, a drawer or whatever. He forgets everything about it, forgets everything he just finished writing. And he starts writing a new fragment. After finishing as many materials as possible in this way, he brings them out and connects them together.

SE: I think that's the way a lot of writers write. But because my books verge on the disconnected, and because my books are not linear, it's important for me to write them in a linear fashion, because I want to have a sense as I am going along of how the book is unfolding for the reader. And I've always worried that the reader is going to get so disoriented that he or she loses track and loses interest. I want to draw the reader in and keep the reader, and therefore I need to write from the beginning to the end and have a sense of how the book is developing for the reader and what the momentum of the book is. And I've written all of my novels like that. Every single book has been written from the first page to the last, and rewritten as I go along.

YK: It's a service for the reader, to help them follow you.

SE: Exactly.

YK: But what kind of rewriting is it? Checking the words and phrases or revising the early version completely?

SE: Yeah, I'll go back and rewrite. I may rewrite some things. I may cut things. I may embellish things. I never—well, I shouldn't say "never"—I rarely do a drastic rewrite. I mean I have very rarely thrown out things completely and started over. I can't say that my books are seriously rewritten.

YK: So that is to say you carefully write your first drafts?

SE: Well, I'm not sure how carefully. I write fast.

YK: You write fast? How many pages?

SE: I wrote *Rubicon Beach* in eight months, and *Tours of the Black Clock* in about the same time, eight to ten months.

YK: You mean without stopping? A few hours every day for eight to ten months?

SE: Right.

YK: How about *Days Between Stations*?

SE: *Days Between Stations* took me the longest actually. *Days Between Stations* was over a year of writing.

YK: And *Arc d'X* took that long?

SE: The basic writing of *Arc d'X* took eleven months.

YK: Don't you think it's much quicker to write on a computer?

SE: Oh, it's much quicker. The main thing is that while I'm writing this novel I've had to do some journalism on the side to pay bills. And the computer is much easier. It saves so much time because it's much easier to shift from one thing to another.

YK: That's a lovely aspect of the computer. You can shift words and phases so easily.

SE: The only thing, I must say, is that it also indulges my compulsiveness. With a computer it's really easy to fool with stuff, to go back and change stuff, and as a consequence the book could be rewritten more often and tend to get a bit longer.

YK: Generally speaking, which comes into your mind first when you write, characters or scenes?

SE: I think the first thing that comes is a character in a situation. And then it grows out from there.

YK: But don't you have the main characters in mind, at least a couple of them, when you start writing? The reason I ask that is you deal with very complicated human relationships in your fiction.

SE: Well, in *Tours of the Black Clock*, in my head I started with an American writer in the thirties who winds up becoming Hitler's pornographer. That was the crux and then it kind of spread out from there. By the time I started that book, I had about 85 percent of it in my head. And that's generally true of *Arc d'X*, too. I don't write from an outline. I don't write from notes. I make no notes at all. I make no outline. Because I don't want the novel to sound as if it was written from an outline. I want it to be written from my head and from my heart.

YK: Yeah. Reading your fiction, I understand that. Reading your novels, we enjoy your nonlinear narrative digressions, which embody many ideas and emotions.

But how about the titles of your fictions? Genichiro Takahashi told me he usually has the title before he starts writing. If he has a title, at least a working title beforehand, he feels safe and can go on writing. Sometimes it can be difficult to give a title to the work you've just finished.

SE: Well, I have found it varies. I didn't have the title *Days Between Stations* until the book was completely finished. I could not come up with one. I had a bunch of working titles, none of which was right. I had finished the novel and I came up with that title. And *Rubicon Beach* and *Tours of the Black Clock*, I had both those titles in my head before I started writing. I came up with *Arc d'X* about a third of the way into the book.

YK: Okay. Could you explain about the title *Arc d'X*? It sounds very mysterious, profound and symbolic. It reminds me of the arc above the sand dune as presented in *Days Between Stations*, and it also seems to refer to the paradoxical phrases of history, where facts and fictions, the past and the present, all intermingle and become changeable.

SE: In the book there's a section about a French scientist named Seuroq who's trying to find a missing day at the end of the millennium. His calculations are based on history's denial of the human heart, and history's secret pursuit of the heart's expression. The heart's story is the pursuit and denial of love; history's is the pursuit and denial of freedom. The X is the intersection of the arc of love and the arc of freedom.

For the Future

YK: This is the final question: I heard you're doing a collection of essays. I imagine the book will be based on your "Guerrilla Pop" columns in the *Los Angeles Reader*. Can you tell me about it?

SE: I hope to publish a collection of pieces on American pop culture, defining the term very broadly. Because I would want the book to represent where I am now as a writer, those would not be the "Guerrilla Pop" columns I published in the early eighties but rather essays written since *Leap Year*—before, during, and after *Arc d'X*. Nothing about this is definite, but it's possible such a book could come out next year.

An Interview with Steve Erickson

Larry McCaffery and Takayuki Tatsumi / 1995

Originally published in *Contemporary Literature* 38, no. 3 (1997): 395–421. © 1997 by the Board of Regents of the University of Wisconsin system. Reprinted by permission of the University of Wisconsin Press.

During the past decade, Steve Erickson has published six remarkable, visionary books of great stylistic virtuosity and thematic ambition. These include *Leap Year* (1989) and *American Nomad* (1997)—highly personalized accounts of the 1988 and 1996 presidential elections that mix journalism, political commentary, and wild flights of fancy—and five visionary, post-apocalyptic novels: *Days Between Stations* (1985), *Rubicon Beach* (1986), *Tours of the Black Clock* (1989), *Arc d'X* (1993), and *Amnesiascope* (1996). These books all combine features of the magical realists' exaggeration of the familiar with Faulkner's mesmerizing rhetoric and ability to explode time and space. The end result is a haunting and grotesque evocation of the shattered nature of twentieth-century life and its ongoing love affair with fascism and violence.

Steve Erickson's work has been decisively informed by the experience of having grown up in one of Los Angeles's innumerable suburban communities, where Erickson witnessed a mind-boggling series of physical transformations; equally significant was the impact on his sensibility of the wider cultural, political, and social upheavals that occurred during the late sixties and early seventies, while he was working on a film degree at UCLA. Collectively and individually, his novels have captured more convincingly than any writer since Nathanael West Los Angeles's peculiar ability to disorient and deceive with its glitzy, seductive facades and illusions. Erickson's Los Angeles differs from novel to novel in terms of its particulars, but it is always a surreal, utterly fluid landscape where volcanoes belch fire and brimstone, rivers and enormous condo developments appear and disappear from one day to the next, and characters become lost within their own

houses and memories as they wander through bizarre, subterranean labyrinths in doomed efforts to find love and make sense of their existence.
It was the presence of these seemingly futuristic, dystopian narrative
elements that led to Erickson's finding a home for his fiction within the
relatively insular science fiction publishing scene: his first five books were all
published by Poseidon Press, a respected SF publisher best known for having
released early, seminal works by William Gibson, Bruce Sterling, and Joanna
Russ. But although Erickson's association with SF at least permitted his
fiction to be published when commercial presses showed no interest in his
work, it has ultimately been unfortunate and misleading in a number of ways.
A literary descendant of William Faulkner, Gabriel García Márquez, and
Bob Dylan in his midsixties visionary period, rather than of Ray Bradbury,
Isaac Asimov, and the cyberpunks, Erickson has never been embraced by
SF readers and critics, most of whom are bewildered by his works' daunting
formal difficulties, their emphasis on passion and psychology at the expense
of rationality and science, and their fiercely moralistic treatment of self and
society. The disorienting spatial and temporal features of Erickson's fiction
are created not in the service of attempting to describe some possible future,
but as a formal means of capturing a sense of Los Angeles's dizzying ability
to alienate its citizens from each other and from themselves, and to wreak
havoc on time and space. Likewise, the nightmarish dystopias that recur in
Erickson's novels are not SF trappings but literalizations of his sense that
the ideals of the American Dream have withered in the harsh desert of the
real. For Erickson, as for Nathanael West and Thomas Pynchon before him,
Los Angeles is much more than a sprawling, smoggy megalopolis: it's the
end of the Yellow Brick Road, the world's dream dump, the place where
all the original promises of the American Dream find their most vivid
incarnation—and their most traumatic betrayal.

What has not yet been recognized by reviewers or critics is the degree to
which Erickson has used his setting, characters, and plot materials as a means
of metaphorizing, exorcising, and otherwise projecting outward aspects of
his own psyche, a region of blasted hopes, confusion, idealism, self-lacerating
guilt, and perpetual isolation. His fiction thus becomes a kind of magical
looking glass reflecting back to himself and his readers a dark, troubling,
but extraordinarily vivid self-portrait of an artist struggling to strike through
the mask of illusion and self-deception and uncover the real. Always this
struggle is linked to efforts to find love and some source of personal security
in a world whose spatial and temporal coordinates have become warped by
psychological forces as well as those of technologically driven change.

This interview was conducted on a rain-drenched afternoon in Steve Erickson's apartment in central Hollywood in January 1995. Now in his midforties, Erickson is initially likely to strike people as boyish and somewhat reserved. Throughout the interview, he responded to our questions thoughtfully, his replies delivered with a hint of the stutter he's had to live with since childhood. As an affliction that constantly threatens to compromise self-expression, stuttering has an impact on people's lives that is often far greater than the relative severity of its symptoms might suggest. In *Amnesiascope*, Erickson's most recent novel, stuttering becomes a dark and troubling abyss whose personal and metaphorical dimensions are simultaneously projected outward and inward. But as is the case with all his work to date, approaching this abyss proves to be a liberating rather than paralyzing experience, for Erickson and for his readers.

Q: Do you see any radical departures, either formally or thematically, from your earlier books in what you've been doing in your new novel, *Amnesiascope*?

A: That's not an easy question for me to respond to because I'm really not much aware of either the differences or similarities in my work. For instance, people sometimes find my fiction and my journalism very different, which is something I'm not aware of at all. I guess my first five novels culminated in *Arc d'X*—that's what they were all evolving toward. On the other hand, *Amnesiascope* is probably either the end of something or the beginning, or both—a coda or a prelude. It's the bridge between *Arc d'X* and my first novel, *Days Between Stations*, and turns the meaning of the earlier books inside out. It seems entirely possible to me that it could wind up displeasing everyone, dismaying the readers who have liked my work in the past while failing to convince those who haven't. For better or worse, it's not necessarily what people expect from me.

Q: What makes it so different from what you've been doing?

A: Well, it's a much more personal book than anything I've done. It's a much more naked book. It takes the landscape of my earlier novels and places on that landscape someone who rather unabashedly bears a resemblance to myself. It's set in Los Angeles and is much more contained in time and space and point of view.

Q: Of course, all your books have been set in some version of LA, even if it's not identified as such.

A: This is identifiably Los Angeles, although transformed—a "post–Los Angeles," with fleeting similarities to the one we know, where all the cultural immunities have collapsed, so that any random influence permeates the city's membrane. A somewhat fantastic backdrop against which I've addressed more personal concerns. Writing this particular book was trying in a way the others weren't, though both *Arc d'X* and *Tours of the Black Clock* were completely exhausting. Sometimes I felt very good about it and sometimes I despaired. It was a more subjective experience than the others, because it's personal and also quite sexual. But I always felt reasonably confident that, for better or worse, it was the book I was supposed to write, so when I started worrying about what people were going to think of it, I just had to set those worries aside and keep going. What people think is beyond my control.

Q: And yet all the things you've just said about this new book—how personal it is, its sexuality, that it's set in a transformed LA that serves as a backdrop that allows you to explore your own life—haven't they really been true of all your books, though maybe not so obviously?

A: Well, exactly. What makes this one feel different is that I relied less on the intermediary of fiction.

Q: So you're not relying here on any hints of the magical realism of your previous books?

A: I doubt anyone will call this magical realism. Surreal perhaps— there's a kaleidoscopic quality to the structure and the storytelling. But the big shifts in time and space and point of view that have characterized my earlier books are gone. The people who like mainstream fiction aren't likely to consider it very mainstream. Like my other books, it's not really fish or fowl—not mainstream enough for the mainstream and not avant-garde enough for the avant-garde.

Q: It's interesting that you say your new book is surreal but not magical realism. You've said that you don't consider your earlier books to be sur-realistic. Why not?

A: Surrealism was born out of a preoccupation with the irrationality and illogic of the subconscious, and a view that human relationships are fundamentally absurd. Whatever else my books may be about, they don't express an absurd view of existence. The form of the books, and the strange juxtapositions of their narratives, may strike people as surreal, but the central concerns that drive the stories are traditional ones. I don't think any true surrealist would consider me a surrealist, in the same way no hard-core science fiction fan would consider me a science fiction writer, since the basic concern of most classic science fiction is the relationship between man and technology. Philip K. Dick and Theodore Sturgeon and a few others are exceptions. Technology is a completely valid and important topic to write about, but it just doesn't happen to interest me. And my books aren't "experimental" because my priorities don't involve reinventing literary forms, and they're not fantastic because they're not characterized by the sense of wonder that fantasy evokes. I think it's been hard for my novels to find a niche.

Q: Do you see your books as being postmodernist?

A: You know, I've never been entirely clear what "postmodern" means. But to at least some extent postmodernism seems to involve a cultural or aesthetic self-awareness, and an insistence on art recognizing and tweaking its own artifice. My aim isn't to call attention to the artifice of my books but to make readers forget the artifice, to persuade them to exchange their reality for the one I've created. I'm aware that trying to get readers to give themselves over to another reality is always doomed to failure. On the other hand, that's the job of the novelist, to fail and fail again. The great hope isn't to succeed—I'm not sure what success would really mean—but to risk everything, and perhaps to fail by narrower margins, until there's nothing left to fail with.

Q: That sounds admirable but inevitably frustrating—knowing you won't ever break on through but taking consolation from the act of trying. It seems related to something else I sense in your books that's difficult to explain—a masochism or self-laceration that seems to emerge.

A: Oh, I'm big on guilt. Scandinavians are big on it—just watch a few Ingmar Bergman films. My mother, who is not Scandinavian, is almost guilt-free—she can't understand where all my guilt comes from. One of my friends has a theory that in every family each member is designated to carry a particular burden, and that in my family I am the designated guilt-bearer.

Q: Could you talk a bit about the process of how your books actually get written? What is it that seems to get you started with a new book, and then what sustains it if you don't know where it's going?

A: With each of my books there's always been something that, for one reason or another, was unresolved, which led to the next. After *Days Between Stations*, there were still things I wanted to say about Los Angeles, so I wrote *Rubicon Beach*. After *Rubicon Beach*, there were still things I wanted to say about the twentieth century, so I wrote *Tours of the Black Clock*. After *Tours*, there were still things I wanted to say about history and politics, so that led to *Leap Year*, where the sections about Sally Hemings led to *Arc d'X*. For me the surprise of *Arc d'X* were the passages that suddenly lapsed into the first person—or into a third person that had the effect of first-person confession—and I realized that was where I was going next.

Q: So you more or less plunge into the writing of your books without knowing where they are going? For example, were these first-person voices in *Arc d'X* unexpected?

A: I don't outline the books, because I want to leave room for the surprises, particularly since I tend to be a little compulsive and obsessive, and so I want to counteract those tendencies by not plotting things out too much. If anything, *Amnesiascope* was less defined in my head than the others. You know, I had a vague sense of how it was going to end—unless I changed my mind—and for the first time I made some notes, because the book is fragmented, something like a memoir, and because as I get older I don't seem to remember things as well. But essentially the writing process was the same. I wanted to leave myself as much room as I could for the unexpected. Sometimes I went back to the notes, and, often as not, sometimes I wound up ignoring them altogether.

Q: You reportedly destroyed a number of book-length manuscripts that you wrote almost fifteen years ago. Did those early manuscripts contain any of the unresolved issues that led you to later books? Or do you find yourself incorporating aspects of those destroyed texts into anything now?

A: Every once in a while something from one of those early novels, that's been buried in the seabed of my unconsciousness for twenty years, pops loose and floats to the surface. I destroyed those early manuscripts because once I finally became a published novelist with *Days Between Stations*, I knew I was at a point where I was going to go forward or backward, and I didn't want to go back. And at the risk of sounding really presumptuous, I also didn't like the idea of someone rummaging through my garage after I dropped dead and finding these things and putting them out. I'm not saying there aren't connections between the forms and concerns of my early books and what I've done since. But I was aware when I destroyed those books that when I wrote them I wasn't good enough to pull off what I was trying to do.

Q: Were those earlier books written in a more conventional manner?

A: Not necessarily. In some ways they may have been less conventional.

Q: While you were a student at UCLA you were awarded a Samuel Goldwyn Award for one of those early novels. Is it available at the library?

A: No. It was never published. You know, the Goldwyns were usually awarded to screenplays and television scripts, and so the decision to give it to fiction was pretty controversial. They wound up suspending the prizes for a year or two afterward, and then when they brought them back fiction was no longer eligible.

Q: Your generation of writers has been assimilating various formal features—for example, ways of structuring and organizing narratives—from different sorts of nonliterary media such as film, rock music, and television, and of course you started out at UCLA as a film student and have been a film reviewer. Do you feel that your literary sensibility has been influenced by film or other media forms?

A: Sure. I don't think there's any question that I've been influenced by movies and rock 'n' roll. After all, at the point when I was first starting to think seriously about being a writer—back in the sixties—the postwar era of mainstream fiction in America seemed pretty dismal. For whatever reason, John Updike and Saul Bellow didn't mean all that much to me. Maybe they should have. As much as the fiction writers who had a formative influence on my writing, it was Dylan and John Lennon and Van Morrison, Neil Young and Lou Reed and Bruce Springsteen who had a big impact on me. Pretty much the usual suspects. I've said before that in some ways Ray Charles may have changed me more than any single artist of any medium. I grew up in the San Fernando Valley, a very white-bread childhood, and I didn't hear any rock 'n' roll or rhythm and blues when I was a little kid in the fifties. I didn't have any brothers or sisters to expose me to it, and my parents certainly had no use for Elvis Presley, for instance. I was pretty much raised on Frank Sinatra and Tony Bennett and Nat Cole, and I still like all those guys—the Sinatra of the late fifties, in particular the torch albums like *Where Are You?* and *Only the Lonely*, still move me as much as anyone. But to my folks' credit they liked Ray Charles, and hearing him when I was ten or twelve, around 1960 or 1962, was a shock. It rearranged all the furniture in my head. All my rigid, refined ideas about what art was supposed to be, all my most formal notions, were profoundly shaken, and all the things I valued, as a kid who probably took school a little too seriously for his own good, were replaced by new values—refinement by passion, polish by energy. Again and again over the years the art that's moved me in some cataclysmic fashion has been that which unsettled my most rarefied, elitist ideas, and musically that included *Highway 61 Revisited* and *Otis Blue* and *Astral Weeks* and John Lennon's first solo album and the Stooges' *Fun House* and Patti Smith's *Horses* and "Anarchy in the U.K." It seems obvious to me that Dylan is the single most important writer of my generation. Those albums he put out in the midsixties, from *Bringing It All Back Home* through *Blonde on Blonde* and *The Basement Tapes* and *John Wesley Harding*, are really the great American novels of the time. They're mystic journeys through frontier towns and women's bedrooms and mythic cities of the American imagination. Those records reclaimed for popular culture the kind of visionary surrealism of the soul that surrealism abandoned later in various sorts of nihilistic piques, and I'm sure they had a similar influence on a lot of other American writers of my generation. I'm not talking just about Dylan's words but the *sound* of those albums—the organ and guitars and drums and above all his voice.

Q: What about films—weren't you actually planning on a film career at that point?

A: Pretty quickly I realized that my temperament and whatever talent I have were more suited to writing novels. Since I often fear that fiction is an obsolete art form, it would have been nice to have been a filmmaker or rock 'n' roll musician, but, for better or worse, I was probably born to write novels. There's no doubt films and television were formative influences on my work, but what writer of my generation can't say that? When I was growing up, *The Million Dollar Movie* would play *Invaders from Mars* on Channel 9 every day for a week, and every day for a week I watched it, and things like that shape the way you conceive of narrative in ways that are difficult to explain. Reviewers have referred to my fiction as being "cinematic," but the truth is my work doesn't take place so much in the camera's eye as in the mind's eye, or maybe the mind's version of the camera's eye, and in the last days of the twentieth century, distinctions between the artifice of the media and the artifice of the mind become more difficult to make. I suppose I became a film student at UCLA because by 1968 it was clear to anyone with open eyes or an open mind that movies were the great emerging art form of the twentieth century.

Q: You've mentioned in earlier interviews that your talent and temperament aren't suited for having to work collaboratively, the way filmmaking demands. What did you mean?

A: That from a personal and creative standpoint I would just as soon never leave my apartment. What suits me best is sitting alone in a room talking to myself for twenty-four hours a day and having as little civilized social intercourse as possible. In college I realized I couldn't be both a filmmaker and a novelist because either one would require a complete commitment, so I had to make a choice and while I had some reason to believe I might have the kind of sensibility necessary to write novels, I had no reason to believe that might be true of making films. Also, the novel is one of the few creative endeavors over which the artist has something approaching complete control.

Q: In *Arc d'X* you deal directly with the problem of slavery, but even as early as *Days Between Stations* you were already exploring it.

A: Slavery has been a running theme in my books. The slavery Sally has to deal with in *Arc d'X* exists as much in her head as it does socially—she struggles against how her sense of identity has been bound to the men in her life and their expectations of her. Related to this are the themes of submission and domination. These things are part of the dynamic between people, and there are times to liberate yourself from that dynamic and times to creatively use it.

Q: Any time you fall in love with someone, you give yourself over to a form of slavery. You have said that your work is not overtly political, but many people assume it is. Certainly the last two books were specifically concerned with fascism. But I've sensed that the political dimensions that are so apparent in your books are only part of what's going on—that perhaps these books are even more fundamentally about personal relationships and the control and submission that goes with them.

A: There are two ways to look at it. Some argue that all emotional, psychological, and sexual concerns are, at base, political. Others argue that all political concerns are, at base, emotional, psychological, or sexual. I fall into the second group: I think politics is a manifestation of psychology and sexuality, rather than sexuality being a manifestation of politics.

Q: How would you describe the evolution of your work? To what extent have your formal and thematic interests changed over the years?

A: I suppose that over the course of my books the dark and the light have each pushed farther out from the center. It's not something I consciously strive for. My books pretty much chart their own trajectories.

Q: In January [1995] you published a piece in the *Los Angeles Times Magazine* called "American Weimar," about totalitarianism and politics in contemporary America. The appeal of totalitarianism is something you've examined in different ways in several of your books—it's obviously central, for example, to both *Tours of the Black Clock* and *Arc d'X*. Is there a sense in which you think Americans have voluntarily given themselves over to authority? I've begun to come to the conclusion that the long-term effect of "postmodernism"—the attack on dogmatic attitudes, the recognition that values and meanings aren't absolutes but really do arise out of contexts—has been to strengthen the appeal of fascism. In the absence of values and any sense of higher purpose, Americans seem to be increasingly willing to give up their freedom. Rather than being exhilarated by postmodernism's program of deconstruction, there's a nostalgic longing for submission and the shiny boots and being able to give yourself to something so you can march in step—a great, troubling irony.

A: It seems Americans have come to feel more burdened by freedom than invigorated by it, and at the crux of this profound disillusionment is the illusion of innocence. Whether it's assassinations or political scandals or O. J. driving down the freeway, it seems like nothing happens in this country that isn't interpreted by the media or the culture as the end of American innocence, and it's a little odd, since America has never been an innocent country. It's not possible for a country that was born out of the twin experiences of wiping out all the people who were originally here and bringing over people in chains in the hulls of boats to be innocent. Which isn't to say that America isn't a genuinely idealistic country, and which isn't even to say this idealism is necessarily hypocritical. The great paradox of America has been the conflict between its true idealism and its false innocence, and this pathological contradiction is at the root of the country's current cynicism and spiritual bankruptcy. When we began to come face-to-face with the fact that we're not an innocent people, one of two things was going to happen: America was either going to grow up or begin to die because it couldn't stand the truth, and because everything it believed about itself was based on a delusion. Lately the country's been dying more than growing. There certainly remains a lot of denial in America. The most popular movie of 1994 was one in which the quintessential American was portrayed as noble precisely for how dimwitted he was. *Forrest Gump* was a pretty neat manifestation of America's ongoing struggle to hang on to this idea of itself as innocent.

Q: Of course, these contradictory impulses were already being exposed back in the nineteenth century by writers like Melville, Hawthorne, Poe, and Twain. So what is responsible for this massive increase in disillusionment? Are we collectively acting any worse now than we were back then? Or does the media today make it more difficult to maintain the denial mode?

A: It's an accumulation of things that were born out of the Puritanism and repression that were part of this country from the start. Americans are now fifty years removed from the redeeming experience of World War II, where we could say, without any real fear of history contradicting us, that we were the good guys, and in that fifty years we've had nothing but experiences that taint that sense of righteousness. The media has played a big part in this— its growing omnipresence has forced us to see aspects of ourselves that previously could just be conveniently ignored or disguised. We're caught in a series of profound and deeply disturbing paradoxes: We've won the Cold War and we don't feel good about it, the economy is empirically improving and we don't feel secure in it, crime is statistically declining and we don't feel safe, we live in an age of sexual repression while being exposed to a constant cultural barrage of sexuality, albeit an artificial sort of sexuality. All of this has alienated us from ourselves in fundamental ways. The violence we dread we also glamorize. The sexuality that our Puritan roots condemn we live out vicariously through the media, even while AIDS makes sexual contact less tenable and accessible. These are paradoxes of experience we're unable to resolve, and Americans aren't people who have much use for ambiguity. We like to see things in clear-cut terms, whether they're clear-cut or not. Of course, as you pointed out, things in this country have never really been clear-cut, but the American antipathy to ambiguity is finally catching up with us.

Q: The Vietnam War was one of the defining moments in post–World War II America—and it wound up affecting not only the American men who went over there but those who didn't as well.

Even those of us who didn't go—I know you got a high lottery number—and who were convinced it was a good thing we didn't go—as I gather you were—had to deal with the fact that we didn't go while others around us did. There was a sense of guilt, or at least ambivalence, that you can still see being played out today in how emotionally charged the debates about Clinton's antiwar sentiments are.

A: Before Vietnam, American men grew up with the idea of war as a crucible. The experience of war was one in which you passed from being a boy to a man and found out who you were. Those of us who didn't go to Vietnam obviously didn't have that experience, and those who did were so shattered by the experience that what identity they had left they had to pick up in pieces. As a country we still haven't come to terms with the fact that Vietnam was a perfectly useless war. Ronald Reagan tried to sell the idea that there was something noble about it, and we almost intuitively assume that the grief we feel about it has a redeeming quality all its own. But thirty years later, particularly given the collapse of Communism, no one can offer a single sound argument why that war had to be fought. To come to terms with Vietnam, America would have to accept that fifty-eight thousand Americans died for nothing, not to mention perhaps hundreds of thousands of Vietnamese. That kind of acceptance is not something we're good at. In fairness, I don't suppose any country would be very good at it. So Americans continue to try to revise the story of the war, because the nihilism that's the true lesson of Vietnam is something we recoil from. That's part of the problem with Clinton. The great moral and political failure of his 1992 presidential campaign was that he didn't or couldn't or wouldn't speak forthrightly about his opposition to the war. So part of the country—the part that still supports if not the war then the impulses that lead to it—feels more comfortable with the position of a Dan Quayle, who dodged the war but supported it anyway as a fine war for someone else to die in. In the eyes of many Americans, somehow the hypocrisy of Quayle's position absolves him, while Clinton's refusal to serve out of opposition to the war is a restatement of the argument that it was a bad war. So while the country elected Clinton, it abhors the meaning of having done so. If that isn't profound national confusion, I don't know what is.

Q: This fundamental ambiguity surrounding Vietnam seems to be related to what was happening in the programs of deconstruction and postmodernism; it would have been nice if Vietnam "made sense," but it didn't—just as a lot of other dogmas we used to believe in were revealed to be constructs. Getting rid of those dogmas was a great "victory," but it's also created a huge hole or void for Americans—all we seemed to have left to fill it with in the eighties was hyperconsumption.

A: But the dogmas that have collapsed about so many other things still haven't collapsed about sex, for instance. The sexual argument in this country remains one between repression on the one hand and promiscuity on the other.

Q: You wrote in *Leap Year* that America is a country founded by sexual neurotics.

A: George Washington was in unrequited love with his neighbor's wife. There's circumstantial evidence, the protests of Jefferson scholars notwithstanding, that Jefferson may have had a long sexual relationship with a slave. In Paris, Benjamin Franklin was rumored to be sleeping with everything from little boys to sheep, and a very twisted relationship with a prostitute blew up in Alexander Hamilton's face, almost ending his career.

Q: Can one read a figure like Gary Hart into this mold then?

A: The appetites that disqualified Hart from the presidency characterized a lot of the people who founded this country. Personally, I found Hart's reckless sexual behavior less dangerous than Nixon's reckless asexual behavior.

Q: In *Leap Year* you credited Gary Hart with what you called a "nuclear imagination." What is that?

A: An imagination that's liberated by the abyss, that finds a measure of freedom in confronting the abyss rather than being terrorized or paralyzed or overwhelmed by it.

Q: In *Leap Year* it seems that you were not only dealing with political issues but also talking about your own literary imagination, your own poetics—do you see any analogies between the nuclear imagination and postmodernist rhetoric?

A: I certainly wouldn't limit the nuclear imagination to the nuclear era, let alone the postmodern one. I mean, Dostoyevsky is as good an example of nuclear imagination as any. When working on *Leap Year*, preposterous as it sounds in retrospect, I was under this weird spell in which I thought 1988 was going to be a watershed year for this country. I actually thought 1988 would be a really fascinating and fun presidential election to write about. I mean, here you had the end of the Reagan era, with no incumbent seeking the presidency for the first time in twenty years, and it also seemed that, as far as the United States was concerned, the twentieth century was about to play itself out in spectacular fashion. I thought it was going to be Mario Cuomo against Jack Kemp, which is to say two serious men of intellectual integrity, whether you agree with them or not, and that people would be forced to make choices that would either lurch us into or withdraw us from the future. It was only after I was well into the book that I realized this premise was totally insane, since it turned out that 1988 was a year when people put big decisions about the country on hold.

Q: Why wasn't America ready to make that great leap forward yet?

A: We weren't ready to leap because we still had one more impulse left to exhaust, after the others of idealism, realism, heroism, confidence, and naïveté that had characterized the previous half dozen elections. That was the impulse of cynicism. George Bush, of course, was the perfect vehicle for this impulse—in fact his cynicism was ultimately *too* naked and complete for Americans to accept, which is why Clinton won the 1992 election. By 1992 Bush's cynicism was so manifest that Americans couldn't deny it even in the midst of all their other denials. To have elected Bush again would have been to have denied the future and accepted the inevitability of betrayal, and that would have been spiritual death, because it would have meant we no longer dared to have faith. 1992 was the first important American presidential election of the twenty-first century, which is almost certainly going to devour itself even faster than the twentieth century has. In 1992 Americans were faced with the prospect of departing this century revealed as a country for which cynicism was the only identity left, but some constant of American faith was intact enough not to allow that to happen.

Q: At what point did Sally's voice begin to emerge in *Leap Year*? Where did that voice come from?

A: I honestly don't remember. I do know that I heard her talking pretty early on, and as it became more and more apparent that the election was going to be a lot more dismal than I could stomach, I got more interested in her voice. The truth is that the Sally Hemings episodes in *Leap Year* are the least satisfying parts of the book. I didn't do as much with her as I would have liked, in part because the concept of the book didn't really allow for it. Afterward I felt like I needed to go back and reexplore things that had presented themselves to my surprise, especially the contradictions in Jefferson. This is a good example of the kind of unfinished business in one book that carries over into the next. With *Arc d'X* I wanted to get more deeply into the impossible conflict between Jefferson's ideals and his passions. Here was a guy who, as a young man and member of the Virginia legislature, tried to pass a number of measures that would have loosened the bonds of slavery in America, but later, as his power and reputation and moral stature grew, his passion for abolition diminished, just about the time he became the only man other than Washington who might have addressed the issue of slavery and gotten away with it. I became fascinated with the idea that perhaps Jefferson loved Sally and that, in America at that time, the only way a free white man could love a Black woman was if he owned her. If Sally had been free, the culture and society would not have accepted their relationship, but because Jefferson owned her as a slave, society turned its head, at least until he got down to the business of running for president. It was the fascination of placing Jefferson within that kind of web that initially inspired *Arc d'X*.

Q: Your ancestry includes Swedish relatives on your father's side and French-Indian on your mother's. I'm wondering if your own Native American heritage might have had some influence on your decision to focus *Arc d'X* on issues like slavery and genocide.

A: I'm conscious of my Indian background, but I feel presumptuous making too much of it. I would feel like I'm trading on some kind of trendy ethnic glamour. I was aware of it distantly, because I'm just enough Indian to be on the rolls of the Bureau of Indian Affairs and receive a tribal newsletter every once in a while. I don't think my children would be enough Indian to qualify unless I had children by a woman who was at least as much part Indian as I am. So I don't have a great deal of Indian ancestry, and yet it's enough that I've been made officially aware of it through the years. And I used to get some residual money from tribal oil lands in Oklahoma.

Q: It may be just a coincidence, but I've noticed a lot of references and allusions to *The Wizard of Oz* in recent works I'm interested in—they're there in Salman Rushdie's last story collection, in David Blair's *Wax, or the Discovery of Television among the Bees*, and of course in your own books. What's the basis of your own references?

A: I grew up with the *Oz* novels. I read most of them. I particularly remember *Ozma of Oz* and *Rinkitink in Oz*. They were very strange books, dark in a way the movie just hints at—not particularly light-hearted children's fantasies. They were as close to early American surrealism as they were to fairy tales, and you can see the influence they had, for instance, on Philip K. Dick. As I got older, it was a natural evolution from the *Oz* books and *Arabian Nights* to comics and science fiction and crime fiction, and all of that was just part of a larger stew. By the time I got to so-called serious fiction, it was only one more component of what interested me, whereas I guess that for the generations of writers that preceded mine there was still a strong sense that the recipe for serious literature couldn't possibly include what the elite would consider trash.

Q: You were saying earlier that your writing isn't so much specifically cinematic as it re-creates the "mind's eye"—which has been influenced by your exposure to visual media. I've noticed that a lot of writers I'm talking to recently have admitted that their imaginations are deeply informed by forms that they encountered as kids—comic books, for example, and especially cartoons. Critics haven't spent much time examining these sorts of influences, but the long-term effects, at least on some artists, seem undeniable to me. For instance, cartoons are very surrealistic—there's a certain plasticity to the form, a physics of cartoons, which is akin to surrealism. When I interviewed Mark Leyner, he said that the experience of watching Bugs Bunny and other Warner Brothers cartoons had a major influence on his narrative imagination. You mentioned earlier that you don't work from an outline, so that you don't necessarily know where your novels are heading. Did you know in the case of *Arc d'X* that it would start in the past and jump-cut to the present?

A: Yes.

Q: One way your work differs from science fiction is precisely these sorts of unexplained leaps that are never logically or scientifically explained. Do you introduce mysterious events because that's how you think the world works? Or is it an aesthetic choice or an aesthetic device? A different way to put this would be, Why don't you write in a more mimetic, "realistic" manner?

A: There's never been much calculation on my part to write this kind of book over another kind. That just isn't part of the way I work. I write the way I do because I seem to have to write that way. I honestly wish I was more naturally inclined to write a linear story. I certainly don't mean for my books to be difficult. Actually, if there was any calculation in *Arc d'X*, it was to try to make it more accessible than my previous books.

Q: For all the "difficulty" of your fiction, your works are also real page-turners—there's a kind of compulsive feel to them that draws the reader along, despite the leaps in time and space.

A: Partly because my stories are not very linear, I try to follow a linear, sequential process in writing them, by which I mean that I start at page 1 and write to the end, because I want to have the same sense the reader has of being pulled along, as you say. I'm certainly not looking for ways to make the reader's progress difficult or confusing. I want to involve the reader as deeply as I can in what I'm talking about, which is really all the old stuff—love and freedom, sex and history, redemption, obsession and idealism, identity, self-delusion, and—

Q: Memory.

A: Especially memory. As the title would indicate, memory is a big theme in *Amnesiascope*. The main character wants to transcend the memory that seems to have overwhelmed or paralyzed him. He looks at Los Angeles as a wide screen empty of memory and all its meaning, and he strives to forget the unforgettable, in order to go on.

Q: You've said elsewhere that this emphasis on memory in your work has to do partly with how you grew up—the way things kept changing so radically and repeatedly.

A: I'm sure the way my narratives work so disjunctively has a lot to do with growing up in Los Angeles, watching the landscape change constantly. I grew up in the San Fernando Valley in the 1950s, before it became the perfect metaphor for modern American suburbia. My neighborhood was very rural—there were ranches and horses and orchards and strange white mansions standing alone out on open plains. We moved into a tract house in one of those neighborhoods that were springing up all over the LA suburbs, and then within ten years the neighborhood was gone—the dust and horses and orchards and eucalyptus trees that had totally disappeared and were replaced by lawns and pools and malls were all finally replaced by a freeway. Later I went back to see the house where I grew up, and the house was gone but the swimming pool was still there, along with my next-door neighbor's house—the new freeway had just missed it. So there you had the ultimate symbol of my relationship to my childhood—only part of it was still there at all, this patch of blue shimmering in the twilight, and it was claimed by the next-door neighbor's chain-link fence, while everything else seemed like a dream. The point is that while I was growing up, this kind of radical change simply was part of my experience of the way things operated. And these metamorphoses weren't occurring just on a year-by-year basis but day by day, until by the time I was a teenager there was literally nothing around me to connect me with what I had known as a child. Later when I went to Europe, at the age of twenty, where I found myself surrounded by buildings and streets that hadn't changed for hundreds of years, I recognized that this acceleration of time and physical change was unusual. That's when I realized what a truly peculiar place Los Angeles is.

Q: I see in your work a blend of Faulkner and Márquez, both of whom were also obsessed with memory and with developing a formal means to convey this obsession. Have these writers been important influences?

A: Faulkner was the most significant. Faulkner taught me how reality ticks not to the clock of time but the clock of memory—in *The Sound and the Fury*, the idiot Benjy begins a sentence in the present, and by the time the sentence is halfway finished we're thrust into the past, and by the time the sentence is over we're back in the present, or maybe we've gone somewhere else, all of this conveyed as part of the continuum of consciousness. Faulkner's structures were brilliant, revolutionary. His greatest characters exist both as grand symbols or metaphors and people possessing intricate, poetically evoked psyches that emerge from specific human circumstances. What's remarkable is that the ways in which these characters are abstractions never detract from their humanity—Faulkner keeps both aspects coexisting somehow, so that Joe Christmas, the crazed, lost, enraged figure of *Light in August*, who literally doesn't know if he's a Black man or white, comes alive for the reader as someone very real and yet also as the embodiment of everything that's hopeful and damned about America. Henry Miller had a big impact on me, not because of the sexuality of his work but because of the nakedness and emotional intensity. He was willing to reveal himself utterly, no matter the consequences, and in the process he wound up breaking through a lot of artificial distinctions and integrating things we're usually told to keep separate—lyricism and vulgarity, the body and the spirit, the cosmos and the gutter. Whitman did the same thing, obviously. I'd say that Márquez, on the other hand, was more of a crystallizing influence than a formative one, mostly because I came to his work later. When I read Márquez I saw how he had been able to apply the lessons of Faulkner to his own particular experience, and all this helped to bring into focus issues or concerns that were lurking somewhere in the back of my mind, but which I wasn't mature or talented or sophisticated enough to grasp or work out for myself.

Q: Obviously people today have a different relationship to memory than people had even twenty or thirty years ago. People today don't seem to have memory so much as *constructed* memories that are provided for us by the media, photographs, and other technological sources.

A: Given the media and the movies, we remember things that we never personally experienced. I have very clear and vivid memories of the forties because I've seen all those movies. The movies have created a collective memory for us.

Q: Has using a computer to write your books changed the writing?

A: I'm afraid the computer just indulges my most obsessive, anal tendencies. It gives me a chance to keep going over things, fiddling and fine-tuning, until at some point the process becomes potentially destructive and I have to make myself stop.

Q: Do you have any plans to deal with computer culture in your fiction?

A: Computers don't really interest me. The whole computer culture is something I just don't care much about. Online? Why? So I can talk to people I don't know or like? Half the time I don't want to talk to the people I *do* know and like. The idea of sitting at a computer all day writing a novel, and then conducting a social life on it as well—honestly, it almost makes me ill. When I'm done working I want to get the hell away from the computer, read a book or watch a movie. Don't get me wrong—I realize that cyberreality, if you will, is a completely valid area for fiction, and I have nothing but respect for pioneers like William Gibson who have been visionary enough to chart the new zeitgeist. But these people are writing about all this with a lot more intelligence and insight and imagination than I ever could, so nobody needs to hear from me about it.

Q: The epigraph to *Days Between Stations* by Pablo Neruda struck me as a perfect choice. Neruda's work represents to me many of the same things your own work does—he was someone who was trying to write about the inner through some exteriorization.

A: Neruda may be my favorite poet. The fantastic, surreal nature of his imagination somehow never lost its passion or soul or sensuality.

Q: You've mentioned Miller and Faulkner as writers you admired early on. Were you aware of what was going on in American fiction at that point—the fiction being written by people like Pynchon, Donald Barthelme, and Robert Coover?

A: You know, thirty years later I've still never read Coover. I've still never read Barthelme. God knows, I'm sure I should have. It's a huge lapse on my part. I've never read a lot of the writers I get compared to—Angela Carter, for instance. I didn't get around to J. G. Ballard until after I'd finished my second novel, *Rubicon Beach*, and people said, "Ah, right, Ballard," and pointed out that he had written a novel called *The Terminal Beach*. Honestly, I just never realized. I admire Don DeLillo for the integrity and intellectual adventurousness of what he does. Of course Pynchon, more than anyone else, is the novelist who found a way to express a post-Einsteinian literary synthesis and make it vital, and his influence today is pervasive almost in the same way Joyce's was seventy years ago, which means that if you're a serious novelist you have to come to terms with him one way or another, whether you like it or not. Now and then a few people have made comparisons between his work and mine, but we're not really that much alike. He's a slapstick anarchist on a cosmic scale, and by comparison I'm a cheap sentimentalist.

Q: Your writing also seems more emotional. But I have sometimes felt like comparing your character Dania in *Tours of the Black Clock* to Tyrone Slothrop in *Gravity's Rainbow* because whenever Dania dances someone seems to die, whereas whenever Slothrop has sex with someone, a V-2 rocket lands there.

A: I wasn't conscious of the similarity. In *Tours of the Black Clock* I apparently failed to make one particular clear. The real point of Dania's dancing has to do with voyeurism and obsession and men transforming women into their fantasies. In the scene when the detective Blaine is out on the little house on the river, he finally meets Dania, after all the time he's been watching and following her, and says to her that every time she dances, someone dies. And she says back, "Don't you see, it could just as easily have had nothing to do with me. It could just as easily have had everything to do with you. You thought someone was dying every time I danced, but maybe that wasn't it at all. Maybe someone was dying every time you watched me dance."

Q: What you've just said about voyeurism and sexual obsession in *Tours of the Black Clock* sounds almost like a gloss on some of Alfred Hitchcock's films, like *Vertigo* and *Rear Window*. Hitchcock was someone who was also taking deep, obsessive, and very personal themes and transforming them into art.

A: It's interesting that you would bring up Hitchcock in this connection because *Vertigo* is my favorite movie. And at the end, when Kim Novak falls to her death, who finally bears the responsibility for what's happened? Where does James Stewart's victimization end and hers begin?

Q: This notion of victimization seems related to what you've said is your favorite work of Natsume Soseki's, *Kokoro*.

A: Twenty years ago, in a little beach house I was subletting one hot July, I read *Kokoro* and *Wuthering Heights* back to back. That made for a very weird summer. Both books astounded me for how they were so ahead of their time. If *Kokoro* had been written by a writer in the West, first of all it probably wouldn't have been published, and if it had it would have revolutionized fiction two decades before the existentialists did. I guess it's indicative of Western chauvinism that we celebrate Western writers for doing something twenty years after a Japanese writer did it better. I only read a translation, of course, but even so the psychological precision of what Soseki was doing was extraordinary to me.

Q: But the real appeal of that book for Japanese readers was that it dealt with suicide. Japanese readers love that kind of thing—suicide, disappearance. For example, right now at the top of the bestseller list in Japan is a suicide handbook—a practical guide to disappearance. On the other hand, the Hollywood idiom seems to suggest that Americans prefer happy endings for their stories.

A: That's certainly true these days. These days you simply can't end a movie any other way. Even while Hollywood tries to revive noir, for all the wrong reasons, the studios would never allow for an ending as in *Out of the Past* or *Double Indemnity*, the two films that may best embody the spirit of noir. Something like *The Last Seduction* is exceptional for how, among contemporary movies, it actually manages to get close to the noir spirit. What Hollywood loves about noir is the style and glamour of it, not the desperation it expressed. Now it's all escapism, for which we have George Lucas and Steven Spielberg to thank, since they're the ones who have done it on a very popular and accomplished scale. This isn't taking anything away from Spielberg, who has obviously made some very good films, but with the exception of *Schindler's List*, whenever he's tried to make darker films the audiences have rejected him. *Empire of the Sun*, his most underrated movie, is the best example of that.

Q: By escapism, you mean something with a happy ending, not an alternative universe?

A: Fantasy, action, adventure, entertainment—I'm not putting any of that down. I love films like that myself, and there will always be a place for them. The problem is that nobody today in America can seem to make anything else, or at least get it financed and supported at a studio level.

Q: But it's important to retain a sharp sense of the ways different cultural sensibilities receive and create such forms. Americans seem to embrace these Hollywood fantasies of escape because they appeal to deep-seated cultural beliefs and desires.

You described *Kokoro* and *Wuthering Heights* as revolutionary. Georges Bataille once described *Wuthering Heights* as the "cruelest" novel ever written.

A: For a woman to have written a book so relentless, uncompromising, even cruel, as you say, in the mid-1800s was an utterly revolutionary act. Brontë was depicting the bonds between lust and hatred, the dark, utterly irrational and contradictory impulses that join people, in ways most Western authors weren't able to present so explicitly until well into the twentieth century. She subverts just about everything Western culture likes to believe about love and personality. That's a little of what I felt when I was reading *Kokoro*. But of course I don't know whether that book was revolutionary in terms of Japanese culture.

Q: In fact, contemporary Japanese readers see it as being the opposite of revolutionary—they see it as being traditional, even sentimental.

A: This just illustrates your point about how cultural differences shape the responses of audiences.

Q: Kobo Abe is a writer whose works seem very existentialist and who deals with the topic of disappearance in a dry, hard-boiled manner. And in fact I found some resemblances between Abe's *Woman in the Dunes* and your own *Days Between Stations*.

A: I saw the film of *Woman in the Dunes* not long after writing *Days Between Stations*, and I still have a vivid recollection of it.

Q: The Japanese people have long been obsessed with self-obliteration, self-effacement, a kind of "creative masochism." When I came across your comment that *Kokoro* was one of your favorite books, that got me to thinking about why your books appeal so much to Japanese audiences, why the Japanese seem to feel a great deal of sympathy with your sensibility.

A: I never thought of that.

Q: You mentioned earlier that you hadn't read many of the postmodern American writers. How much reading do you do?

A: For one thing, I'm a very slow reader. Secondly, I don't usually read fiction when I'm writing. Instead I read history, maybe some poetry or criticism. Lately, which is to say over the last six months, in the intervals between finishing *Amnesiascope*, I've been reading patches of *The Alexandria Quartet*, Carl Hiaasen, Neil Gaiman's *Sandman* graphic novels, a galley of Richard Kadrey's new novel, and a trilogy by Philip Kerr called *Berlin Noir*, about a private detective in Nazi Germany. If you can figure out the rhyme or reason of all that, I'd love to hear it. I start out with this rather grand reading plan and then it sort of falls apart, and I get drawn to things for reasons I don't understand.

Q: In one of your *LA Weekly* pieces where you were discussing Public Enemy, you said something very interesting about ambition: "Ambition is never ambiguous. By its nature ambition laces all art with the uncertainty of convictions that collide with megalomania, epic aspirations that meet grand pretensions." Would you say that applies to you?

A: You know, when his last novel came out, Martin Amis was quoted as saying something to the effect that he thought he was as good as any other novelist around, and better than most, and—among all the other things that they were mad at Amis for—people got very angry at that. They thought it was incredibly arrogant and egocentric, which I suppose it was. But I understood it completely, because unless you're just a hack or a careerist, given all the outer obstacles and inner doubts a serious novelist has to deal with, you're just not going to do anything good unless, at some level, you believe in yourself inordinately. It's not too easy to keep going otherwise. Once my publisher said to me, "I'm going to make you rich and famous," and I said, "I don't want to be rich and famous, I just want to be immortal." And it was a joke. But she repeated the line to a writer from *Publishers Weekly* who was doing a profile on me, and the writer asked me about it, and I confirmed that I had said it but added, "If you're going to print it, at least make clear it was a joke. At least make clear that I laughed when I said it." Well, of course the story came out and the writer didn't make that clear at all—the story just said, Steve Erickson wants to be immortal. And I probably looked like the same sort of arrogant asshole that Martin Amis does, and I think I may have paid for it in a review or two of *Arc d'X*. And even though as I've gotten older I find myself just trying to get by, just wanting to figure out what my work is supposed to be about in the final analysis, and hoping I'm not completely inconsequential in the process, and even as time passes and it begins to cross my mind that I'm not going to be as great as I one day hoped, that little dream is still there; those of us who do this never stop wanting to be immortal.

The Infrequency of Liberation: A Conversation with Steve Erickson

Ron Drummond / 1996

From *Steam Engine Time*, no. 2 (November 2011): 12–20, ed. Bruce Gillespie, Paul Kincaid, and Maureen Kincaid Speller. Reprinted by permission.

Steve Erickson's writing career began in the early eighties with "Guerilla Pop," a weekly column in the *LA Reader*. His first novel, *Days Between Stations*, was published in 1985, followed by *Rubicon Beach* in '86. During the late eighties/early nineties, Erickson was a film reviewer and staff writer for the *LA Weekly*, long the home of another brilliant LA essayist and novelist, Michael Ventura (both men quit the paper in 1993, in protest over the firing of its editor in chief). Erickson's other books include *Tours of the Black Clock* (1989), considered by many to be his finest novel; *Leap Year* (1989), a surreal travelogue and exercise in political fabulation that proved a dry run for his 1993 novel, *Arc d'X*; and *The Sea Came in at Midnight* (1999), a novel.

On June 8, 1996, Steve Erickson and I met in the bar of the Madison Renaissance in downtown Seattle. Erickson was promoting his then-new novel, *Amnesiascope*. He was also in the middle of writing a book on the 1996 presidential campaign, *American Nomad*, later published by Henry Holt. In the fall of '95, Erickson had been hired by *Rolling Stone* magazine to cover the 1996 election, but was fired in spring '96 after publishing only three articles. I began our conversation that June by asking him what happened.

Ron Drummond: Uppermost in my mind, what's the story with *Rolling Stone*?

Steve Erickson: We were never really on the same wavelength. *Rolling Stone* approached me and basically said, "We want a novelist who will cover the campaign like it's a novel." I said, "That sounds like it's kind of up my alley." But I don't think it was a concept that Jann Wenner ever understood. I don't think he was ever clear in his own mind what he really wanted.

Everybody at the magazine seemed to like what I was doing a lot, except him. I don't know exactly what he didn't like, except that I think he wanted something that was more straight reporting, and it was a battle from the very beginning. The first piece really came the closest to what I had conceived the assignment as being about. Then from that point on there was the sort of insidious pressure to become straighter and straighter, more and more conventional. And I bent about as far as I thought I could. I wound up writing five stories, of which he killed two.

At one point he flatly ordered me to cut something from one of the pieces that ran, and I just as flatly refused to do it. And it wound up running the way I wrote it, but I'm sure that that took a toll on our relationship. It was a battle, really, from the beginning, and they fired me. I probably thought, several times, during the month or two leading up to that point, about quitting. But it wasn't my style to quit. I'd been hired for the job, and I wanted to try to see the job through, if I could. But Wenner did not feel the same way.

RD: Which article was it that he flatly demanded that you cut and you refused?

SE: It was the piece I wrote about the Christian Right. The part where Alan Keyes—who was this Black, conservative talk show host—is addressing this convention of white Christian conservatives in Florida. It comes toward the end of the piece, the point where the piece stops being theoretical, and stops being a collection of interviews, and takes shape in the form of some kind of scene, some kind of human drama, and I just thought he was wrong. He never gave me a reason for cutting it—he just said, "Cut it."

RD: Did you ask him why?

SE: Sure. But I was informed that "Jann does not give reasons." Maybe he had a very good reason. I somehow doubt it, but it's possible.

So I wouldn't cut that, and I think they probably had no choice but to run it at that point, because the magazine was about to go to press. Now I'm writing a book instead. I do have a contract from Holt to write a book that is—I'm reluctant to call it a campaign book—it's part memoir and part travelogue through the year in which the country is having the last election of the millennium, and in the process there are these meditations about the meaning of America, sometimes as viewed through the context of pop culture, so the book will go off into discussions about Frank Sinatra or

Oliver Stone or Bruce Springsteen. And, you know, this book will be the one that I wanted to write for *Rolling Stone*, essentially.

RD: And you're probably gonna deal with the whole trip with *Rolling Stone* as well?

SE: Yeah. It's part of the story.

RD: So, it was more Wenner's head trip, as opposed to his corporate masters putting pressure on him or anything like that?

SE: No, this was Wenner. In fact, I think Wenner was getting pretty good feedback. He got a letter from, I think, Stephanopoulos at the White House saying he really liked the coverage, and that probably saved my job for a couple months. But he didn't know what to make of it, and without getting into a long, protracted psychological analysis of Jann Wenner, I get the feeling he's the kind of person who doesn't feel in control of things he doesn't understand.

RD: The second article, the one that was rejected, did that change the nature of the third article?

SE: Sure. The third piece—which wound up being the second piece that ran—was the piece about the Dole campaign in New Hampshire. They had killed the second piece, which was about the Republican straw poll in Orlando, and the convention that was held there, and the ways in which Orlando's both a very strange and very appropriate metaphor for American politics in general right now. It was flatly killed, and they had a hole in the magazine, and I sat down on a Friday night and, between seven and midnight, knocked out that Bob Dole piece, and sent it in the next day. And that too probably saved my job for a couple months—in fact I know it did.

RD: With *Arc d'X*, your *LA Weekly* gig ended three or four months after it was published; your *Rolling Stone* gig ended a couple of weeks before *Amnesiascope* came out. Doesn't it say you're covering the campaign for—

SE: Yeah, the jacket had already gone to press. I actually told the publicity people, "Don't go to press with this *Esquire* thing yet." After *Rolling Stone* fired me, *Esquire* put out the feelers, and said they'd like me to cover the campaign for them. And then that wound up falling through—I think in that case for reasons that had nothing to do with me, or *Esquire*, but for reasons that had to do with the campaign—the way the primary part of the campaign was over before it began.

What was originally fascinating about the campaign was that it looked like it might reflect the way the country was fracturing, that you might actually have a campaign that had four or five major candidates. Clinton and Dole and Powell and Perot and Buchanan, maybe. That is not going to come to pass, at least not on that scale. It's not as interesting or as cataclysmic as it looked like it might be.

RD: It must be a little frustrating for you, because you were kind of bankrolled by *Rolling Stone*, weren't you? They were flying you all over the country, you had the credentials, you could get to interview these guys, and then suddenly your economy of scale has shrunk considerably, I'm sure.

SE: Well, it shrank, and a certain credibility is gone. I'll tell you this, and it's between you and me until this thing runs: My idea for this book, the working title for which is *American Nomad*, is to continue to pass myself off as a *Rolling Stone* writer. I've got the *Rolling Stone* business cards, I've got the *Rolling Stone* stationery, and since *Rolling Stone*, in a story that's too petty to get into, basically cheated me out of twenty-five hundred dollars, I figure they owe me twenty-five hundred dollars' worth of credibility.

RD: But you've got to wonder, though: Couldn't they sue your ass?

SE: I don't know, I suppose if I'm not careful, it's possible. On what grounds would they do it, though?

RD: I don't know—misrepresenting yourself?

SE: The way I've been presenting myself is, "Hi, I'm Steve Erickson, and I've been covering the campaign for *Rolling Stone*." Not "I *am* covering the campaign for *Rolling Stone*." So there's a little legalistic loophole that Bill or Hillary Clinton would appreciate, and I figure I'll wiggle through that. And besides, it'll make for a good story in the book.

RD: Well, it sounds like you've thought it through rather carefully; obviously, you wouldn't even be doing it if you hadn't.

SE: Maybe not as carefully as I should. But there is a way in which both the entrée, not to say the money, were big losses when I left the *Rolling Stone* job. Now, with the book contract I wound up getting with Holt, I'm actually making more money out of the whole deal than I would have just with the *Rolling Stone* job.

RD: Okay, here we have *Amnesiascope*. It's a memoir, essentially.

SE: Right.

RD: I mean, it's autobiography. But it is a novel, it's abundantly obvious within the first couple of sentences that technically, by definition, it's a novel. Which strikes me as probably the most honest way to write an autobiography—just let's call this a novel up front.

At the same time, anything you write is a matter of making choices about what to include and what to leave out, and you always leave out far more than you include. On that basis I consider all language, whether spoken or written, to be fiction. I feel that when you start calling something nonfiction, it starts becoming dangerous in a negative way. I think the greatest monsters of history have been people who said, "I know the truth, and I alone am able to speak it." When they believe that, it can suddenly start justifying all sorts of atrocities. So calling something a work of fiction up front—which isn't quite the same as calling it a pack of lies—frees discourse on some level to express truth in a way that something that claims a certain authority to itself cannot.

The running cliché among writers is that "I'm a paid liar." Which I wonder about, because one of the things I was realizing is that part of the definition of a lie has to do with how it is presented. A lie is a non-truth that's being passed off as a truth. So what's a non-truth that's being passed off as a non-truth? Well, I guess it's fiction.

SE: Well, this book is certainly a novel. There's an imaginary context in which I can address certain things that seemed important. I'm probably getting further and further to the point where the novels each seem less like distinct entities to me, and more like an ongoing, continuing story, and each novel now winds up addressing something that was unfinished in the previous novel. As you know, two-thirds, three-quarters of the way through *Arc d'X*, there was suddenly a character named Erickson, who appeared quite to my surprise—I hadn't planned on him presenting himself—and a few pages later, the book killed him off, also quite to my surprise. It wasn't I who killed him off, it was the book who killed him off. And that seemed interesting to me, and I realized after a year or two that that was where the next chapter of the story was going to pick up for me, with that character, that character who was at a certain emotional and psychological ground zero, and even a certain ground zero of the imagination. I was suddenly less concerned with a lot of the things that earlier books had been concerned with, the construction and the shifts in time and space, and I wanted to talk about this person who was in the middle of basically a crisis of faith in his own vision, if that's not too crammed a word. And who's basically existing, at least for the time being, by his sensuality and nothing else. And doing so on a landscape that really reflects that. A landscape where all of the semblances of order have just fallen to the wayside—there's nothing resembling authority to be seen anywhere. And it's a highly eroticized landscape.

At the outset, I was *sure* this was going to be my longest novel. It took me longer to write this, or it took me nearly as long to write this, as it took to write *Arc d'X* and *Tours of the Black Clock* combined.

RD: So, what, pushing two years?

SE: No, but a year and a half. As I went along I started calling it *The Incredible Shrinking Novel,* because the more I wrote, the shorter it got, because I kept cutting stuff. And it seemed to me that this book in particular could especially ill afford anything that approached becoming too self-indulgent. It's so self-absorbed in places that I was making it tighter and tighter and tighter and condensing it more and more and more and more. And I worried about that, you know, I worried that the book was too short, but I guess I worried about that just a little bit less than I was worried it was gonna be too long, that people would not be willing to put up with a book of this nature for four hundred pages, that this particularly was a book where I had to say my piece and get out.

But it's not a calculated thing, at this point. I don't know that it—

RD: What do you mean, "at this point"? You mean, the novel is not a calculated thing, or what you're doing with your life or with your writing?

SE: All of that. I don't know that it ever was. But it's more and more instinctive, it's less and less a matter of me making a decision to write *this* kind of novel instead of *that* kind of novel. The only thing about this book that was probably calculated was the humor, because I knew the book was gonna get so personal in so many ways, I knew that it had to be funny, at least, to balance that out, or people would lose patience with it.

RD: How can you describe your relationship with the narrator of the book?

SE: The narrator of the book is a guy who is a lot like I have been at various points in the last five years. And he's probably less like I am right now than I was a couple years ago, and even a couple years ago when I started writing the book, he was not as much like me as I had been a couple years before that. So it is a memoir in that sense.

RD: So it's a memoir of who you were as opposed to who you are, quote, unquote, when you were sitting there writing.

SE: Right. But of course it's a memoir of a guy who does not want to remember—hence the title. And a guy, a memoirist, trying to free himself of his memories so he can survive, instead of being swallowed up in pain or guilt or fear or whatever.

RD: In *Amnesiascope,* and then the Erickson sections of *Arc d'X,* did it have a healing aspect?

SE: I think it did. The only thing that obstructed the healing was that I was riddled with doubt about this book from the minute I began writing it. Halfway through it, I said to myself, "Oh good, I'm writing a book that not only will sell badly, but that the critics will hate on top of it." And yet this was the book that I had to write. You know, aside from the question of whether it's a good book or a bad book or my best book or my worst book, it was the book that I had to write. And I'm finally starting to make my peace with that. But, for instance, I have told my publisher and my agent, I've told all my friends, I am not reading reviews of this book—I don't want to hear about them. I've taken myself out of that part of the process completely.

RD: How are people reacting to *Amnesiascope*? I mean, like the hometown boys—for instance, here's Michael Ventura as a fictional character in your new novel.

SE: Well, the truth is, in terms of "man on the street" reaction, in some ways I'm getting the best initial response to this book that I've gotten. I think for a lot of people, it's the most accessible book. It pulls them in. I worried at first that I was just getting that response from people who knew me, and therefore would be taking an interest that most people wouldn't take. But that doesn't seem to be the case—I'm meeting people who don't really know me very well at all, who really respond to the book. I think that for people who are not longtime readers of my work, this book is an easier entrée than a lot of my books usually are. I mean, I think they found *Arc d'X* generally difficult. You know, I never set out to make the books difficult; I never set out to be arcane. I want to be as readable as I can be. But these things dictate themselves, you know? And so the more populist reaction to the book has been good, and that's probably why, like I say, I'm starting to finally make my peace with all the doubts that I had about the book, in large part because the book is too subjective for me to objectively assess.

RD: Is that still true? I mean, have you reread it since it—

SE: No, I try not to spend too much time rereading the stuff that I write. Obviously, on the tour I wind up reading from the book. When I finished the book, I had it in my head that there was something missing, and I set it aside for three months before I sent it in to the publisher. And even after I sent it in to the publisher, I told the publisher, "I feel like there's something missing." And the publisher said, "Well, I don't know what." And as time has gone by, there are still times I feel that way, but I don't know what it is, and I'm coming to the conclusion that because the book is as personal as it is, there is always going to be something missing for me from this book, that somebody else wouldn't necessarily notice. I mean, I think it's true of all my books—all my books try to get at something that they never get at.

RD: Is that a failure?

SE: Well, yeah. But it may be that it's an inevitable failure. And I know I'm not the first writer to feel it. Where you start out with this thing in your head, and it's not completely formed—but you've got this really big thing in your head, and then a year later that's what comes out and it seems much smaller than what you had in your head.

RD: It's more like a flavor or something.

SE: Yeah. A flavor or a smell or some scent of something that, um . . . [*resignedly*] yeah.

RD: But as a fan of all kinds of things—other artists, singers, whatever— I'm constantly struck by that dichotomy. Growing up, as a teenager, certain things blew me away—I was just like, "Oh my God, this is gonna change my life." And of course it doesn't. And then down the line, as I get older, they don't have the same impact that they used to.

SE: And not only the new things don't, but if you go back and read the books that blew you away—books that are considered great books . . . this will probably sound like an incredibly presumptuous thing to say, but I hope it's taken in the right spirit: I can read Faulkner, and I see all the flaws now. I can see all the places where the young Faulkner was overwriting, or didn't really carry this off. And it doesn't change for two seconds that he's a great writer, and ten times the writer that I would like to be. But he's not a god, he was just a guy, working. And so, yeah, I think we lose our sense of wonder. And that may be a process of getting older, it may be a function of the fact that a lot of the things that make a great impact are done by younger people, younger artists, younger writers, younger filmmakers, and you start to get too old for them. I mean, at the age of forty-six, how many Nirvanas are there going to be, how many young rock 'n' roll bands are going to come along and make that kind of impact on you, that they did when you were that age? Fewer and fewer. Because a lot of times they're dealing with concerns that you've outgrown. That sounds incredibly patronizing, but that's not the way I mean it to sound.

RD: It may very well be that your best work is already behind you. I don't know, but even if so, it doesn't really matter: that fact would not necessarily diminish the quality of the work you're doing now, or of the work that you have yet to do—it's still worth doing. But what I am finding is an appreciation of the humanity of it, flaws and all. There's something warm and simply, nakedly, real in it.

SE: Exactly. And I find myself caught up with the artists who were coming of age when I was coming of age, and now growing old with them. Okay, Bob Dylan's new album is not great, and it's not the album he made when he made *Blonde on Blonde*, but I'm growing up with the guy, and it becomes fascinating to watch him follow this road to the end, wherever the end is. Or whether it's Lou Reed or Neil Young or—

RD: You sort of sidestepped my question: How did Michael Ventura respond to your new novel?

SE: Ventura liked the novel. I gave it to him and I said, "I won't change anything, or cut anything, with one exception: If you want me to change your name, I will change your name." But he didn't.

RD: Has *LA Weekly* reviewed the book yet?

SE: Not that I know of. I know that they're not happy with it.

RD: You heard this through the grapevine, your old friends from the paper?

SE: Yeah.

RD: So is it the people that you still feel close to at the paper that aren't happy with it?

SE: I don't know. I was sure that the publisher wouldn't be happy with it. I don't know if the other people are people that I knew or not. I have to assume they are: I assume it's people who were there when I was there, and that they seem more inclined than I would have necessarily expected them to, to assume that the shoe fits their particular foot. Since with only a couple exceptions I didn't speak in terms of specifics—it was just sort of this general characterization of the paper, which I didn't think was really any more or less harsh than the rest of the book.

RD: Did you ever find yourself feeling gleeful, like, "This is a novel, so I can tell the truth"?

SE: With the exception of the portrait of the publisher, I wasn't settling any scores.

RD: But with the portrait of the publisher, you were?

SE: Well, I don't even know that I would put it in terms of settling a score—it was part of the story. My leaving the *Weekly* coincided with a time, much like in the novel, when a lot of things were coming crashing down. So that had to be part of the story, and if that was part of the story, then everything that preceded it had to be part of the story. If it's part of the story that the narrator quits his job at this newspaper, then I had to kind of fill in the details of that.

RD: There's been a lot of curiosity about what happened there, and why.

SE: I guess I just assumed that, outside of a small circle of people, nobody really gives a fuck. And so from that standpoint, you can't write it like it's nonfiction—you have to make it serve the story. You've gotta make it matter in terms of the story to people who don't know anything about the *LA Weekly*.

RD: I was wondering if you could define hysterical cinema for me.

SE: Well, the idea was, a cinema that was beyond rationality, that was ur-rational, as opposed to irrational. I think the line in the book is, "These are movies that make no sense at all, and yet we understand them completely." And movies seemed appropriate for the time and place of the book, for the landscape of the book. Films that, on a literal level, make no sense at all, and yet we instinctively understand them.

I mean, you don't need me to expand on the Cinema of Hysteria, if you go out tonight, after the reading, and rent *Vertigo*. That will sum it up. And films like *Vertigo*, or *In a Lonely Place*, or *Shanghai Gesture*, or *One-Eyed Jacks*—if you start to think about them at all from the standpoint of what happens in the film, they're patently absurd movies, and yet there is an essential truth about them. They get at something in the subconscious that we understand, and for which we are willing to suspend rationality.

Did Orson Welles know that *Touch of Evil* was as weird as it turned out to be? He probably knew that it was kind of a strange film, but he probably thought he was making a pulp film. Have you seen it? These are great movies. Not all of the films I cited are great films. In fact most are not. But *Vertigo* and *Touch of Evil* are. And they're films that will define what I'm talking about probably better than I can.

RD: Are there any recent examples that you would call hysteria?

SE: Maybe *Last Temptation of Christ*. Maybe *Twin Peaks: Fire Walk with Me*, a film that got totally ripped. I think I am probably the only critic in the country that championed that film, and I did it with great indignation, because I had planned to write a feature on it. All the critical word came over that it was a turkey. I canceled the feature. I went to see it just to write one of the little blurbs that the paper runs. For the first twenty minutes, it's David Lynch's worst movie, and then, forty-five minutes into it you realize that something's going on here, and that the party line among the film critics missed it. Everybody fell into lockstep to dismiss the film in ways it did not deserve. It's a pretty good example of Cinema of Hysteria.

It was funny, because I wrote this thing, thinking, "Well, I'm really going to be a fool." But then I started to hear from people who had had the same reaction, and, when I got a card from Greil Marcus telling me that I had gotten it, I realized that maybe it wasn't just me.

RD: It seems like that's part of the risk of what you're doing—just being willing to look like a fool.

SE: I talk about that in the book—I found myself becoming the champion of films that completely embarrass themselves. And that became a basis for the Cinema of Hysteria.

RD: Part of what threw me was just your use of the word *hysteria.* I almost wish . . . is there another word?

SE: I like *hysteria,* actually. That's the word, because it's a hysterical word, you know? It's over the top, it's out of control, it's shrill, it's messy, it's—

RD: Human.

SE: —it's irritating. And that was exactly the word I wanted to use.

RD: When Krzysztof Kieślowski died recently, *The New York Times* obituary said: "In 1994, Kieślowski announced his retirement from filmmaking because, he said, he believed that literature could achieve what cinema couldn't. But Zbigniew Preisner, who wrote the music for most of his films, said the director was planning future projects at the time of his death. Mr. Kieślowski did, however, take a cautious pride in *Red.* 'I think we have shown a way of thinking a little bit different than film normally does,' he said. 'In film, every moment is clear, but in literature, everything becomes clear when you finish the book.'"

Which I thought struck up a strong contrast not only with your comments but with the comments of a few other people, about film being *the* art form of the twentieth century. I'm not sure I agree with what he says.

SE: Film just seems the natural culmination of all the other arts, because all the other arts are at play in some form or another in film. There's no doubt that fiction can do certain things that film can't. *The Sound and the Fury* can go certain places that the movie version doesn't go. And I think there are chords of memory or emotion that music can strike—so the comparisons are probably less qualitative than quantitative. It's because film winds up employing so many of the other arts in creating the whole world that it creates that I made that statement. Which is not to say that it is the best art form, but it is probably the most relevant—at this point in time.

RD: Each of the forms can do things that the others can't. And the usual trope about film, vis-à-vis novels, is that you've only got one film up on the screen, but with a novel you've got all these different films running in our heads, but that's a twentieth-century metaphor. That's a film-based metaphor.

SE: Film by its nature has a certain literalness; fiction is not bound. That's what I mean when I say there are interior landscapes that fiction can get at that film cannot without externalizing the internal landscape.

RD: Which is interesting, because to a certain extent that's what you do in your novels—externalize the internal landscape—and yet your novels strike me as eminently unfilmable.

SE: Yeah, I feel the same way.

RD: I'm curious about the impact not only of film but of photography on the human imagination and on memory itself, because to a certain extent, it's a voyeuristic medium. You're sitting there in a darkened theater and you've got this gigantic twenty-foot-high face filling a screen. And it's an unimpeded gaze: you can gaze at a lovely face without feeling self-conscious or embarrassed or whatever, and savor it. And I think about how my own memory works—often in snapshots. And I'm wondering: Did somebody 150 years ago remember in snapshots? Or are we trained to it?

SE: Yeah. And we now have more of a collective memory, because of film, than we used to. I mean, we all have—or, at least, I think we all have—distinct memories of the thirties and forties, thanks to the movies. I have a very strong sense of what the thirties and forties were like, not just visually, but psychically. I can almost at times feel it, like I was reincarnated from it, but I think that that's the effect of film—creating that collective memory. More than oral history used to do, or folktales, or wandering minstrels.

RD: There's this furious stasis that we're reaching now. I mean, the whole trip of television eliminating history, which you've talked about at length. But despite the fact that we can see these movies, I wonder how accurate it is. We're remembering a 1930s that never existed.

SE: Well yeah, right.

RD: I'm sure you've had the experience of talking to somebody who's twenty-two years old, and you're going, "I'm not even in the same universe as this kid."

SE: They don't have the same reference points at all.

RD: And the sets of reference points are changing much more rapidly.

SE: Right. And in the process, history is being lost, and the collective memory we're talking about gets more and more distorted. I'm not sure our memory of things was ever especially accurate, and so the way that film has made our memories inaccurate is probably not that much different from the way collective memory always used to be, with the exception that our collective memory has become stylized in a certain way that it didn't used to be.

RD: Or just from an imagistic standpoint. We share it from the standpoint of seeing the same images, having access to the same images over and over again.

SE: Right.

RD: One of the things that happened when I was drafting "The Frequency of Liberation," my article for *Science Fiction Eye* on your work, was that I wrote a lot of the sections of it from memory. I'm really glad, because that ended up being the key of the piece. I pretty quickly realized, as soon as I started following up on the passages from your books that I had written about purely from memory, that I'd gotten them wrong. And in about half the cases I decided to rewrite them and get them right, and in about half the cases I went, "No, no, this says more about it wrong than it does just to get it clinically correct." And that just evolved or emerged out of it. So much of your work is about distortion, that the better way to honor it is to distort it.

SE: Or it's about the secret truth that kind of lurks beneath, as you put it—the clinical truth.

RD: Exactly. And I felt, or hoped, that to a certain extent my distortions were doing that. The one that bugged me the most, that I really wrestled with, wrote and rewrote and endlessly rewrote before finally going back to the original version, was the paragraph about the Big Man, Blaine, who chose between letting Jainlight go or capturing him on the docks in New York. And Blaine winds up dreaming, out on the platform over the nameless river, about the two different worlds that arose from him choosing to let Jainlight go and from him choosing to keep him. That whole thing, I wrote from memory. And when I started zeroing in on the passage—part of the whole thing is that question of men dying when they're watching her as opposed to when she's dancing—and, what I realized, looking at that, was the reason why. Why is it that men are dying when they're watching as opposed to her dancing? And when I looked at the answer, I realized that I had gotten it wrong in my description, that there weren't two different realities where in one Blaine lets him go, and in the other, Blaine says, "No, you're mine, and we're taking you in." I got that wrong. In *every* reality, Blaine would have made the same decision, in every reality Blaine would let Jainlight get on that ship—his decision would *not* change. Whereas, a lot of these other people, they would have gone ahead—

SE: There were forks, yeah.

RD: —and made the opposite and mutually exclusive decisions. So of all these people, only Blaine was pure of choice, whether or not he was pure in any other way. Only Blaine would have made the same choice every single time. And so I kept trying to rewrite my description, but the words didn't want to be changed; they kept fighting back. Finally I realized, "Wait a minute—he's dreaming. And of course, there's nothing in *Tours of the Black Clock* about Blaine dreaming on the platform, before that platform's torched. So this is him dreaming about What If—what if I had made a different choice?"

SE: That was your dream about his dream, you know? That was your interpretation of his interpretation, and it seems completely valid. And I would probably leave it at that.

RD: Writing that article was very weird for me. There were times where I thought, there's stuff in this that only you will get.

SE: I liked it a lot, because it was a more impressionistic piece at times than an analytical piece, or it was analysis on such a subterranean level as to resemble impression. And it seemed really appropriate.

RD: And so I had a feeling of recognition reading Ventura and Hillman's book, *We've Had a Hundred Years of Psychotherapy and the World's Getting Worse*, because Hillman talks about seeing your life from the end backward. You know, Einstein was such a genius that at first it could only silence him, and hence he didn't start speaking until he was five years old. He was totally mute till he was five, and when he started finally speaking, he spoke in complete sentences. That kind of thing. And I feel like, I can do this, you can do this, you can have the future that you want. And I'm just wondering, Has that had any relevance in your own thinking? Cause I almost see Erickson in Berlin in 1999 being . . . you're exorcising the future that's *not* gonna happen.

SE: Right. I think that with this book, I got to a point where I needed to try and live as much in the present moment as possible, that I was getting tangled up on the past and the future, and choosing my past—which couldn't be chosen, because it was done—and, because I was tangled up in the past, I was having a hard time choosing my future. And so I was in this place where I had to live in the present moment. The paradox, of course, is that the present moment I chose, in this book, is not our present moment. I don't know if it's the future, or what, but it doesn't really resemble our present moment. For me to address the things that I needed to address in the present, I still had to move the character to a present of the imagination, an imagined present rather than a "real" one. And of course the process you're talking about, where you're struggling with a thing for a long time, and suddenly it's just sort of there, because you make some choice, or you make some leap of faith, and the past and future and present all kind of flow into the same moment—that's a big part of what writing's about. And keeping, maintaining, sustaining the creative energy for that to happen is difficult. I find it harder and harder as time goes by. Which is why the span between books gets longer and longer.

RD: Going back a little bit, you were talking about being in a place where what you needed to do was to focus on the present—but, in the novel, the present of the imagination. But I'm wondering how—you know, I assume that that's hooked to where you were at as a human being.

SE: Sure.

RD: Were you going through a period of stripping away all the accumulated habits?

SE: Sure. The guy is at ground zero, he's at ground zero of his memories, and his psyche, and so a lot of—

RD: Steve, where were *you*?

SE: I was in a place just a little farther down the road from where the character is, at a place where my father had died, and I hadn't quite come to terms with that, and a very important relationship had ended, and I hadn't quite come to terms with that. A marriage had ended, aside from the relationship, and there was all that back there. And a job ends, and also the realization that I'm never going to be a hugely famous author. And trying to accept that in as existential a term as possible, even though my whole life has been defined by that dream, and that chosen future. And coming to terms with the fact that sometimes the biggest future of all which you've chosen is not going to be the one that life presents you.

RD: Right: there's limits to that idea of falling into the gravity . . . And at the same time, though, I'm sure a lot of your illusions about what it would *mean* to be a big famous author were shattered too.

SE: Right. Exactly. I'm finally old enough to realize how ephemeral and transitory all of that is. What does it mean to be a hugely famous author, that I get a good review from the *New York Times*?

RD: Or to have nubile young women recognize you on the street.

SE: Yeah, right. I think that illusion, especially, passed early on. Or the importance of that, passed early on.

RD: Do you actually get laid as often as your doppelganger on the printed page?

SE: No. I am settled in a relationship going on four years.

RD: Is that the relationship that the relationship with Viv is based on?

SE: Yes. But there was this period where I was sort of sexually bouncin' around, you know? And not doing it nearly as well as he does it—and he doesn't do it that well. You know, halfway through the book, all his sexual fantasies start pulling the rug out from beneath him. You know, he's gonna make this porn movie, and be surrounded by all these naked women, and he winds up the only naked person in the movie, you know? He fantasizes about the teenage hooker standing on the corner, she winds up taking over his apartment, and he's too guilt-stricken to even take advantage of it.

In the years since my conversation with Erickson, I have at long last seen *Vertigo* and *Touch of Evil*, in their respective big-screen restorations. I found they silenced the inner monologue better than most films; if that's hysteria, I'm all for it.

As for the recent US presidential election, I can only note that Steve Erickson has been predicting this election for at least twelve years, an election that may yet stand as an epitaph for America, if not the United States. Or blame it on Coyote, who once upon a time sprayed his rankly hopeful spoor in Theresa LePore's dreams.

Finding a Way to Obliterate the Barriers: An Interview with Steve Erickson

Yoshiaki Koshikawa / 1997

From *The Rising Generation* 143, no. 6 (1997): 294–302. Reprinted by permission.

Amnesiascope and "I"

Yoshiaki Koshikawa: Since I've already interviewed you twice in Los Angeles, I want to ask you now about *Amnesiascope*, your latest fiction, and hopefully, if we have time, about *American Nomad* as well. First, I want to ask about the form of *Amnesiascope*. The narrator of this novel is "I." This "I" reminds me of you, the author, confessing or telling a story of himself in a fictitious, tricky way. And you never used the first-person narrator in your fiction before. This narration seems to be a new enterprise, a new challenge for you. Could you tell me how you chose to write this fiction in the first person?

Steve Erickson: It's true that *Amnesiascope* is the first novel that is written in the first person from beginning to end. But there are parts of *Rubicon Beach* that are written in the first person. And the central part of *Tours of the Black Clock* is written in the first person, in the first person from the point of view of a clearly defined third-personal character, if that makes sense. But it's a first person's voice, and I think any time an author employs a first person's voice, even if he's telling the story ostensibly through another character, his voice becomes part of that voice. I think what happened with *Amnesiascope* is that this was the first time that the first person's voice has been used consistently in a sustained way from beginning to end. It was also a voice that was, at least to the reader, identifiably mine—the author's voice, rather than Banning Jainlight's voice in *Tours of the Black Clock*.

There were brief moments in the previous book, *Arc d'X*, where suddenly a first person's voice presented itself. And every time it did, it surprised me. I hadn't planned on that happening. And, as I think we may have talked about before—the other times we have spoken—a lot of times my novels wind up addressing something that was unfinished in previous novels— something that presented itself in previous novels in some spontaneous way that I didn't anticipate and had not calculated as part of the schematic of that particular work, so that when the work was over and I've had some time to think about it, I think to myself, "Well, that's kind of interesting." There was something new that came out there that I hadn't planned on. And that becomes the seed for the next book. That's what happened with *Arc d'X* and *Amnesiascope*. *Arc d'X* was, at least on the face of it, a very imagined work. It became a more personal work as I was writing it than I had anticipated. And that led to *Amnesiascope*, where most of the pretenses were dropped. As you say, a lot of it is cast in clearly fictional terms, but the intent became more overtly confessional.

So it's always a process of evolution. It's rarely a process of calculation. It's rarely a matter of my saying, "Okay, now I'm going to do this," and following some kind of preconceived strategy. The work usually takes me where it wants to go. At the beginning of a novel the author is the boss, but at some point during the writing of a novel, the novel becomes the boss. The novel starts dictating its own terms and starts telling the author what it's about. And if it doesn't do that, then the novel is probably not very good, because it hasn't taken on a life of its own. And that's what has happened in virtually all of my novels.

YK: I understand that's why you said to me before that you were a "spontaneous and unconscious" writer. But in an interview by Takayuki Tatsumi and Larry McCaffery, you said *Amnesiascope* would be a very personal novel. Unfortunately, many readers misunderstood you because of that. They suspected you were going to confess your own guilt or bad deeds in the fiction. They imagined it wouldn't really be a novel, but just a self-confession. After reading it, I still believe you wrote a novel instead of indulging in self-confession.

SE: I think that all of the work is an expression of imagination on the one hand, and experience on the other. A work comes out of what one imagines or what one has experienced. And through all of my novels that has been true. There has been a component of each, imagination and experience. It's just that the balance shifts from book to book. Some books are more imagined and some are more experienced. And some are more clearly the vision of imagination, and some are clearly the voice of experience. But one never completely dominates the other. With *Amnesiascope*, the voice of experience probably took over to an extent that it hadn't in any of my previous books. But, as you say, it is still being cast in terms, hopefully, of some imaginative vision. That's what makes it a novel. And that is what makes it something more than just self-indulgent. Using the means of art, the author takes something that has happened to him and casts it in terms that are going to mean something to the reader who doesn't know him, who is not there partaking of the experience. And that's where you find some sort of universal compatibility with the reader. Does that make sense?

YK: Yes. But aren't you interested in creating a character named Steve Erickson in *Arc d'X*?

SE: Yes.

YK: Why is that?

SE: I don't know. The section that I'm going to read from *Arc d'X* when I'm in Japan, which is written in the third person, but about a character named Erickson, was a complete surprise. I hadn't anticipated it. It was one of those decisions my creative intuition made that I never stopped to examine very closely. I'm not sure it would be a good thing for me to examine very closely. All I knew was that at the end of that particular section of *Arc d'X*, not only had I introduced a character named Erickson, but I killed him off. He died, and that's that. And *Amnesiascope* is the story of that character after he had been killed.

YK: You didn't name the narrator Erickson in *Amnesiascope*.

SE: It would have closed off too many interpretations. It would have narrowed the meaning of what I was doing. *Amnesiascope* was already close enough to the bone, if you know what I mean by that. Then to stick my name on the character on top of that not only seemed superfluous, but almost narcissistic. And so I wanted to give the reader a character to whom the reader could apply a name he or she chose.

YK: I've enjoyed your works, but *Amnesiascope* is somehow more interesting to me. That's probably because I know you personally. It's kind of difficult to distinguish you from the character.

SE: That was part of the point. That was sort of the idea. And you are not the only person who had that difficulty. It was emotionally and creatively a conducive place to put myself, if that makes sense. By putting the character somewhere between fiction and autobiography, I was then free to say the things that I needed to say in that book. And it helped me find whatever courage I felt I needed to find to write the book. But that too was an instinctive decision that I haven't really figured out.

Apocalyptic Vision of America

YK: Does *Amnesiascope* contain some personal, nonfictional elements even though it is called fiction?

SE: Yes.

YK: On the other hand, *American Nomad* could be called "fictional nonfiction," though it is labeled as nonfiction. So, these two books are very close to each other.

SE: Yes, these are kind of a yin and yang of the same book. And it's true that *American Nomad* has an almost novelistic quality to it, and as you will see when you have a chance to take a look at it, it even picks up where *Amnesiascope* leaves off. The character of Viv in *Amnesiascope* is in *American Nomad*, too. So the book starts where the novel of *Amnesiascope* leaves off and then moves gradually into literal nonfiction history and some examination of the political and cultural zeitgeist of America right now.

YK: The last time I interviewed you, you told me that you revised this novel so many times it became shorter and shorter. Was it that difficult to finish the book?

SE: Yes. It's my shortest book, and it took the longest to write. And at one point, when I started it, I assumed it was going to be my longest book. The more I worked on it, the shorter it got, instead of getting longer.

YK: Did you use some of the deletions for *American Nomad*?

SE: No. When I say, "I picked up where *Amnesiascope* leaves off in *American Nomad*," I mean that at the outset of *American Nomad* the narrator is clearly the same narrator as the one telling the story of *Amnesiascope* at some point later on. So there is a clear transition from *Amnesiascope* into *American Nomad*. Getting back to the question you asked, the lines between the fiction and the nonfiction are deliberately blurred and difficult to distinguish.

YK: I've read *Amnesiascope* as a story of the unconscious confusion of a literary persona named Steve Erickson, even though you didn't give him that name. I've also read the novel as the narrator's surreal vision of a monster he is living with, called Los Angeles. You are obsessed with the apocalyptic image of the monster city that is now decaying. In the first scene of *Amnesiascope*, LA's airport and the city's major highways are destroyed, and people lose their homes and wander about starting fires in the streets. This ruin reminds me of the key image of the Armageddon, the end of the world, which can also be found in Pynchon's *Gravity's Rainbow.*

SE: The Los Angeles of *Amnesiascope* is a ghost city. It's a landscape that approximates the emotional apocalypse that the character has lived with; that is, it is the appropriate landscape for what the character is feeling emotionally and psychologically.

YK: So the LA landscape was reflected by his emotion?

SE: It's what is inside the character expressing itself in an urban apocalyptic metaphor. And so for that reason, I always wanted the LA landscape to be secondary in *Amnesiascope.* I didn't want to call too much attention to it. I wanted to fix the character in that landscape and then look at the character, and sort of forget about the landscape. The comparison with *Gravity's Rainbow* is something I would have to think about, because *Gravity's Rainbow* is conceptually a much more outward book. You start at the center and move out. In my book, you kind of start with the landscape and move in toward the character. It's a smaller book. *Amnesiascope* could be a mere chapter in *Gravity's Rainbow.*

YK: I was just observing that the nightmarish vision of your novel was very similar to that of *Gravity's Rainbow.*

SE: Yes.

YK: Not the size, of course. You have presented a nightmarish image of metropolis in your fiction. Los Angeles, Paris, and Venice have all gone wild in *Days Between Stations*—

SE: Vienna in *Tours of the Black Clock,* and Berlin in *Arc d'X.*

YK: All these cities become a ruin, a desert, or a bleak desolate landscape.

SE: It's a motif that comes naturally to me from some reason. I suppose at least unconsciously it must be part of my view of life, because I seem to keep returning to it. But the appalling thing is that there are ways in which the desolation is also liberating. The character in *Amnesiascope* feels liberated in his ghost city. He feels alive in it. He even says at one point, "The thing about a dead city like Los Angeles is that it can make you feel more alive than you have ever been." I think that's a very fleeting life, because by the time you get to the end of *Amnesiascope,* the character has been emotionally and psychologically exhausted; he has defined himself by his sensuality, which has become displaced by a certain amount of nervous breakdown. At the end of the book, he has left Los Angeles, he has lost everything he had, his car was stolen, his woman has left, he has quit his job, his dreams as a novelist are gone, and he gets in a car and he gets out on the American highway and he kind of cracks up. And he has a sort of epiphany out in the hinterlands of America and pulls back from madness at the very end, for we don't know how long. And it's not enough to live by his sensuality anymore. He's going to have to find another reason for being alive. He's going to have to rediscover the courage to embarrass himself, as the old filmmaker advises him to do at the end of the novel.

YK: Adolphe Sarre says that.

SE: Yes.

YK: I like that last scene. The narrator is driving on the highway so fast he's lost control of the car and himself.

SE: He keeps piling up one speeding ticket after another. He can't slow down.

YK: You mentioned his epiphany "at the margin of insanity." That's the point. You are doing this, compelled not by your mind, but by your emotions. That moves the reader. And the nightmarish cities in all of your fiction seem like wild nature, which you can't control at all.

SE: Right. Nature keeps swallowing these cities up, whether it is the desert outside Los Angeles or the winters in Paris or the animals that have escaped from the zoo in Berlin. All of these forces of wildness, all the primitive forces that cities are constructed to keep at bay, come back to take over. The city can't keep that wild nature at bay forever. Sooner or later, the city loses the battle with nature with the passing of time.

YK: So does it mean you are a primitivist?

SE: I don't know. Maybe it does. Or apocalyptic enough to assume that decay and breakdown are inevitable, that the caprices of civilization don't last forever.

LA as a Free-Associative City

YK: Take the Hotel Hamblin in *Amnesiascope*, for instance. I think it's your favorite image of the anarchic, free world for the pleasure of the unconscious.

SE: Yes.

YK: That hotel seems similar to a place from the previous novel called the Arboretum, where you can see so-called nefarious activities, like "a theater, TV arcade, book outlets," and "forbidden artifacts." In the Hotel Hamblin, you have a manager, Abdul, who is a Palestinian terrorist, and a weird radio station named Station 3. This radio station is owned by a Moroccan religious sect who believes in an SF version of Islamic fundamentalism and plays Moroccan jajouka music all the time. How do you get this kind of image?

SE: Los Angeles is very conducive to that kind of image. Los Angeles is such a pluralistic, eclectic mix of influences and cultures and sort of random associations. It's the free-associative city, if you know what I mean, free association being where you think about one thing and it just automatically conjures up the image of something else that may be totally unrelated. But the subconscious makes a link. And Los Angeles is the subconscious city. And it's very easy to imagine that kind of strange conglomeration that you are talking about. I have never actually made the parallel between the Arboretum and the Hotel Hamblin. I think it's really appropriate.

YK: I thought you took the key note of the Hotel Hamblin from the Arboretum.

SE: I probably did, but it wasn't something I was conscious of.

YK: Maybe I was attracted to the anarchic aspect of these places.

SE: That kind of enclosed system of strange conglomerations does seem to pop up in my fiction now and then, so I've got to assume that there's a reason for it, that there is some connection.

YK: Do you have a model of this Hotel Hamblin?

SE: Yes. It was modeled after the apartment building that I lived in for five years, right in the center of Los Angeles.

YK: Is that the one I saw? The building with a kind of old Gothic atmosphere?

SE: Yes, exactly. When it was first built in the 1920s, it had an Art Deco motif to it, but as time has gone by, it has gone from Art Deco to Gothic. It originally was a hotel where aspiring movie stars stayed when they first came to Los Angeles. They were looking to break into the movies, and they would stay in that hotel. Legend has it that John Wayne stayed in that hotel. Jean Harlow stayed in that hotel.

YK: The hallways are very dark even in the daytime.

SE: In this country, do you know the movie *Barton Fink*? If you see the movie, which takes place in Hollywood in the 1930s, people who have seen the movie and have gone into that building that you saw are always reminded of *Barton Fink*. It's very much like that.

YK: Who's Barton Fink?

SE: Barton Fink is the name of the main character in the film. He's a playwright from New York who has been brought into Hollywood to write for the movies, and they put him up in this old strange hotel, which always reminds people of the apartment building that you saw and I lived in. And that became the model of the Hotel Hamblin.

YK: When I went to the apartment four or five years ago, there lived a bunch of punks.

SE: All kinds of people lived there. There were people who had lived there for a long time, and then there were punks and there were young starlets, beautiful women who had come to break into the movies. There were always beautiful women around the building.

YK: I envy you.

SE: They would be there for a month or two. They would move in, they were there for a month or two, and they would be gone. And you never knew what happened to them—if they took up with some producer, had become successful, found a husband or boyfriend. But there was a steady stream of beautiful women through the hotel, who would come and be there for a month and then would be gone.

YK: So, those beautiful women came from all over the United States.

SE: Exactly.

Animal Logic and Compulsive Drive

YK: In *Amnesiascope* you wrote a sentence like this: "I've thrust myself forward not out of faith or even will but the sort of primal force of habit that moves an animal to the place that nature commands it, to graze or mate or die" (p. 151). When I read this passage I remembered another novel, by a Japanese woman writer named Amy Yamada. The novel is titled *Animal Logic*, and it is set in New York City. It has what is called a "lecherous" female protagonist named Jasmine. Though she has many sexual encounters with American men—Black and white—she doesn't seem to be a "loose" woman. In fact, she is a vigorous, strong woman. Though she is not aware of this fact, she has an uncontrollable virus inside her body. That creature helps her survive the wild jungle called New York City through its power, wisdom, and "animal logic."

SE: I understand what you are saying about that character, and it is very similar to this particular sentence of mine. But in this context, the character is talking about writing. He is talking about being a writer. But that is the same kind of compulsive drive. In that way, writing is pretty sexual. It's the same kind of compulsive drive that transcends faith or will, that is not an expression of transcendence. It is an expression of compulsion.

YK: Both books deal with such compulsive drive of the main characters, and they are similar, fable-like novels in the sense that they give the reader some humanistic or antihumanistic advice for getting by in this chaotic world. We'll, this isn't a question, but a comment on your book and Amy Yamada's.

SE: It sounds like a good book. Has it been published in English?

YK: It has been published here recently. I doubt there is an English version out yet. But sometime later maybe they will publish an English version. Apparently Amy Yamada plans to have it translated into English. The title seems American.

SE: Yes, it does. It's a good title. That writer's name sounds familiar to me.

YK: One more thing I found interesting in *Amnesiascope* is that there is a new aspect of yours as a novelist which has never appeared before. You may be aware of this radical comic aspect of your writing, but I'll just pick up one example from the novel. The narrator of this novel desperately calls up many different women at one time and has sexual relations with them one after another, but paradoxically this only deepens the desolation of his soul, and his mind goes even more out of control. This scene is very sad, and very funny at the same time.

SE: That's good.

YK: I think this is new in your fiction. You are a serious writer, not humorous or comic in your writing, but in this particular scene you are extremely funny.

SE: I was saying just a little while ago that there was not much about my work that is calculated. But it was certainly intended that this book would hopefully be funny, because I felt like the confessional aspect of the book would be too difficult for the reader to accept if there were not some corresponding humor to it. If you found the scene both funny and sad, that's good, that's what I would have hoped.

YK: I hope to see more humor of this sort in future novels. Could you explain the title of this novel, *Amnesiascope*? Why did the narrator's girlfriend try to build "the Memoryscope"? Was it because she believed that to remember the past would cure her soul? And why did the narrator try to build "the Amnesiascope" in order to forget the past to cure his soul? In my interpretation, the novel itself provided a kind of cure for you when you were writing it.

SE: The novel itself becomes a kind of amnesiascope. The title *Amnesiascope* obviously refers, as you say, to "the Memoryscope" that she was building. And because the book had—I thought—a kaleidoscopic quality, amnesiascope sort of plays upon kaleidoscope. It's very fragmented, a lot of different colors and shapes. And finally, it was a takeoff on CinemaScope. At one point the narrator even says, on page 124, "Under a moon the color of flesh, that shines behind the smoke and a cloud that appears about to explode, LA surrounds me in amnesiascope." So, it's a play upon Cinema-Scope, the wide-screen movies, the panoramic spectacular visions in films. Instead of CinemaScope, he sees Los Angeles in amnesiascope. So, it's a way of seeing things.

Stuttering and Writing

YK: If you don't want to talk about this, it's okay, but could you tell me about the relationship between your stuttering experience and your motivation to be a novelist? Somewhere in the novel you say that if you didn't stutter you would not have been a writer.

SE: I assume that's true, because I stuttered when I was a very small child. And when you stutter, you are immediately severed from the rest of society in a certain way, in terms of communication and in terms of verbal exchange. And when it happens to you at a very young age like four years old, it's a traumatic thing. And so that experience cut me off from the world around me, and as a result I lived a lot inside my own head. And because I had a verbal facility, it was going to find some expression in some other way. It couldn't express itself in speech, because the speech was impeded. So I became a writer. It's a very common thing for writers to be stutterers. A lot of stutterers have become writers. Lately I have begun to wonder if I had it reversed. I have always assumed that a stutterer becomes a writer. Lately I have begun to wonder if the writer becomes a stutterer, if a writer is born a writer—if there is something about the writer from the very beginning that makes him a writer and that's what gets in the way of his speech. Do you understand? I don't know which comes first, which is the horse and which is the cart. But there is definitely a relationship.

Joe Christmas, the Ultimate American Character

YK: Let's talk about *American Nomad*. The book has not come out yet, and I've just read excerpts of it you wrote for *Rolling Stone*. Would you explain the meaning of its title? You mentioned the name of Joe Christmas somewhere in one of the *Rolling Stone* pieces.

SE: Joe Christmas in the novel *Light in August* is a man who literally does not know if he is white or Black. And it makes him literally crazy. I've always thought that, along with Huckleberry Finn, Joe Christmas is in some ways the ultimate American character, because of that madness having to do with his racial identity, and because the identity of America was born out of the moral confusion and moral bankruptcy of slavery. *American Nomad* refers to the way in which it seems to me the country is fragmenting, the way the people are becoming disenfranchised from the common idea of America. The irony is that in some ways that was what America always intended. In some ways, America was always intended to be a country where everybody was a country unto himself—or herself—a sort of "anti-country," in which there is not one American but 250 million Americas. Each American is America, but now I think that's begun to catch up with the country today, because people have become disenfranchised from the idea of America. And it has made them nomads. They're not physical nomads. They are spiritual nomads. They are wandering this huge collective American psyche, looking for where they belong, because the country seems to be breaking up.

As we were saying at lunch yesterday, we've got little fascistic enclaves of these right-wing militia groups out in the hinterlands of Montana or Utah. And you've got these guys blowing up government buildings in Oklahoma City, and there's some insidious crisis, I think, going on in America right now, where Americans are exhausted by the effort of being Americans. They are exhausted by how much work it takes to make America work, to make the American idea work, because without the American idea there is no America. America is not a country of common traditions or common heritage or common language. It's a very young country, and it's a country that was born out of the idea that it could break loose from history and memory—it could break loose from the past, it could break loose from all of those thousands of years of history that exist in Europe or the Old World. And whereas other countries were born out of common borders and common language and common tradition and common history, America was not born out of that. America was born out of this very elusive idea. And once the idea is gone, the country is gone. There may still be a United States, but there is not an America. And that's where the title *American Nomad* came from.

YK: Incidentally, this year is the hundredth anniversary of William Faulkner, who created what you would call the ultimate nomadic character of the US.

SE: Really? When was he born?

YK: September 25, 1897.

SE: I think Faulkner is the great American novelist of the twentieth century, and most Americans still find Faulkner a difficult and inaccessible writer. His books are very hard for most Americans. His influence has probably exceeded his actual readership. And I don't know how the literary establishment regards him now, because certain writers sort of come in and out of vogue. In the early part of the twentieth century, Hemingway was considered the great American novelist. Then I think in the second half of the twentieth century, Hemingway was sort of displaced by Faulkner in terms of his status in the hierarchy. I don't know how Americans feel about him now. You talk about the internal landscapes and the external landscapes—Faulkner, in the same way James Joyce did in European literature, knocked down the walls between the internal and the external and made a big impact in terms of the way time ticks not to the clock on the wall but to the clock of the psyche. And even though I didn't completely understand him when I first read him as a student, he changed me completely.

YK: As I mentioned earlier in this interview, your writing in *American Nomad* is clearly that of a novelist. You use metaphors and allusions to describe politicians not only as participants in political events but as characters in mass cultural events. This kind of writing is very challenging to readers of conventional nonfiction because they have to read between the lines, just as when they are reading fiction. These fictional strategies are much more pronounced in *American Nomad* than in *Leap Year*, so I hope readers don't get confused.

SE: I hope so too. And I especially hope it is not confusing for the Japanese readers for whom I am going to read part of *American Nomad*. My impression is that the Japanese readers are more creative readers—they are willing to make the associations, and they are not confused when something does not stay inside its little niche. In America, when something does not stay inside its niche, Americans get confused. It has become a culture of specialization, and it has become a culture of specificity. I anticipate that some readers are going to wonder why I am talking about Bill Clinton and Bruce Springsteen in the same book, whereas, to me, it seems completely natural, especially because I think popular culture really says more about America right now than the political culture does. The book is more about the political culture, just because that's what the book is about. I couldn't imagine writing a book about the political culture and not talking about the popular culture. And so I hope that all of these allusions or these momentary diversions in *American Nomad* about Bruce Springsteen and Oliver Stone and Frank Sinatra and F. Scott Fitzgerald will be reference points that illuminate the political discussion rather than confuse it—if the readers are just open-minded enough not to become panic-stricken when the book suddenly takes a turn that he or she is not expecting.

YK: As you said earlier, *American Nomad* is the twin sister of *Amnesiascope*. Both books are very unconventional. We have a lot of conventional works of fiction or nonfiction, but "fiction" and "nonfiction" are just labels after all.

SE: That's the way I look at it. And when I was originally hired by *Rolling Stone* to write the presidential piece I did, *Rolling Stone* said to me, "We want a novelist who will write about the campaign like it's a novel." Those were their exact words. It turned out that was not what they wanted. They thought that was what they wanted. And it sounded good to me. But when they got that, they started becoming very confused and anxious about it. It seemed to me to be a natural way to write about the country—kind of a novelized, narrative-driven story about what is going on in America.

The Novel as an Interior Journey

YK: I am not sure if Japanese are more creative readers than Americans, but it seems true that you have more enthusiastic readers here. Why do you think your works are so popular in Japan?

SE: Boy, I'd like to know the answer to that myself. If I knew the answer to that, then I could do the same thing in the United States. I don't know. All I know is that I give a number of interviews to a number of journalists, and the few interviews that I have given to Japanese journalists or Japanese professors have always been more challenging, more complex. I think you would have to tell me why, because I have no idea. I would not have expected it. And yet now it doesn't surprise me, for some reason.

YK: It's funny, but there was a rumor last year that Bob Dylan was a candidate for the Nobel Prize for Literature.

SE: Well, Bob Dylan is one of the similar influences in my life: Henry Miller, William Faulkner, and Bob Dylan. Bob Dylan changed me as a writer in 1965 the same way reading Faulkner for the first time changed me. Having said that, I think that Bob Dylan's greatness is as a songwriter rather than as a poet. I think Bob Dylan's words work with his music and his voice. In a way, they do not work as well just on the printed page. I would have no problem at all giving Bob Dylan a Nobel Prize for Literature, but then we would have to redefine literature, which is okay with me. But if you give Bob

Dylan a Nobel Prize, then the next year you have to give it to Ray Charles, and the year after you have to give it to the Beatles, and so on. Because all of these people have had more impact than novelists have. It's sad but true. Or it might not be sad. It might just be the way it is.

YK: Some of my friends, editors of literary magazines, often worry that people are losing interest in literature.

SE: Well, the same thing is happening in the United States. People are reading less and less and less. I worry that the novel as an art form is becoming obsolete. There is nothing that I can personally do about that. For better or worse, I was born to be a novelist. And I actually can understand why. As life gets faster and faster and as the consumption of information multiplies tenfold, a hundredfold, just the time and patience it takes to lose yourself in a novel demands a lot, I think, in contemporary life.

I'm not sure that on a mass scale the culture can be conditioned to love literature the way it has been conditioned to love TV, because there are ways in which reading a novel is still very much a private thing. And it's supposed to be a private thing. It's not like going to the movie theater, where you are sitting with a lot of people and watching a movie. Or even sitting at home in front of your TV set alone, there are still other people on that TV set. And so it is not the utterly private experience that reading a novel is. And there is the question of whether the age still has room for something like that. And there are plenty of times that I despair that it doesn't, when I think that the novel is a vanishing form—eight thousand copies of *Arc d'X* is not bad, but eight thousand CDs, eight thousand people going to see your movie, you've got a problem. The scale of success and the measure of success is so completely different, and so miniaturized, as time goes by, for literature.

But I think that each art form has its own individual idiosyncratic potential. Music is capable of communication in ways that no other art form is. The movies communicate in ways that no other art form does. I still think that the novel is capable of doing it, that the novel still takes people places, especially into the interior landscapes, that other narrative art forms cannot. And what I would hope to do with my fiction is find a way to obliterate the barriers between the exterior landscapes and the interior ones. That is what I want to do, because it seems to me that this is what a novel can do that no other art form can do. And hopefully that is still going to be important. And as long as that is still important, as long as those sorts of interior journeys are still important, the novel is going to be a worthwhile endeavor. But I think that people have to find that for themselves.

Steve Erickson: Uprooted from the American Idea

Ron Hogan / 1997

From Beatrice.com. Reprinted by permission of Ron Hogan.

Steve Erickson was hired by *Rolling Stone* to cover the 1996 presidential campaign, although he's not entirely sure why. "They thought they wanted to cover the 1996 campaign in an unconventional fashion," he explains in his living room in the hills above Los Angeles, "a novelist who would cover the election in a novelistic fashion." But Jann Wenner also wanted a political correspondent like the *New York Times*'s R. W. Apple. "So he hired me to be R. W. Apple, which made no sense to me, and in the final analysis, I guess it made no sense to him, either." After all, if you're looking for straightforward mainstream political journalism, why hire the man who wrote about the 1988 election (in *Leap Year*) with frequent commentary by Sally Hemings, Thomas Jefferson's slave and mistress?

When *Rolling Stone* finally cut him loose, Erickson decided that there was still something to be said. The final result is *American Nomad*, a portrait of a nation whose soul was in danger of falling apart. Although the book chronicles Erickson's cross-country trek, it draws upon films, music, and literature, as well as current events, to show, as Erickson says, how "we're all American nomads because we're uprooted not from the land, but from the American idea."

RH: For a book that's ostensibly about the '96 election, there's a much broader take on American culture. The election gets pushed to the background on a regular basis.

SE: I thought of it more as a zeitgeist book than a political book. Obviously, the campaign is the main highway that runs across the book's terrain, but more of the interesting stories take place on the detours, the side roads. I wanted to write a book, especially as the campaign became more and more dull, and more and more soul-killing, that dealt with what I thought was going on in the psyche of the country.

RH: The choice of Philip K. Dick as an author that addresses the core issues affecting the American psyche is really apt.

SE: Dick seems to me as close to a millennial American writer as I could think of. The motif of the joined twins that reasserts itself—sometimes wittingly and sometimes unwittingly—throughout his writings became a natural theme for this book, particularly when we're talking about a country that is literally and figuratively dealing with matters of Black and white, dealing with its own dual identity defined by the American promise and the American betrayal.

RH: For somebody who can easily be viewed as an enemy of the conservatives, you also nail liberals pretty hard at some points. Your chapter on abortion, for example, has enough ideas in it to get both sides extremely pissed at you.

SE: I never saw myself as the enemy of the right wing, although the right wing probably sees me as an enemy. It says a lot about the right wing that they tend to see things in those terms. I think the Left would have been just as prone to see me as the enemy thirty years ago, and probably would be today if it wasn't so frantically grasping for survival.

A lot of the issues in today's politics get defined by the extremes, by people who bend the truth to their biases rather than the other way around. That's probably the fault of the rest of us, who absolve ourselves from taking responsibility for seizing the political debate and conducting it on more reasonable terms. Abortion is probably the best example of that. As I say in the book, it seems as if the debate over abortion is controlled by people who would allow any and all abortion, right up to the moment of birth, and people who would outlaw any and all abortion, virtually back to the moment of conception. Because abortion makes so many people, including myself, profoundly uncomfortable, because it's something people really don't want to talk about, it's easy for the so-called pro-life and pro-choice movements to seize the debate and polarize it in a way that's bad for the country and for any fair, honest examination of what the truth about abortion might be. Of course, it's an issue that by its nature defies knowing what the truth is, because that would entail knowing the spiritual and metaphysical certainties we can't know. But it wouldn't hurt to contemplate the uncertainties of the issue rather than scream about it.

RH: In the first half of '96, the political debate wasn't between Democrat and Republican so much as between moderate Republican and extreme right-wing Republican.

SE: All presidential campaigns have some degree of in-party conflict to them. It's becoming more true lately of the Republicans. In 1968 and 1972, the Democrats went through their version of what the Republicans went through in 1992 and 1996. It happens to parties that reach a certain plateau of political power and strength. Having achieved a certain amount of success in obtaining power, parties feel a need to purge the ranks, to distill who and what they are down to some notion of political purity.

RH: But the "renegade" elements within those parties now have the option of forming their own faction. When George Wallace ran as a third-party independent, it was considered revolutionary. Now, third-party splintering has become accepted as a legitimate event within the political process.

SE: I thought it was going to be more pervasive in '96, actually, which is why I thought the campaign would be more interesting than it turned out to be. While Perot was discredited after '92, I was sure that the political impulse that produced Perot would still be strong. America doesn't have a majority party. People care less about political parties, have less faith in them than ever before. I can't think of another time in this century when political parties meant less to the American people. That invites political fragmentation, but it's also a manifestation of a broader fragmentation throughout America.

RH: That fragmentation plays itself out in the book very experientially. It's a portrayal of a nation lurching around trying to find something to cling to.

SE: There's a void now, especially as we near the year 2000. Even people who are not superstitious or religious have some subterranean psychic resonance with the millennium, and the country finds itself at increasingly loose ends. Having in some ways succeeded all too well and in other ways failed all too profoundly to achieve the American idea, the country is looking either to find some new faith in that idea or, more terrifying, find a new idea.

RH: That leads us to find our political consciousness not in politicians, but in popular culture. You, for example, end up writing about Bruce Springsteen and Oliver Stone.

SE: Those kinds of crosscurrents make complete sense to most people at some level, but to the political establishment, or those in power, they make no sense at all. To the people who make the big decisions about our media and our culture, those sections of this book are confounding, yet I couldn't imagine writing about what was going on in America without writing about Stone or Springsteen, or Philip Dick or Frank Sinatra.

RH: The fragmentary experience of the campaign has a lot in common with your novels. They all present a state of existence you've obviously been contemplating for some time.

SE: At this point, it's all turning into one ongoing novel, or rather one ongoing story. It made perfect sense for me that *American Nomad* would pick up in a certain sense from where my last book, *Amnesiascope*, left off. At this point, I don't step out of one frame of mind into another just because I'm moving from fiction to nonfiction.

RH: It reminds me a lot of the latter Philip K. Dick, especially *VALIS*.

SE: *VALIS* is certainly the clearest case of that in his later work, where he includes a character who sort of is Dick, but isn't, and who might be the author of the book, or might not be . . .

RH: Writers seem to get to this point where you can either filter your experience or your consciousness—if you're trying to constantly write from a place that close to your own identity—through an alter ego, like Philip Roth has done with Nathan Zuckerman, or you can simply write about Steve Erickson.

SE: That's an advantage when you're traveling along the not very well enforced border between the conscious and the subconscious. While I just got through saying that I can't step in and out of a frame of mind, I can step in and out of certain notions I may have about my own personal identity and my own literary identity, if I can make that distinction. As a writer, I know that the public and private and literary identities are never all that far apart, but they may be perceived by others as being far apart, and that gives you certain advantages. In the eyes of others, I can step into new roles through my writing when I'm not really stepping into a new role at all. I can create an identity within the context of my work that's the other side of whatever dual or fragmented identity all writers have, the secret identity we all possess, our own conjoined twin.

RH: Given how confounded people get by the type of political and cultural analysis you're conducting here, do you see any future opportunity to pursue this type of journalism in magazines?

SE: I don't know. The state of magazine journalism is pretty bleak. Magazines are not about ideas and voices. They're about concepts and packaging. *Rolling Stone* is a classic case, a very different magazine from what it was twenty-five or thirty years ago. I assume people who publish magazines and advertise in them believe that those magazines accurately reflect what people in America are thinking, and maybe they're right. But it's not an adventurous endeavor to write for magazines today. And that's scary. The situation doesn't bode well for writers who have any sense at all of who they are. When I get hired by magazines, I increasingly feel that it's on the basis of whatever small reputation I may have rather than on the basis of the way that I actually write and think.

RH: And the alternative press has become almost completely corporate.

SE: That's an ongoing process that's been happening over the last ten years. The *LA Weekly* became increasingly corporate, and now it's owned by the *Village Voice*. The *Village View* and the *LA Reader* were bought and merged together by the New Times chain, which is supposedly the new wave of corporate alternative journalism, if that isn't a complete oxymoron.

RH: Are you working on anything now?

SE: I've started a new novel. But I don't like to talk about ongoing projects, especially at the beginning. My confidence is always precarious at the outset, and writing is, in part, a process of coming to believe in the work. To put any part of it out there for people's response before it's really ready is dangerous. To be honest, even when a book is finished, I find it difficult to talk about. Even when people ask me what a finished book is about, I'm at a loss as to how to distill the experience of writing it down to a line or two, without it coming off as completely pretentious horseshit.

Surfing the Slipstream: A Mini-Interview with Steve Erickson

Ellen Datlow, Robert K. J. Killheffer, and Lawrence Person / 1999

From *Nova Express* (Fall/Winter 1999): 16–17. First published on Event Horizon, May 6, 1999. Reprinted by permission.

This interview was first conducted online at the Event Horizon website through the auspices of Ellen Datlow and Robert K. J. Killheffer and appears here with their permission. Since it was conducted online in an open forum using chat handles, not all of the participants could be identified by name.

Robert K. J. Killheffer: Your work clearly roams beyond the usual confines of "mainstream" fiction. It's surreal, phantasmagorical, dream-filled, and anything but strictly mimetic. In some cases, such as *Tours of the Black Clock*, you've used common SF devices such as alternate history. Are you a reader of SF? Or has your work generated these ideas and approaches without such influence?

Steve Erickson: Well, I was drawn to SF as a kid, books and movies and comics, but as you can imagine, there were certain writers who spoke to me more than others. Heinlein, Asimov, Herbert, those people never meant much to me, whereas Dick, Sturgeon, and Bester did. It wasn't that far a leap, strange as it might sound, to Faulkner, Márquez, and Pynchon.

RK: To what extent have you followed (or even been aware of) your following among SF readers?

SE: I'm not real clear on it, to be honest. I know that really interesting bookstores like Dark Carnival up in the Bay Area, for instance, have carried my books among the more predominant SF and fantasy, and I know my books have occasionally been reviewed in SF magazines. One of the single smartest reviews I ever got was in the English SF magazine *Interzone*. So I'm happy to get my readers wherever I can. God knows I can use them.

RK: You seem to be the kind of writer who revisits a variety of central concerns in book after book—the weight and meaning of history, the metaphorical power of time, the anguished search for identity. Your novels are of a piece on one level, yet utterly different from one another. Are you aware of revisiting themes again and again?

SE: Well, as I get older, those concerns that you've identified exactly, among others, are informed by new experiences and, I would like to think, new insights. I did finally become aware, somewhere around the third or fourth novel, that in a way I was writing one long novel, with each book a chapter.

RK: That sounds like a comment by John Crowley, who has been working on his *Aegypt* sequence for years and has come to realize that most of his life will be dedicated to this huge single novel, in several parts, reflecting and refracting a finite selection of concerns. He seems resigned to it, though a bit disconcerted. Do you ever think about trying something wholly different? Or are these issues the very reasons why you write in the first place?

SE: At the risk of this sounding like a lot of mystical wah-wah when it comes to the creative process, I don't think about it that much. I don't choose the book; the book chooses me. And I suspect that's true for a lot of writers. I write about the things I write about. They're there, and they demand to be written.

RK: In *The Sea Came in at Midnight*, you depict Tokyo as a mystical ur-city and epitome of late-millennial material culture all at once. Did you visit Tokyo? Or did you weave that out of secondhand knowledge?

SE: I spent some time in Tokyo. It's a very strange city. It makes LA look positively authentic. I thought, "This is the true *Blade Runner* city," and then everyone in Tokyo told me the true *Blade Runner* city is Hong Kong.

RK: It seems that the times have caught up with you, in the sense that the concerns you've been writing about for years are now being discussed in the wider culture. Have you felt ahead of your time all these years?

SE: I don't know. That sounds awfully pretentious for me to say. You can say it though. It may be one reason I wanted to write about the millennium not so much in cataclysmic terms, but in psychic terms, or even—if I may put it this way, because it's become a bit of a cliché lately—spiritual terms. In the new book, the millennium is not only something of an anticlimax, it's basically an anti-millennium, arguing that in historical terms the millennium began thirty-one years ago almost to the day, and in personal terms that we are each our own millennium.

Lawrence Person: Are you familiar with the term *slipstream*, and do you think it applies to your work?

SE: I am familiar with it. I think it's probably as good a catchall phrase for my work as any, and besides, it reminds me of a line from the greatest album of all time.

Ellen Datlow: Which line? What album?

SE: Knew you couldn't resist. "Venture in the slipstream," from *Astral Weeks*.

Cole (unknown): At times you use crystal clear, really tight images and phrases, and at other times, it's vast and overwhelming. Do you feel this tension, and what do you make of readers struggling with that vastness?

SE: You know, at this point it's really all so instinctual. These people in their stories are caught between the certainties they have to redeem, and the chaos they can't understand. I always hope I can convey both to the reader. Your question about the extent to which the reader is in my mind is particularly hard to address. I'm always aware of the reader, but to write I free myself of him or her too. *That's* the tension.

Jimbo (unknown): I wanted to ask you about your interest in politics. What's your take on the scene for 2000?

SE: I was writing about the Monica thing for *Salon*, and I got so burned out. I just can't face it right now. I think potentially it could be a really interesting election, because the Republican Party will have to come to terms with who they are. And that will be bloody. The more I hear about George W. Bush, the more I keep thinking about George Romney, way back in the ancient history of the sixties. 1967, everyone had decided he was going to be the next president. Come 1969, the next president was Nixon.

Jeff (unknown): Your novels have complex plots. When writing, do you feel you're constructing them, or that you are accessing a full-blown, alternate reality?

SE: Oh, it's more accessing, for sure, because here's the twisted, sick, fucked-up truth: I make them up as I go along. They come to me in the writing. I don't outline, or make notes—it's just the way my brain naturally works. And I have to admit it drives me a little crazy by the time it's done.

LP: One of your primary themes seems to be that of an ordinary man meeting, or even glimpsing, a woman so compelling that it changes not only his life but the fundamental fabric of reality. What is it that makes this theme so central to your work?

SE: Well, I guess that was one of the variations on earlier work in this most recent novel. As you say, in virtually every earlier book, there's been a woman who was a catalytic component, setting things in motion. And this novel is populated by women, really, leaving aside the Occupant and Carl the mapmaker. Kristin, Lulu, and Angie dominate the book, and that was new for me. I don't know why: it just felt natural.

LP: Another label, besides slipstream, that gets slapped on your work is "postmodern." Do you think that label is apt, and do you think anyone really knows what "postmodern" means?

SE: What a good question! I don't know what the fuck it means! Someone out there explain . . .

ED: It belongs in the trash with semiotics.

RK: It's been used so indiscriminately that it hardly means anything anymore—if it once did.

SE: It seems to allude to the artificiality of art, and an inherent irony. Maybe a permanent detachment of the experiencer from the experience, or an overt use of experimental language. And I don't see how either of those things apply to my books. But, you know, it's like anything else: if other people want to call me a postmodernist, I don't really care.

RK: I think the aspect of your work that brings down the "postmodern" epithet is the mingling of tones and scales, which Cole alluded to earlier. That's one of the things critics usually point to in work they term postmodern, and there's certainly some wild mixing that goes on in your books. But what such critics seem to miss is the seriousness of your books—as you said, there's nothing ironic about your juxtapositions—and in that sense you're as far from postmodern as it gets.

SE: Well, I'm certainly influenced by the pop culture of my life, and maybe that's what gets called postmodern. But I really don't mean to call attention to the artifice, or to make a point of it as so much postmodernism seems to. Exactly the opposite. I hope that I pull the reader into the reality of the work, and in that sense I couldn't be more old-fashioned. The last twentieth-century-guy's Emily Brontë, basically.

J (unknown): Do you live in LA still? And is that where you've lived all your life? To what extent has LA contributed to your particular vision of reality?

SE: I still live in LA. I was born and raised here. For a period in the seventies, I lived in Paris, Amsterdam, Italy, NY. LA has probably contributed to the way I see things in that it doesn't define your vision for you. LA is the blank slate of consciousness, as cities go. Don't misunderstand me: there's much about it I feel very ambivalent about. I love how in New York or Paris, you can go to a restaurant and overhear people talking about politics, books, whatever. In LA all you hear is people talking about the "industry." And I love the movies, but I don't want to live and breathe them all the time.

Still, I think there are certain ways LA leaves one the freedom to define his own creativity.

LP: Loaded question: What is your primary motivation in using the fantastic and nonrealistic elements that are so central to your work?

SE: They come to me very naturally. I think LA has something to do with that: there are ways it's a very surreal city. And I think growing up in the time I did, influenced as I was by movies and rock 'n' roll, contributed to that too. So it's not a question of motives, really—it's my natural bent.

LP: *The Sea Came in at Midnight* is a partial departure in that, for the early part of the novel, it is possible to believe that the fantastic events all happen inside someone's head, or can be chalked up to the mental state of the characters. Are all nonrealistic events in this and your other books "real" within the confines of the book universe, or are some of them attributable to your characters' mental state?

SE: The obliteration of the line between "reality" and "non-reality" pretty much comes with the territory in my books—the obliteration between the "dream" and whatever is not a dream. In that sense, nothing is just "happening in someone's head," if that makes any sense. Does that quite answer the question?

LP: Yes. In his *Nova Express* interview, William Browning Spencer said, "It's all real!" And I think your answer is similar, if more roundabout. Or, to put it another way, it's all as real as anything else in the novel can be said to be real.

SE: Yes, I think of it as all real too, and therefore, when people find my books difficult, honestly, I think they're trying too hard. My books should be read as quickly as possible, and thought about as little as possible while you're reading.

LP: What do you think is the most essential "cognitive fracture" in the reality of the twentieth century that makes real and unreal so intermixed? The madness of the twentieth century (Hitler, Stalin, Pol Pot, Mao, etc.), or the furious upheavals of late twentieth-century cultural and technological change, or something else?

SE: I suppose the "fracture" you're talking about is a natural outgrowth of the way time has sped up. The way the human race has crossed the terrain of the imagination more in one century than all the centuries before it put together. And you see the madness of it everywhere.

An Interview with Steve Erickson

Michael Silverblatt / 2005

From *Bookworm*, KCRW-FM (April 14, 2005). Copyright © 2005 by KCRW-FM. Reprinted by permission.

Michael Silverblatt: From KCRW Santa Monica, I'm Michael Silverblatt, and this is *Bookworm*. Today I'm happy to have as my guest Steve Erickson. His most recent novel is *Our Ecstatic Days*; it's published by Simon & Schuster. He is the author as well of several other novels, beginning with *Days Between Stations, Rubicon Beach, Tours of the Black Clock, Arc d'X, Amnesiascope,* and *The Sea Came in at Midnight.* Two of his earlier novels, *Days Between Stations* and *Tours of the Black Clock,* have been republished in paperback by Simon & Schuster. Now, whereas some novels are addressed to the head, and some novels are addressed to the heart and emotions, I think that Steve Erickson's novels are addressed to the unconscious and to our dreaming state. And in order to have us respond from these depths, he's invented all kinds of writing techniques that help displace the so-called intelligent mind to move into the realm of intuition first, and then a kind of deep unconscious area. What are some of the ways in which these books move the reader into that strange and largely unexplored place?

Steve Erickson: Well, I think, Michael, that a lot of it comes out of the way I write the books. I don't know that I consciously set out to write unconscious, dreamlike books, although I agree with that characterization and I think most people do. These are sort of the books that, for whatever reason, come naturally to me, and I don't—I'm always careful, at least in the early writing, not to overthink it too much. I'll start with a situation or an image in my head. In the case of the new novel, you've got a single mother who is living in Los Angeles in the early twenty-first century and one day a lake appears in the middle of Los Angeles, and she gets it into her head that this lake has come to take her child from her. And I would say that out of that initial image or glimpse of a dream, if you will, the stories kind of unfold organically. You know, I don't make outlines of books. I like for the book to take me on whatever journey it's going to take the reader, and therefore, I'm less conscious, frankly, of any technique involved, than in just following the book where it's going to go.

MS: Now, at the same time, though, there are things that, for a reader, become very felt. Because that image of a lake filling Los Angeles becomes eventually a version of the amniotic sac bursting.

SE: Right.

MS: And so an image gets embodied. And I often think that one of the ways in which magic works in literature is for the senses to be addled or confused. That something that you begin with, the image of a lake filling up a city, which is a visual image and something in the head, becomes the woman's growing pregnancy, and it becomes a physicalized image. And I think that frequently that drift between the head and the body becomes part of the way in which the reader gets involved in a new relationship to the prose.

SE: Yeah, I agree with that. And I think part of the reason for that may be that the writer gets involved in a new relationship with the prose. At some point in the early writing of this, I thought of the lake as, as you say, the earth's water breaking at the moment of labor. But that wasn't a metaphor that I began with in any conscious way. So I tend to, I like to leave myself open to the possibility that the images in my books and the characters in my books and the stories take on a kind of metaphorical dimension that I didn't anticipate, hopefully without it ever getting overly symbolic, because I don't particularly believe in symbolic fiction in the sense of characters and stories and metaphors being used, functioning in terms of symbolizing certain themes in the books. I guess the point I make is that for me, the process of writing the book is probably not that much different than the process of reading the book is for the reader.

MS: Now, I would say that the reader is following these images as magical narrative. A pregnancy gives way to the pregnancy of the earth. The earth turns out to have a birth tunnel. If there is something that is going to come out of the pregnant woman's body, it's going to—something is going to go into the body of the earth. There's a kind of strange, magical algebra that goes on.

SE: Right.

MS: In fact, this is going to be like finding Wonderland. There's an access route into an inverse world, I guess more like the looking glass world in Alice, and we're not going to really know whether that's a dream world or a real world. It's going to be both.

SE: That's right.

MS: And part of, I think, the excitement is the multiplying of possibility rather than the limiting of it.

SE: That's right. Yeah, I would hope that's part of the excitement, and it's probably part of the challenge too. As I got deeper into the story, it seemed to me more and more clearly that to a certain extent, this was a story about a mother who wants to protect her child from the chaos of the universe, which a mother can't do. At the end of the book, again without giving too much away, the mother will find a kind of order. But I think we're left with the question of how real that order is, and I think that the mother, having taken the sort of long journey through the book, has had to reconcile herself to the uncertainties of life that every parent who's in the thrall of his or her love for their child has to reconcile herself to.

MS: Now, I'm speaking to Steve Erickson about his new novel *Our Ecstatic Days*, published by Simon & Schuster. And one of the things that I find about your books is that a situation that, on its surface, might be ordinary—a mother's love for her child—becomes subjected to a kind of myopic intensification.

SE: That's right.

MS: And then played against the background of the catastrophes of our time.

SE: That's right.

MS: What's interesting to me here in *Our Ecstatic Days* is that it's almost as if a woman has a child, there's not a father on the scene, and it's hard to be a parent. Now, the contrast, the other thing available, is not to be a parent. What would it be like, it's almost as if she's wondering, if I were my anti-self? What if I were without a child, and in fact, a dominator of men, not the victim of a fatherless situation?

SE: Right.

MS: And so, in the other world, she is a dominatrix. Her circumstances are the opposite of family and order. It's depravity and the unsettling of the bourgeois psyche. It's almost as if this book, in order to tell itself, she has to imagine the extreme opposite of what she's experiencing in order to accept the fact that she is a mother and that the child, willy-nilly, however endangered, will ultimately be as safe as any other child.

SE: I think that's all exactly right, and I can't say that I had thought it through to that extent when I was writing it. But this young woman was a character in a previous novel, which I don't think you necessarily have to read to read this one. But she was a character in a previous novel called

The Sea Came in at Midnight, that takes place at the end of the last millennium. And in order to survive, she gets herself into a situation of sexual subjugation, and it's out of that relationship that—rather, it's *in* that relationship that she becomes pregnant, and it's out of that relationship that she has a child. And so when she loses the child, when he vanishes one day during an afternoon when she's tried to stop the thing that she was afraid was going to take the child, it seemed natural to me that her response, that her way of dealing with the chaos that has swept away her child, would be to put herself into a role of sexual domination, to essentially turn upside down the situation that made this child in the first place. And then, you know, as the themes of chaos and order become manifest in the book, I think that, as you say, that choice she makes takes on other metaphorical implications along the lines that you've just described.

MS: Now, the listener will recognize by now that I'm not talking about an ordinary kind of novel. And it's my feeling that this novel, that these novels that my guest Steve Erickson writes, the most recent of which is *Our Ecstatic Days,* are beautiful poetic attempts to make a sphere or globe out of fear and dread. And to allow one's worst fears to, in a sense, come true, or at least to grow into a mandala-sized thing, so opposites join. Projections occur. The girl that we know as Kristin becomes Lulu Blu, the dominatrix. And there is a certain sense in which I think these novels put the reader through a thrilling and harrowing experience of the worst possible. Characters dream of what they're about to lose. In *The Sea Came in at Midnight,* it's the loss of a marriage. In *Our Ecstatic Days,* it's the loss of a child. It's almost as if the terrors besetting daily life become the subject, blown up here into a point where it can really be seen.

SE: Yeah, I think that's a really good observation, and it occurs to me that perhaps in the same way that, in this novel, Kristin rushes to the source of her fear in order to stop it, in my novels I suppose I rush to whatever is my own unconscious source of fear or anxiety or loss. If you can sort of meet it head-on, maybe you can, in the process, head off whatever is coming to take away the thing that you value. The thing, of course, is that in the novels, that effort is often futile. In the case of *Our Ecstatic Days,* in Kristin's inability to find a way to live with chaos and to find a way to live with uncertainty—and the feeling, I can tell you as a parent, the feeling of uncertainty becomes manifest a hundred times over once you have a child—in her rush to try to head off that uncertainty and meet it head-on and somehow seize control of it, *that's* when she loses the child, because when she returns from that confrontation, if you will, her little boy has vanished from the boat where she left him.

MS: Now, this is a female world that she's entering. In fact, when she goes into the other world, the songs that she hears are largely by female singers: Patti Smith and—who's the writer of "Opal Moon"?

SE: Merrie Amsterburg.

MS: And the walls of houses, when the ear is held to them, they echo with the resonance of female singing and female sorrow. And there's even a house doctor who is almost the psychoanalyst figure of the novel, and like most psychoanalysts, she has a sad background herself.

SE: Which involves relationships with other women.

MS: That's right. Now, this would be a classic area for someone to say, well, how did you know what it's like to carry a child, to miscarry a child, to go through the birth process? You've demanded of yourself not just some empathy, but entire participation in female desire and fantasy here. How did you go about it?

SE: Well, I'd be a liar if I said I didn't have some trepidation about that, and if you asked me how would I know what it's like to carry a child, the answer is I don't. In the case of this particular book, you're completely right—at some point it was very clear to me this was a feminine book. It was dominated by a female sensibility and, in fact, the book talks about [how] the lake is full of melody snakes, and at one point I had a list of all the melodies that the snakes were associated with. And I was going to publish it with the book and I decided not to because I wanted people to hear their own songs. But they were all songs by women, so that was a very conscious choice. In the case of Kristin, because she's a character from a previous book, I felt like I knew her. And it wasn't so much a matter of writing from the perspective of a woman, but writing from the perspective of somebody I knew who happened to be a woman. There's another prominent character who comes into the book later named Brontë, and she was more of a challenge because she functions in the role, if you will, of a male fantasy. She's kind of a protégé to Kristin, who's now called Lulu, and that's kind of how she makes her living. She's a professional male fantasy, and I had to find a way to try to write about her not like a male. I mean—

MS: From inside.

SE: From her standpoint, from her perspective, in her voice, thinking about the things that men might think about differently from the way that a woman would think about them. And I was very conscious about that, and I was very—I was a little concerned about it, because in some ways, I think, it's a rather presumptuous thing to do. But it seemed obvious to me that this was what the book was about, that it was about women.

MS: I've read this book three times, because I was transfixed by its mysteries. And I enjoyed it every time, but on the third time, I began to trace some of its patterns, between the upper world and the lower world, and the appearance of certain toys, in particular a toy monkey in this place, in that place. I saw several different families, disparate and exiled, join into a crucial family, although they are not in fact related by blood. There are projections and fulfillments of a very deep longing for family and order. Now, if those feelings come through, how much do you need the reader to follow the details as they go on through the book? It's a very ebb-and-flow and tidal novel. And how much is based upon a reader's trust that the writer is taking care of the details invisibly?

SE: I would hope the latter. I would hope the book convinces the reader to put his or her trust in it. While the book is written intuitively and instinctually on one level, it's more carefully written on another level. But I never believed that the reader had to grasp every single detail. I would rather that the reader just let himself or herself go with what I'll call the dream logic of the book. And the details and the loose ends that tie up and the ends that would seem to threaten to tie up that then don't—that's all kind of going on, if you will, beneath the surface of the lake, and it's part of the journey that the reader takes. But the reader doesn't have to know every single thing beneath that surface.

MS: Because I feel that the reader really needs to let this book be an experience of life, that this book is a trip through life, and that it's meant to supplant ordinary consciousness.

SE: Right.

MS: And to rely on the reader's crazily higher transformed consciousness—a transformation that you make in the process of reading the book—so that when you come out of it, you've gone through something that allows you to be more whole than you were when you started.

SE: Well, that would be the ideal way to read the book, and I think that if the reader just has faith in his or her own response to the book, and if the reader forms a kind of emotional and psychological alliance with the book, that's the way the book succeeds.

MS: I've been speaking with Steve Erickson, author most recently of *Our Ecstatic Days*. Thank you, Steve, for joining me.

SE: Michael, thank you very much.

MS: The books by Steve Erickson have been being discovered by writers like Thomas Pynchon. Well, this reader has been following him since his second book. To my mind, they're the real event. They're the excitement of what reading is presenting right now. If catastrophe and chaos has become the tenor of our days, and our daily lives have had to find a way of placing themselves against that incredible roaring background of an unstable, unstabilizable time, these are the books that describe the conditions of people in our time. They're the new realism.

Steve Erickson: Ecstasy, Chaos, and the Last Battleground

Andrew Hedgecock / 2006

From *Interzone*, no. 205 (August 2006): 4–7. Reprinted by permission.

My first encounter with the works of Steve Erickson, almost a decade ago, seemed to be guided by something more than chance. I'd read something by Nick Royle, praising Erickson's originality, the power of his dreamlike imagery, and the precision of his description of the horrors and possibilities of our era. "Must read him," I thought but, typically, within days all I could remember was the surname had sounded Scandinavian. Luckily, the next time I walked into a secondhand bookstore, the first thing that caught my eye was a Futura paperback featuring a deserted cityscape (drawing heavily on de Chirico) with Nazi flags, a boat washed up on an orange tide, and a ghostly image of Hitler set against a blazing sky. This was one of the books Royle had been so passionate about—*Tours of the Black Clock* (1989).

And he was spot-on: Here was a searing examination of the horrors and depravities of the twentieth century; a mesmerising blend of bleak comedy, literary metafiction, dystopian SF, alternative history, mythology, and detective noir. This stylistic alchemy is a defining characteristic of Erickson's work. John Buckley, writing in the *Wall Street Journal*, called Erickson "modern fiction's genius caddy, reaching when necessary for just the right club."

Erickson's own assessment of his fusion of literary tropes and forms is reassuringly devoid of golfing allusions:

"This is just material that comes naturally to me. Why the genre stuff speaks to me I'm not sure, except I think sometimes there's more psychic truth in melodrama than 'high' culture wants to acknowledge. The surrealism is somehow part of my view of things. This may have something to do with growing up in a landscape—Los Angeles—that naturally bends notions of time and place, because it's entropic and doesn't impose itself the way other cities do. But there's never been any conscious, conceptual intent to blend anything: it came to me naturally."

From Erickson's first published novel, *Days Between Stations* (1985), to his most recent, *Our Ecstatic Days* (2005), Los Angeles, his home city, is repeatedly reimagined. It's a rich and malleable source of history and mythology for Erickson. I ask if he shares the view of the socialist sociologist Mike Davis who, in the hugely influential *City of Quartz*, suggested the city constituted a prophecy for the future of all cities. Or does LA hold a different kind of fascination for Erickson?

"Mike's LA is very much a sociological laboratory, and he does a brilliant job of translating it through the prism of that agenda. I'm sure I have my own agenda, and if I can't really describe what it is, it's not Mike's, although he did an insightful job of writing about my work and how it pertained to LA in his follow-up book, *Ecology of Fear*. Of course the 'real' LA is neither mine nor Mike's. It eludes the cohesive identity of other cities that lend themselves to simpler definitions. I see it as a terrain of possibility and madness. There's no getting around the fact you have a lot of functioning lunatics in LA, and I don't just mean those lying in the street muttering to themselves: I mean people driving Jaguars and living what other people would consider exceedingly successful glamorous lives, who in fact are entirely off the rails and don't have a clue who they are."

Promises, Betrayals, and Myth-Mining

Days Between Stations set out Erickson's stall in terms of style and concern. It's a haunting odyssey through fragmented and colliding time streams, provoked by a mysterious fragment of film, taking readers from a sand-swept, near-future Los Angeles to a post-catastrophe Paris, where the lights are out but bonfires blaze. I ask if these layers of dreamlike consciousness are a product of authorial design, or if his stories demand to be channeled in this form:

"When I start writing the story, none of that stuff is conscious at all. I feel compelled to write it, usually for reasons I don't understand myself—for me they're more visceral than cerebral, and I hope they're more visceral for the reader as well. Otherwise I've failed. At some point, I do step back and begin asking questions, and some of the answers to those questions get incorporated into the work. But the work never becomes about those answers. It remains about the visceral thing the story was born from. A writer writes to find out what it is he or she is thinking—that is, the book is as much a discovery for the writer as for the reader.

"I know I deal in imagery that's primal and subconscious, but none of the things that happen in my stories are a code for anything. When readers find my work difficult, it's because they think they have to decode it. They read reviews that are very flattering but suggest the work is impossibly daunting. I'm the most literal writer on the face of the planet, and if you just take everything I write at face value and not worry about all the complexities or strategies attached, any one of my novels is easier to understand than any *Harry Potter* book. Compared to anything I've written, the simplest novel by John le Carré—whom I admire but whose stories my pea-brain finds extraordinarily convoluted—is *Finnegans Wake*."

It was with Erickson's second novel, *Rubicon Beach* (1986), that the theme of America—its history, its mythology, its politics, and its collective psyche—started asserting itself in his work. Like some strange brew of Borges, Kafka, and Ballard, the story involves a numerological quest; a political dissident under surveillance in a flooded Los Angeles, part of a Balkanized America; and the mysterious odyssey of a modern-day siren.

"Since it was founded, America has been about *meaning*. I think *Rubicon Beach* concerns itself with that too."

And the theme continued to develop in *Leap Year* (1989), a searing blend of political campaign diary and fictional myth-mining that put the boot into America's liberal Left and conservative Right, and *Arc d'X* (1993), a dystopian extravaganza involving alternate history and visionary fantasy. Both *Leap Year* and *Arc d'X* reveal a fascination with eighteenth- and nineteenth-century American history. Erickson's stories and journalism have been informed by a stark—almost paradoxical—duality of thought about his nation. He's crushingly disappointed by the trajectory of America's recent history but, at the same time, believes it can rediscover just, tolerant, and freethinking approaches to social organization. So how have these competing feelings of hope and despair determined the complexity and ambiguity of Erickson's narratives?

"Rather quaintly, I still find the American Idea thrilling in spite of all the ways we've betrayed it from the beginning. The people who founded the country refused to deal with the issue of slavery, which was an affront to the Idea as obvious as it was horrific. That said, I hope it doesn't sound unduly jingoistic to point out that, for all that's wrong with it, this is still the country that people risk their lives to get into, and that there's enormous

pressure to build a wall around it to keep people out, as opposed to countries that spent the last hundred years building walls to keep people in. The
Idea is still powerful enough to represent a promise so electrifying to people
that it doesn't seem to matter to them how many times the promise is broken. And from the outset the promise and betrayal have been there in the
original DNA of the country, a helix—it's what the Civil War was fought for,
which really involved a recasting of the country in terms of its meaning. It
also says something about the country, on the other hand, that even now
relatively educated, enlightened white people in the American South won't
acknowledge that that war was about slavery."

Ism, Ism, Ism

It's clear from Erickson's interviews and journalism he rejects the whole
array of traditional political "isms." Over the years he has moved from an
independent conservative position to one of almost total skepticism. I ask
if this has meant embracing anarchist traditions, and whether this personal
journey informs his fiction.

"On a psychological level my most profound impulse *is* anarchic, although
my practical and nonviolent side rejects that. At some point I realized
ideology is by definition intellectually dishonest: it involves the embrace
of a single, narrow way of looking at things, and every argument becomes
about serving an ideological interest rather than the truth. The twentieth
century was the century of secular ideology, and the twenty-first is going
to be the century of spiritual ideology, which is scarier because the usual
checks on human behavior imposed by a natural survival instinct are no
longer operational. There are people out there who don't think twice about
the planet and the species going up in flames in the name of some higher
religious ideal; people in fact who find something purifying and righteous
about that idea. I think this sort of religious chaos manifests itself pretty
clearly in some of my novels, including the recent one."

The recent one is *Our Ecstatic Days* (2005), a tale of "the Age of Chaos."
The story features a lake that appears overnight in the middle of LA, ani-
mate buildings that sicken and die, melody snakes consisting entirely of
music, and a shadowy resistance movement. Kristin, the survivor of a lem-
minglike ritual sacrifice of women and children portrayed by Erickson in
The Sea Came in at Midnight (1999), has fled to an abandoned hotel by the
mysterious lake. When her three-year-old son goes missing she sets out

on a quest across fractured layers of reality, in one of which she becomes a dominatrix called Lulu. The book's key theme is the increasingly fragile boundary between civilization and pandemonium. I ask Erickson to what extent the story's strange erasures and chaotic transformations reflect the current battle for the soul of the US and his country's struggle for a new sense of identity:

"On the one hand George Bush is right: al-Qaeda *are* bad people. When it comes to killing children, I don't care how legitimate the complaints about Western policies in the Middle East might be. Terrorism—and this differentiates it from any other sort of military action, including guerrilla warfare—very deliberately targets noncombatants and insists that no one is innocent, including, you know, my eight-year-old. I supported the American entrance into Afghanistan because the Taliban didn't bother denying its alliance with al-Qaeda and its complicity in 9/11. But now the president is willing to use a justifiable war on terrorism to justify the invasion of a country that had nothing to do with al-Qaeda or 9/11, and that presented no documented threat to the US or the West. In the process we've alienated the world, radicalized whatever is left of moderate Islam, created a new staging ground for terrorism, and stretched our capacity for self-defense to a breaking point.

"My revulsion was increased by all the literature that emerged over the last couple of years, showing the government made the decision to go to war first and then constructed a rationale to support it, rather than the other way around. The second big problem is a Christian theocratic impulse, growing in the United States for the last twenty years—an impulse that's not only un-American but, along with our action in Iraq, robs us of moral authority in any battle against religious extremism. The American Right has done a brilliant job of hijacking the *meaning* of the country, and those on the Left or even in the reasonable center have acquiesced."

Deeply Strange and Perverse

"This has had a bearing on several novels, particularly *Arc d'X* and *Our Ecstatic Days*. As well, the collapse of the Berlin Wall certainly played a part in *Arc d'X*, and any careful reader may note the shadow cast by 9/11 on *Our Ecstatic Days*, though that was something I tried not to be too overt about. In the end, my view of history is essentially anti-Marxist. The Marxist view generally holds that politics and societal dynamics define our individual psychological and emotional lives, whereas I believe that our individual psychological and emotional lives define our society and politics, and that, as one of the characters in *Our Ecstatic Days* says, 'history often unfolds for reasons that don't have anything to do with history.'"

Readers will have noted Erickson's fascination with flooding, social breakdown, and the polymorphous possibilities of LA. His other frequently ploughed thematic furrows are amnesia and pornography. The theme of erased, ambiguous, and distorted memory recurs throughout his work—most notably in *Days Between Stations* and *Amnesiascope*. I ask why it repeatedly forces its way into his narratives.

"It may be something as simple as writing *Amnesiascope* in my midforties, when I became distinctly aware that I probably was closer to the end of my life than to the beginning, and when I became distinctly aware how tenuous memory can be. At that point it was a very personal theme, and only over the next few years did it seem to assert itself culturally—suddenly the memoir, or the memoirist novel, is in fashion, and it doesn't seem an accident that it was a fashion born of the late nineties. I think memoirism, if you will, had a millennial aspect to it. It was the secular version of millennialism, apocalypse on a psychic level rather than a sociological or religious one."

Some of the most unsettling and memorable scenes in Erickson's novels manipulate the tropes of pornography and ritualized spectacle. In books such as *Amnesiascope* and *Tours of the Black Clock* he transforms them into symbols of psychic and cultural upheaval.

"Sexuality has become the last battleground. Those of us who came of age in the sixties lived through a brief time when we believed sex didn't have consequences, so when AIDS came along in the early eighties, the idea that sex was dangerous felt unnatural, oppressive. Throughout human history, sex has almost always been dangerous—the brief period when it *wasn't* dangerous was aberrational. People used to die of syphilis all the time. Women used to die in childbirth all the time. Then you add the deeply strange and perverse tendency of the species, as represented by religion, to view sex as evil.

"We live in a time when the artistic depiction of the most mortifying violence is more socially and morally acceptable than the depiction of sexuality; when a guy torturing and killing a woman in a movie is more acceptable than any slightly explicit depiction of sexual interaction between them. As is the wont of my country to polarize every discussion, the discussion of sex is dominated by people who see no middle ground between reckless promiscuity on the one hand and repressive abstinence on the other. In the meantime you have interesting things happening in the culture: more and more mainstream movies—the most obvious example being *Eyes Wide Shut*—inch toward a more explicit sexuality. Meanwhile porn directors like Michael Ninn try to incorporate values of legitimate cinema into their work. At this point I don't see that either is succeeding, but it's interesting. I would hope it goes without saying that I'm talking about sexuality between consenting adults as opposed to something like child porn, which obviously is beyond the pale on any level."

Next Stop, Zeroville

Joshua Chaplinsky / 2007

From *The Cult*, at www.chuckpalahniuk.net (November 29, 2007). Reprinted by permission.

I know many of you are already familiar with author Steve Erickson. In fact, it was on the forums here and at *Cult* sister site *The Velvet* that I was first introduced to his work. I read *The Sea Came in at Midnight* and screamed for more like a hungry child. Erickson fills the void, writing the type of mind-bending genre-less fiction that simultaneously challenges and excites. Less than a year and ten books later, his is one of the first names mentioned when I'm asked about my favorite authors.

Which is why I was thrilled when, so soon after my initial binge, I discovered Erickson had a new novel, *Zeroville*, due in November from Europa Editions. Not wanting to wait that long to read it, I selfishly hatched a scheme to score myself an advance reader's copy. I'd masquerade as a journalist and interview him for *The Cult*! The second the idea crossed my mind I realized how cool that would actually be, and suddenly it was about much more than scoring a free book.

Zeroville is a more straightforward effort for Erickson, narratively, but it is also one of his flat-out best, so there is no reason for longtime fans to fear. It is the story of Vikar Jerome, a film-obsessed ex-seminarian come to LA, fresh off the bus like Axl Rose in "Welcome to the Jungle." The story begins in 1969 and spans the entirety of film history itself. *Zeroville* is a who's who of film references and is truly a treat for anyone who loves the movies. Erickson, who is also a film critic for *Los Angeles Magazine*, really knows his shit, and it is evident on every page.

It literally took one email and I was put in touch with Erickson, who graciously agreed to the interview. He spoke in great depth about *Zeroville*, the publishing industry, his love of film, and his writing career.

Joshua Chaplinsky: There are a number of films important to the characters and to the story line of *Zeroville*. *A Place in The Sun* and *The*

Passion of Joan of Arc specifically play a major role in the novel. Are these films as significant for you as they are for the characters? What are some other films that are important to you?

Steve Erickson: Well, in the end the movies in the novel had to inform the story and characters. The book couldn't just be a compendium of films I happen to like. Some—*Last Year at Marienbad* or, for that matter, *Alphaville*, where the novel gets its title—just naturally lent themselves to being part of the book, without necessarily being any more special to me than real favorites—*The Third Man*, say, or *Jules and Jim*—that are mentioned in passing or barely at all. Most of this was instinctive rather than anything I worked out in a calculated way. I like both *A Place in the Sun* and *The Passion of Joan of Arc*, but that's not why they're important to the book. They're important because there's something about them that's deeply irrational and even rapturous—sometimes in a horrific way—which suited the story and the main character.

JC: I want to ask you about the portrayal of real-life people and events in *Zeroville*. Many of the famous actors and directors you use as characters in the novel either go nameless, or have partial or made-up names. Was this for legal reasons? Because to me, figuring out the references was part of the fun. How much of their portrayal was made up and how much was based on fact, if any?

SE: Legal reasons weren't involved. Maybe they should have been. I'm relying a lot, I guess, on some of the people in question having a sense of humor, and on people recognizing the good faith of my intentions. And I just think the characters have a greater chance of becoming their own characters, and the storytelling has more resonance, when the people in the story are defined in the story's terms rather than explicitly. Sometimes the explicit is more evocative. It's more evocative to, from the outset, identify Elizabeth Taylor and Montgomery Clift tattooed on the head of Vikar, the main character. Other times it's more evocative to let the reader fill in the blanks. I took the facts I knew and more or less made up my own versions of these people, but in the end I have no idea how much they resemble the actual people or don't.

JC: Was the character of Vikar in any way based on real-life persons or events? I couldn't really place him, or his Oscar-nominated film, *Your Pale Blue Eyes*, other than it possibly being a Velvet Underground reference. I like the bit about him finding *The Passion of Joan of Arc* in a janitor's closet at an Oslo mental institution, which actually happened in real life.

SE: Vikar is pretty much a whole creation. I certainly don't know of anyone like him in the movie business, or probably anywhere else. It's never clear if he's a savant or socially arrested or maybe just a bit dim. Someone says he's not a cineaste but "cineautistic." He was a good character through whom to look at a decade when a lot was going on in movies, when a lot was going on culturally. I would have to double-check to be sure, but I believe *Your Pale Blue Eyes* is the only movie in the novel that's made up, and yes, of course you're right, the title comes from the Lou Reed song. Every other movie in the novel is real, including *Nightdreams*, the porn picture. Also, as you say, *The Passion of Joan of Arc* really was discovered, long after everyone assumed it was lost, in the early eighties, in Oslo, in a janitorial closet in a mental hospital. It's just too far-fetched not to be true.

JC: Being both a critic and a fan of film, what are your thoughts on having your own work adapted for the big screen? Have the rights to any of your books been optioned? Are there any directors you would like to see interpret your material?

SE: Two of my novels have been optioned; another came close before I pulled the plug for reasons I won't go into here. Until *Our Ecstatic Days* I always thought my first, *Days Between Stations*, would best translate to film—both have core stories that are inherently cinematic. One is a love story; one is about a mother trying to save her kid. Alfonso Cuarón comes to mind for *Days Between Stations*, because he's a filmmaker who's at once emotional and strongly imagistic, and I can see someone like Jane Campion making *Our Ecstatic Days*. In either case a studio would have to be willing to put up some money, because both would be moderately expensive movies even if the stories are simplified. I think perhaps the most instructive adaptation of a modern literary novel is *The Unbearable Lightness of Being*. I read Kundera's book before the film was made and like a lot of people thought it wouldn't work as a movie, but the director Philip Kaufman broke down the material of the story and built his own version, which no longer resembled Kundera so much in form yet completely caught the book's essence. *The English Patient* is another example. What is it that Minghella told Michael Ondaatje when he bought the rights to the novel? "You realize we're going to fuck up your book." So if you're the novelist selling your story to the movies, you need to let go of it. You need to understand that your novel is your novel and the filmmaker's film is his or her film, and not get too precious about it or too invested. This is why, at least so far, I've resisted invitations to write screenplays of my books. It's better for both me and the movie if someone else does it. If *Zeroville* ever were made into a movie it's likely to be by either a particularly film-conscious director or an actor who sees a good part in Vikar. Obviously someone like Scorsese would get *Zeroville*. Whether he would like it, let alone want to make a movie, is another question, but he would understand it. Some Coppola or other—Francis or Sofia—would understand. Soderbergh. Tarantino, of course. P. T. Anderson. Right now there's a well-known young actor who's interested. We'll see. In Hollywood, "interest" and four bits gets you a morning newspaper.

JC: *Zeroville* initially appeared as a short story in a *McSweeney's* anthology. A lot of key elements from the novel were already present in that story. What made you decide to expand the idea into a novel? Was this always your intention?

SE: Actually I think the short story and novel are pretty different. The plots share a similar "secret," if you will, and the main character in both is a film editor, but other than that they're very different characters and the tone of the two things is different. I wrote the story as a bargain with Michael Chabon, or what I thought was a bargain—I approached him about writing for *Black Clock*, the literary magazine I edit, and he cannily roped me into writing for *McSweeney's*, in what I assumed would be a reciprocal arrangement. So I holed myself up at the Rio in Vegas for five days and knocked out the story. Chabon, sneaky bastard, never came through on his end. I wasn't completely satisfied with the short story because I never got a grasp of that central character. It was later when Vikar came so sharply into focus that the novel fell into place.

JC: Similarly, the characters of Sally Hemings and Thomas Jefferson from the political/pop-culture hybrid *Leap Year* resurface in the novel *Arc d'X*. What was so important about these characters that you felt the need to go back to them?

SE: Jefferson and Hemings are just great characters, and they embody the great contradiction of the country. I wrote *Arc d'X* six years before science more or less proved the two had a relationship, but the fact of their love affair was always clear to anyone who looked at the historical evidence honestly—it doesn't say much for supposedly reputable American historians who for two centuries insisted so vehemently otherwise, offering only the argument that Jefferson just wasn't, you know, that kind of guy. So I was fascinated with the people involved and also with a landscape where it was considered more scandalous that Jefferson slept with a Black woman than that he owned one.

JC: The idea of the female martyr, both literally and figuratively, seems to be a recurring motif in your work. Joan of Arc and immolation are referenced in *Arc d'X* as well as *Zeroville*. The character of Zazi in *Zeroville* also has that potential. I know this is something you have been criticized for in the past. Yet, despite what your female characters go through, many of them seem to retain a certain amount of power. How do you respond to the criticism of your portrayal of women?

SE: Well, I'll have to take your word for it about the criticism. I'm sure there's no getting around the fact that I see my female characters through the prism of a heterosexual guy even when I try not to, with all the hangups and lack of comprehension that go with it. I think I'm drawn to female characters because generally women are more interesting emotionally and psychologically, whereas with guys the train tends to pull into the station by the time they're thirty—that's as far as they're going to go. Whatever else is true about the women in my books, they're almost always defiant figures, and up until *Zeroville* they've increasingly dominated my books, particularly *The Sea Came in at Midnight* and *Our Ecstatic Days*. If someone wants to read those two books back to back with an open mind, I'm happy to accept whatever conclusion they reach about the way the women are presented. While you're right that Sally in *Arc d'X* assumes the role of martyr, I don't see it much in the other books except *Rubicon Beach*, and I must say I don't see it at all in Zazi in *Zeroville*. I just don't think martyrdom is in her future. Her mother, Soledad, maybe. But only if self-destruction counts.

JC: In addition to the aforementioned martyrdom, certain other motifs show up throughout your body of work: the apocalypse, fetishism, punk rock, film, Los Angeles. These recurring themes make it feel as if your characters all inhabit the same world, that they could almost all be a part of the same story. Is this purposeful or unavoidable? Do you feel you are trying to tell variations of the same story, or are using familiar themes to express different ideas?

SE: The recurrence of characters and themes began by accident, or what seemed an accident. It's certainly true that these characters all inhabit the world in my head, and often it's been true that one book would grow out of something that later felt to me incomplete about an earlier book. You're not the first to suggest it's all one book, and to the extent it's a single story I think of it as a round one, where any entry point is good as the other.

JC: You are known for your nonlinear narrative style. Seemingly disparate story lines that share certain characters and ideas, stories which overlap and circle back on themselves. Yet *Zeroville* is one of your most linear novels to date. Was this a conscious effort on your part? Do you generally share Vikar's lack of need for narrative continuity?

SE: I tell the stories in the way that feels natural to tell them. It's not particularly conscious or unconscious. I never try to be difficult, and rather naïvely I'm always surprised when some people find the books hard. Sometimes I think people give me too much credit. In the case of a novel about the movies, and I mean a novel that's really about the movies, rather than a "Hollywood" novel about the business of making movies, it just seemed it should have the pop energy and momentum of a movie, and follow a movie's narrative laws, if you will—linear, told in the present tense and in the externals of action and dialogue and movie references, short scenes that cut from one to the next, with some Godardian numbers thrown in just to make you think I'm smarter than I am.

JC: Most of your novels up until now have been published by major publishers or imprints of majors. Europa is a true independent. How did you wind up at Europa? Were the other publishers finally fed up with you? I find it ironic that coming off the dreamlike narrative of *Our Ecstatic Days* (Simon & Schuster), your first novel at an independent seems to be your most accessible.

SE: Here's the situation. The novel is submitted to a handful of publishers—a couple of the usual corporate behemoths, a couple of the more mid-level places that you would know, and one independent that's only been around a year or so but already has a reputation for really getting behind their books. The bigger publishers say, yes, the novel is great, we'll make an offer next week, and the next week turns into two or three or four, because one of the things that's happened to publishing in the last decade is that no editor has autonomy to buy anything anymore. A decade ago certain editors had that autonomy—it might be limited by what they could pay, but still they could pretty much buy a book on their own that they were excited about. Now even someone as high up in the company as the publisher has to get his paperback guy to sign off on it. So the book works its way through the food chain and as it does the enthusiasm for it gets whittled away by people whose job it is to whittle away enthusiasm—the paperback department, the marketing department, publicity department—and a month later the companies are still dragging their heels because none of them knows anymore how to publish fiction, and all of them are desperate to find reasons to turn books down. In the meantime, while these people are trying to muster up the will just to make a decision, the independent, Europa, is saying, we want it. We want it, we love it, we've already thought about how we're going to publish it. Moreover, the head of Europa here in the States, Kent Carroll, has a very interesting publishing history—before he started Carroll & Graf he was at Grove Press back when they were the vanguard of American literature, and he's published and worked with Beckett and

Mailer, Henry Miller, John O'Hara and Alice Munro and Philip Dick. Not bad company. So no sooner does Europa sign the book than it's got out a press release about it, because for them it's a Big Deal, and for three novels and ten years I've been telling myself I'm going to stop worrying about my advances, even if I really can't afford to, and go with someone who acts as though publishing my book is a Big Deal. I remember when my first novel was published, it was around the time of *White Noise*, and my editor at the time told me, "See, this is how it works—DeLillo had to write nine novels before he broke through." Well, now they don't give you nine novels to break through (*Zeroville* is my eighth). They give you maybe three. The publishing business has become like the movie business—the behemoths like Simon & Schuster, Random House, Doubleday are the big studios that only know how to make blockbusters, with the occasional Oscar-season prestige item thrown in, while the indies, the true indies, are the guys who care about fiction. I can understand it seems ironic but, counterintuitive though it may have been, it was precisely because this novel might find a larger readership that it made all the more sense to go with a publisher that was passionate about it, even if they don't have the resources that the big publishers have but never use anyway. So I don't know if the big publishers are fed up with me or I'm fed up with them or, most likely, of course, it's a bit of both. I should add that with *Our Ecstatic Days*, which wasn't the easiest book to publish from a production standpoint, there were certain things that Simon & Schuster did well. There was a terrific woman there in production named Gypsy who was more conscientious about getting the text right than I was, which I wouldn't have thought possible. Was the decision to go with Europa a gamble? Maybe. So far I haven't been sorry.

JC: When you mention the difficulty of printing *Our Ecstatic Days*, I assume you're referring to the continuous sentence that starts on page 83 and runs through the text of the remaining pages, for the duration of the book. Can you tell us a bit about what led to that creative decision?

SE: It was purely spontaneous. In the story, a lake suddenly has appeared in the middle of Los Angeles and a young single mother becomes convinced the lake has come to take her three-year-old son. And on the page you mention, she dives down into the water and to the hole at the bottom that the lake is coming from, and she goes through the hole and "swims" through the rest of the novel in a sentence that cuts through the remaining text and remaining story and the next twenty-five years or so—and the idea just came to me when I got to that point in the story. I've always steered a bit clear of that kind of thing, of semiotextual stuff or whatever you want to call it, because it seems gimmicky and it's easier and more fun to play around with text than do the hard work of creating characters and telling a story. I hear the word *experimental* and reach for my revolver. I don't consider myself an experimental writer, because experimental writing is about the experiment, and that doesn't interest me. But this was a case, not unlike any other, where the story just dictated to me a certain way to tell it. I admit I would wake at three in the morning wondering, "Fuck, who's going to publish this?" Anticipating the difficulties, I made the pages of the actual, finished manuscript resemble as closely as possible the pages of a finished book, and sure enough, what S&S wound up doing was shooting a PDF of each manuscript page and publishing from that. They literally published the manuscript as I laid it out, and I give them credit for being willing to do that.

JC: When did you first start writing? According to Wikipedia, whose information is suspect at best, you wrote your first story at age seven and were accused of plagiarism. Is there any truth to that? If so, can you tell us anything about that initial story? How about your first novel, which you reportedly wrote at the tender age of seventeen?

SE: For Wikipedia, that sounds pretty accurate. It's a little scary that they know that. That story in the second grade was about some kids who build a rocket out of old car parts and go to the moon and meet the Man in the Moon. I didn't know until years later that the teacher called my mom and asked if she wrote the story for me. I don't remember what that first novel was about. But a good friend in my senior class assured me it was a "masterpiece."

JC: According to the same article, when *Days Between Stations* was published, you destroyed all of your previous unpublished work. I assume this would include the aforementioned first story and first novel. You didn't have any desire to keep those, at least for posterity?

SE: I know it sounds melodramatic. It was definitely a Year Zero kind of act. But I was either going to move forward or dwell on the past, and I wanted to at least operate on the assumption, warranted or not, that whatever I wrote next would be better than what I had written before.

JC: We have a lot of aspiring writers here at *The Cult*. Can you share with us a bit about your writing process? Do you have a set schedule or habits? What kind of environment do you like to write in?

SE: I live with my family in a fairly rural environment—one of the canyons just outside LA—which is problematic, because the truth is I get more creative energy from an urban setting. When I began *Zeroville* I checked myself into the Roosevelt Hotel in Hollywood for four or five nights because part of the book is set there. Usually when I begin a novel, I begin slow—I build up a head of steam until I'm chomping at the bit to get going. Starting too soon, before I'm really ready, throws me off, and about a third of the way into the book I usually wind up having to stop and take a major break and reassess, and often throw out much of what I've done. I begin at a pace that's manageable—maybe a page a day—and take a day off every five or six. Then the pace builds. It took a year and a half to write the first hundred pages of *Our Ecstatic Days*, eight months to write the second hundred pages, three weeks to write the last hundred pages. *Zeroville* is my longest novel and took a total of four months—that's pretty much unheard of for me. *Amnesiascope*, my shortest, took a year and a half, longer than any except *Ecstatic Days*. On a given day, if I can't write, if I sit down to the work and after an hour or two nothing is happening and I can feel nothing is going to, I take the rest of the day off and plan to go back the next day, or maybe I take off the rest of the week or the rest of the month. Use the time to get other things done and resolve to begin again on a certain date—not a deadline, but a goal. I've never been "blocked" in large part because I've never called it that, and have never allowed my brain to get hung up on that idea. You just don't want to make the whole thing into a fucking test. Don't have an adversarial relationship with your own creativity.

JC: When you have an idea for a new novel, how fully formed does that idea have to be before you actually sit down and write? Do you do a lot of outlining, or do you make it up as you go along? For instance, for something like *Rubicon Beach*, which contains multiple sections and story lines, did you envision the entire novel, or did each part of the story come separately?

SE: Look, the right process for any writer is the one that works—it's that simple. Every writer is trying to find the tipping point between productive chaos and necessary order. If the room is a mess and there are dirty dishes in the sink, I have a hard time writing because that's the nature of my compulsiveness, but when I do sit down to write, on the other hand, I don't have an outline, I don't have notes, because that's boring for me. I don't want to write from an outline or notes, I want to live the story with the reader, and I want to be open to the story taking over. I've written every novel from beginning to end, and there have been times I planned—to the extent I plan at all—for a character to do something at a certain point in the story and then I got to that point and realized that the character, as he or she had developed, just wouldn't do that, that he or she wanted to do something else. And suddenly your story wants to go in a different direction from where you thought it was going. And having said all that, I know good writers who outline everything and that's the way they work and they write good books. So don't listen too much to people like me trying to tell you that you have to do it a certain way.

JC: What is your revision process like? Do you do a lot of heavy revising?

SE: I revise as I go along. In theory I think it probably would be better to write the whole thing and then go back and revise, but again, this is the way that I need to work. When I get to the end of the manuscript, it's pretty close to what I want it to be, but then I'll go back again and start at the beginning and revise some more—although at that point, while I may move something around or decide I need to elaborate on something or cut something, it's unlikely the story is going to change in any significant way, in part because I have lived that story with the reader, as a result of my particular process, so it feels organic and like it can't be another way. Somewhere in the revision I can feel when I've reached the point that the perfect becomes the enemy of the good, and continuing to try to make the thing "better" is only going to thrash the life out of it.

JC: How do you feel about touring and publicity? Have you done extensive book touring? Is it something you enjoy, or is it more of a chore?

SE: I'll be honest: it's more a chore. I think this probably is true for most writers. There was a piece in the *Los Angeles Times* recently by Scott Timberg on writers who are famously reclusive, like Pynchon and DeLillo and Denis Johnson—but except for a few who are good at self-promotion and work hard to cultivate a kind of persona, and while all of us would rather that people were interested than not interested, I think most writers become writers because they're reclusive by nature and want to be left alone. J. D. Salinger excepted, the writers who everyone knows as "reclusives" are the ones who can get away with it. Years ago I did a book signing with Denis Johnson, the point being that before he sold books to the movies, he toured and publicized like anyone else. Pynchon once told me that if he had come along twenty years later, he would be doing book tours, because he would have to. He said that's just the way the business has changed. I hasten to add that I get in trouble when I repeat this story—I mentioned it rather off-handedly in an interview once and five years later it showed up in *New York* magazine, in which it was reported that "Erickson says Pynchon is going to tour for his next book," which of course he never said and which I never said he said.

JC: You currently teach writing at the California Institute of the Arts and are editor of the literary magazine *Black Clock*, which they publish. Is teaching something you enjoy? Do you feel compelled to give back, to work with new writers, or is it more of a gig to help pay the bills?

SE: Well, in some measure it's a day job, and as I almost always tell my students, my role in the CalArts writing program—or the way I see it, anyway—is as the teacher who's skeptical of writing programs. Particularly when student work is being workshopped, writing programs can't help turning into creativity by committee, and the only "community of writers" that ever got any good writing done is the community of one. What would any workshop, including the smartest and most well-meaning, have made of the first ten or fifteen pages of *The Sound and the Fury*? There are just built-in problems in writing programs that I'm always trying to finesse in some way, because a writing program tries to socialize what is innately an antisocial activity. Be all that as it may, I do worry incessantly about whether I'm phoning it in when I teach, because these students have come to the program at some considerable cost, financial and sometimes otherwise, and personally I'm at the limit of what I can give. I'm increasingly nearing a point of not only diminishing returns but vanishing ones—I can't be a novelist and a movie critic and publish a literary magazine and teach and raise a family. Very soon something will have to give.

JC: Do you have any advice for our budding young writers here at *The Cult*? Whether it is creatively or on the business side of things? Any wisdom to impart that you've picked up along the way?

SE: That's the problem. The students in the writing program want the same wisdom, and if I were in their shoes, I would too. And there isn't any—not any hard advice that you can use as a five-step business plan. There's the Work and there's the Career, and unlike, say, brain surgery, where your skills in the operating room are quantifiable and are going to have a direct bearing on whether you're a success, in art the Work and Career have nothing to do with each other, and I'm not just making high-minded literary/commercial distinctions here, because I have a lot of respect for a Stephen King, natural storytellers who can grip a reader—there's no doubt in my mind that a hundred years from now *The Shining* will be considered a kind of classic. My point is only that there are really good writers of all stripes who have great success, and really good writers who have little success, and really bad writers of all stripes who have great success, and really bad writers who will never get published. It's all a crapshoot, all pretty fucking capricious. The one thing I can say with certainty is that you want to find an agent who's good at his or her job and who believes in you. That was my breakthrough. After wandering in the wilderness ten years and going through any number of agents, I found the one I'm with now and who I've been with almost twenty-five years. Melanie [Jackson] took a book [*Days Between Stations*] that had been turned down by four other agents and twelve publishers over the course of more than two years and sold it in four months to one of the publishers who already had rejected it. If I'm being honest, and particularly if you are what the business would consider a "literary" writer, I also have to tell you that moving to New York and getting a job at a publishing house isn't a bad move. I didn't do it, and maybe I should have. I don't doubt it would have changed me as a writer and—in my case, anyway—not for the better, but there's the trade-off. The publishing business, as I think I've already said, pretty much is without a clue these days when it comes to literary fiction. But the good news is that in a cyber age the center isn't holding, and a certain potentially constructive anarchy has seeped in—inmates are starting their own asylums—all of which offers writers other options, even if they aren't as financially promising. Just remember that the Career is the Career and the Work is the Work, and if you're going to be a good writer, regardless of whether you're a successful one, you have to keep them straight.

JC: I know *Zeroville* has yet to be published, but what's on the horizon for you? Any upcoming writing or film projects we can look forward to?

SE: I don't know.

JC: You have written two nonfiction books centering on politics, *Leap Year* and *American Nomad*. They cover the 1988 and 1996 presidential elections, respectively. Do you have any thoughts you'd care to share on the current political climate or the upcoming presidential election? Any plans to publish more nonfiction, political or otherwise?

SE: My standard joke is that I write only about boring elections. But I didn't know 1988 was going to be boring—it marked the end of the Reagan era, which seemed momentous, and was the first election in twenty years that didn't involve an incumbent. And for the 1996 election I was a hired gun for *Rolling Stone* before Jann Wenner fired me and I decided to go on covering the campaign anyway. By all appearances 2008 will be the election of a lifetime. It will be the first since, what, 1952, that doesn't involve a sitting president or vice president, and the country appears in more psychic turmoil than in forty years. The current occupant of the White House has squandered the opportunity of a generation to unite the country so that instead he could mire the country in the foreign policy disaster of a generation. And now what's at stake is something that hasn't been at stake since the 1840s and '50s, and which only was resolved when half the country went to war against the other half, and that's the meaning of America, which is bigger than all the notions of Left and Right that are outmoded anyway. When I was a fourteen-year-old for Goldwater, conservatism was about constitutionalism. It wasn't about wiretapping phones without search warrants—that's exactly what conservatism wasn't about. I never thought I'd live long enough to see a debate in the United States Senate over whether it's all right for America to torture people. Not so long ago that question would have been considered beyond the pale no matter what your politics were. Not so long ago we were supposed to be better than that. I'm exactly the traitor to Ann Coulter's America that she claims I am, because I've never believed in her "America."

JC: And finally, on a lighter note—are you familiar with the fantasy novelist Steve Erikson, and have you ever been mistaken for him?

SE: Please, let's not make it even more confusing than it is. He's Steven Erikson, which is to say that we're divided by more than the lack of a *C* in his last name but also the addition of an *N* in his first. I imagine we both cling to such distinctions. The only time I know of that I was mistaken for him was when I chairing a panel at the *LA Times* Book Festival some years ago, and one of the panelists very diligently had done her homework and read all seven volumes of the *Malazan Books of the Fallen*. I could only assure her that those sounded like very interesting novels indeed and that if I had written them, I probably would be richer. There's your last bit of "wisdom" for aspiring young writers, like the guy in *The Graduate* imparting "one word" to Dustin Hoffman. But here it's not *plastics*. It's *genre*.

An Interview with Steve Erickson

Guy Savage / 2007

Originally published on MostlyFiction.com. Reprinted by permission.

Author and film critic Steve Erickson granted an interview to Guy Savage of Mostlyfiction.com. *Zeroville* is Erickson's eighth novel, and he's also written two nonfiction books. Currently the film critic for *Los Angeles* magazine, he is also the editor of *Black Clock*, a literary journal published by CalArts, where he also teaches writing. For more information on this author and his novels, go to www.steveerickson.org.

Mostlyfiction: What inspired you to write *Zeroville*?

Steve Erickson: Well, the movies play a part in a number of my earlier novels—*Days Between Stations, Rubicon Beach, Amnesiascope, The Sea Came in at Midnight*—so they've always been an interest of mine. I actually got my degree at UCLA not in literature but film. A few years ago I was trying to recruit Michael Chabon into writing for the literary magazine I edit [*Black Clock*], and being the slippery guy he is, instead he recruited me into writing for a *McSweeney's* anthology he was putting together, and over five days in Vegas I knocked out a short story called "Zeroville." I realized that at the core of the story was a pretty good idea I could have done more with, and a central character I wasn't really satisfied with. I wrote the story not long after finishing my previous novel, *Our Ecstatic Days*, which was a very intense, emotionally roiling work, and I felt that a novel about the movies should have the energy of the movies; it should move like the movies. It was when the character of Vikar—this childlike, excommunicated theology student who's "cineautistic"—fell into place that the novel fell into place with him.

MF: What is the significance of the fact that *Zeroville*'s protagonist arrives on the very day of the Sharon Tate murders?

SE: You know, there are any number of days that the sixties are said to have "died," but if you lived in LA at the time, that was definitely the day.

It also seems to have coincided with the beginning of an era in Hollywood and moviemaking when, for better or worse, a kind of anarchy set in. For a while things became more creative and people took more chances, and then things became more undisciplined and people become arrogant and indulgent. During the same time you had the punk movement in music, so it was a great period of upheaval to write about, and I was around for a lot of it.

MF: Vikar's shaved head sports a tattoo with images of Elizabeth Taylor and Montgomery Clift in a scene from *A Place in the Sun*. This film is mentioned throughout the book, and at one point it is the focus of some intense analysis. What is the significance of this film to you, the book, and to Vikar?

SE: *A Place in the Sun* is a great example of what I call Cinema of Hysteria. It may be the dreamiest major movie to come out of the studio system of the late forties and fifties, when the studios were coming unhinged for all kinds of reasons. There's a rapture about the film that's entirely irrational—it's very different from *Swing Time* or *Gunga Din* or *Woman of the Year* or almost anything else that George Stevens directed up until that time or afterward—and that exists outside the socially accepted notions of right and wrong. The movie is morally absurd on a rational level, yet on some unconscious level we completely understand it. Zazi, the teenage girl in the novel, puts her finger on it when she realizes it's not a movie that really can be watched with anyone else—it's too private. But having said all that, I would be a liar if I claimed to have thought of all this when I chose it for the novel. Rather it was one of those instinctive decisions that become clear later (like when I'm being interviewed).

MF: There are some parallels between Vikar's life and the life of Montgomery Clift. Obviously this is deliberate. Why did you pick Clift?

SE: Well, Clift was John the Baptist to Brando's Jesus. (James Dean was St. Peter, the martyred disciple on whom a church is built.) And as such, he's at the crossroads of where the dying Classic Hollywood meets the new Nuclear Hollywood. Clift still has the old glamour while anticipating all the neuroses of what being a movie star would come to be about. He was a subtler actor than Brando or Dean and, as the novel says in the opening paragraph, in that terrace scene in *Place in the Sun* he and Taylor may be the two most beautiful people in the history of movies, "she the female version of him and he the male version of her." So there's something very dreamlike about Clift.

MF: Some of the best film criticism in the novel comes from a burglar. Vikar parrots most of this back at critical moments, and manages to either wow or stun the film community—especially when he mentions *Emmanuelle II* in the same breath as *Battle of Algiers*. Vikar seems unable to differentiate soft porn from Pontecorvo's masterpiece. How do you explain that?

SE: I don't want to explain Vikar too much. Actually I don't want to explain him at all. We never understand whether Vikar is some sort of savant or just dim. His passion for movies, his faith in them, is unmediated, unschooled, raw—he may love a movie because it speaks to him spiritually or just because he thinks the lead actress is hot, and in his mind not only is one reason as good as the other but there's no difference between them. The spiritual is sexual and vice versa, and his "aesthetic," such as it is, is entirely personal, entirely intuitive. That's part of the nature of Vikar's belief in film, and it's confirmed by the fact that very few of the people he meets in Hollywood who work in the movies really know anything about movies—or so it seems to him—while at the same time he runs into burglars, call girls in Cannes, and teenage punkettes who are all more insightful.

MF: At the Palme d'Or Vikar's film is hailed as "the creation of a revelatory new cinematic rhetoric." Most of the film community (Cannes, for example) is uncertain whether to classify Vikar as a lunatic or a genius. Do you feel this uncertainty on the part of the film community is an accurate reflection of reality, or is this a satirical representation?

SE: Is it really an either/or proposition? Yeah, it's satirical, but that doesn't mean it's not real. Hollywood is a business where hairdressers become major producers and gigolos wind up running studios because they happened to stumble into Norma Shearer by the hotel pool. Uncertainty is the status quo of the business—nobody has a clue, and it's as dangerous to dismiss the possibility that the fool is a genius as it is to ignore the possibility he's a fool.

MF: Part of the fun of *Zeroville* is trying to guess the identities of the characters who are usually described rather peculiarly by Vikar by certain silent characteristics. For example, there's Margie, "the crazy one with the tits." The book will have a special appeal for film fans. How do you feel about that?

SE: Because I was seeing all these people through Vikar's eyes, I wanted to define them in Vikar's terms, not in the terms of their fame and celebrity that came later and probably wouldn't mean anything to Vikar anyway. The characters have a greater resonance if their identities are not always explicit—except when it's more resonant to be explicit. To be honest, the most reassuring reactions I've gotten so far are from readers who don't know much about movies and still got caught up in the book.

MF: I've got to ask this one: Vikar's film *Your Pale Blue Eyes*. Did you have a certain film in mind here, or is this film a composite?

SE: It's virtually the only movie in the novel that's made up. The title, of course, is from the Velvet Underground song. There's also a brief, passing reference to another made-up movie that was in my novel *Days Between Stations*.

MF: Humor me here. If you could pick someone—anyone—to direct *Zeroville*, who would you pick? Who would play Vikar?

SE: Well, just remember that you did ask, so if this sounds completely grandiose, it's not my fault. For a director you would want someone very film-conscious—not all directors are. The most famous and obvious example is Scorsese. He would understand this novel. Whether he would want to make a movie, of course, is another question. Anyone who's not seen his *Personal Journey through American Movies* doc on DVD should check it out. Soderbergh, Tarantino, Paul Thomas Anderson are all possibilities. So far at this early stage there's been interest in Hollywood from actors who see a good part in Vikar. You want someone with a man-child quality that also harbors a potential violent streak. Ryan Gosling, Tobey Maguire, Joaquin Phoenix—none of them is exactly how I pictured Vikar, but then the image on the jacket of the book wasn't how I pictured him either. I saw him as more angelic. Johnny Depp may be too old at this point (which makes me feel ancient), but that's the general idea.

MF: As a film critic for *Los Angeles* magazine, films are obviously a large part of your life. What are your top ten films?

SE: Round up the usual suspects. Anyone who's read the novel won't be surprised by most of them. *The Third Man, Vertigo, Casablanca, The Godfather Part II, Double Indemnity, Lawrence of Arabia, The Lady Eve, The Passion of Joan of Arc, 2001: A Space Odyssey, My Darling Clementine, Jules and Jim, A Place in the Sun, The Shop Around the Corner*. That's thirteen, I know, but you have several overlapping five- or eight-way ties in there. Sorry, too, it's so English-language-centric. Give me a few more slots and I can easily work in *That Obscure Object of Desire*. Twenty-four hours from now, half the list will be different anyway.

MF: Fassbinder felt that film had lost a great deal of its original content in the process of commercialization. He often deliberately overused clichés in an attempt to show the emptiness of the Hollywood film. Do you think that Fassbinder was correct?

SE: That may be Fassbinder's version of why he used the clichés, but I think the real reason is he loved them. I think he loved all that classic iconography of "empty" glamour and artificiality, and some part of him yearned to make *Now, Voyager*. A gay German *Now, Voyager*, maybe, but still. I think the tension in his best movies comes from that contradiction of loving the clichés even as he tries to deny and discredit them.

MF: In *Zeroville*, the director known as Viking Man who wants to be the "next John Ford" makes oblique references to changes in the Hollywood film industry. What are your feelings about the decline of the movie studios and the rise of the independent director?

SE: Well, the "decline" in the studios mostly has to do with the obvious fact that they make hundreds of millions of dollars that the independents don't. That is to say, the studios haven't commercially declined at all. They've declined creatively for the most part because the people who run the studios don't care about movies or even particularly like them—what they care about is the enterprise of movies. There's probably no point getting overly indignant about this—the studios always have cared about making money—but I do think that in the thirties and forties even the vulgarians like Mayer and Zanuck and Warner loved and understood their product. Harvey Weinstein is probably the closest contemporary example, and he's the godfather of independent film, at least from the production standpoint, so that probably tells you everything. I don't know of anyone like him at the studios today, unless you're counting something like DreamWorks. I know it's a cliché, for instance, to include a movie like *Casablanca* in that list of films you asked me for a couple of questions ago, but it's difficult to find a more perfect movie or a more satisfying one on a scene-by-scene, role-by-role, line-by-line basis, and *Casablanca* is the ultimate example of a studio picture, and something I doubt today's studios could replicate in another hundred years, largely because the studios just aren't like that anymore. They aren't run like that and they don't think of movies like that. I don't want to over-romanticize the studio films of the forties any more than I want to over-romanticize the independent films of the nineties, only to make the point that there was something about the forties—the sensibility, the zeitgeist, whatever—in which the studios flourished, and there's something about the eighties and nineties and zeroes in which most studio pictures are soulless and all the creative energy is with the indies. You see pretty much the same thing happening in publishing today, in which the behemoths like Simon & Schuster, Random House, Doubleday are the big studios that only know anymore how to make blockbusters, with the oc-casional Oscar-season prestige item thrown in, while the indies are the pub-lishers who actually care about fiction.

MF: When I read *Zeroville*, two names came to mind. The British director Greenaway for his intricate, complicated, symbolic films that often focus on the nature of obsession, and novelist Michael Frayn for his highly intelligent, complex, layered novels. Any comments on those comparisons?

SE: Well, I know of both Frayn and Greenaway, of course, and can understand the comparisons, but probably the best way to answer is to say that the writers who had the biggest impact on my work are William Faulkner, Henry Miller, Emily Brontë, Jorge Luis Borges, Gabriel García Márquez, Philip K. Dick, Thomas Pynchon. At least one or two of them are fairly intricate, layered, and obsessive too. On the other hand Hawks and Hitchcock are probably my two favorite directors, just because they made so many great movies between them, yet I don't know that either actually has *influenced* me much.

MF: Are there any new projects on the horizon?

SE: No.

An Interview with Steve Erickson

Angela Stubbs / 2007

From *Bookslut.com* (December 2007). Reprinted by permission of Angela Stubbs.

If there's anything you'd like to know about LA, just ask Steve Erickson. He's the ultimate observer of people, film, culture, and detail when it comes to the City of Angels. Knowing how things work in this crazy place called Hollywood is one of the most valuable assets you can have, and Erickson, along with his characters, all surprise you from time to time in his eighth novel. Whether it's a film buff by day/burglar by night, or the ex-seminarian turned film editor, they always know more about film and its history than many who work in the industry itself.

Zeroville's current acclaim is never-ending. Since its release in November, it's been reviewed by *Newsweek*, the *Washington Post Book World*, the *Toronto Globe*, *Bookforum*, *Bookslut.com*, and *The Believer*, and on the front page of the *LA Times Book Review*, as well as the *New York Times Book Review*. Erickson will be making appearances at the New School and the National Arts Club in Gramercy Park, and his radio interview with Michael Silverblatt on KCRW's *Bookworm* in Los Angeles will air December 13.

In addition to completing *Zeroville*, Steve Erickson spends his time teaching in the MFA program at CalArts in Southern California and is the editor of *Black Clock*, a literary magazine published by CalArts. He also has a website that you will definitely want to check out (www.steveerickson.org) to find his books, essays, and links to other interesting work. Additionally, you can read his critiques in *Los Angeles* magazine, where he's a film critic.

Erickson exchanged emails with *Bookslut.com* over Thanksgiving weekend. Here we discuss music, his multifaceted characters, film, publishing, *Black Clock*, and what it is about Los Angeles that keeps him coming back for more.

Angela Stubbs: This work, like other novels you've written, is set in Los Angeles. I'm reminded of [John] Fante in that he constantly wrote about this city, his love/hate relationship with it, and making a living here. What is it about Los Angeles that keeps you coming back to it as the backdrop and, oftentimes, the focal point of your writing?

Steve Erickson: I was born and raised in LA. I didn't understand what an unusual place it is until I left for a while and lived somewhere else, Europe mostly. Then I saw LA as the ever-transforming landscape, the end of America both geographically and metaphorically, and a psychological blank slate that lends itself to whatever people can imagine—which is why it's a perfect place to make movies. I don't know that I love LA, but I'm fascinated by it, find it more interesting than any other American city, if not as beautiful or dramatic, and at some intuitive level I feel I understand it. Of the eight novels I've written, half take place primarily in LA, two take place partly in LA, two don't take place in LA at all. After the last two novels I can imagine the next having nothing to do with the city. But don't hold me to it.

AS: With each work you approach, do you find your process becoming easier or more difficult to tackle? How long does it typically take you to complete a novel that you're happy with?

SE: My process hasn't changed in any fundamental way. I don't make an outline; I don't work from notes—what I usually have is a strong sense of at least one of the central characters and a strong sense of the beginning, and a vague sense of where the narrative is going, and more than anything else a psychic head of steam, a compulsion to tell the story. If I don't feel so compelled, I'm better off waiting. Beginning too soon only prolongs the writing more than anything. Most novels it's taken me about a year to write, but that can vary wildly. It took me the better part of three years to write *Our Ecstatic Days*. The longest before that was *Amnesiascope*, which took a year and a half—and it's my shortest novel. The longer I worked on it, the shorter it got, because I kept cutting it. It took me four months to write *Zeroville*, which is very unusual: I've never written anything even remotely that quick. I had planned to put off writing it for a year until I had a sabbatical from teaching, but the story was coming so fast, so many scenes filled my head, that I knew I better not wait. I almost feel I can't take credit for it—it was like the cosmos were saying, "Here, you worked hard on all those other ones, so we're giving you this one. It's a freebie."

AS: Tell me how you get to the point where you decide, this is no longer a draft—this is something I need others to consume. Is there anyone that you allow to read your work in the draft stages—colleagues or other writers whose opinions are of great help?

SE: With very few exceptions over the years, nobody sees anything until I'm done. Then I show it to a relatively small circle of people—my wife, my agent, a couple of close friends—and then I may make revisions depending on the response.

AS: In *Zeroville*, your main character, Vikar Jerome, is an ex-seminarian who's completely infatuated with Los Angeles and, in particular, film. There's something really interesting to me about the dichotomy between the life of a seminarian and that of what Vikar later becomes—and at the same time similar. Did the character of Vikar slowly evolve for you or did you have a pretty good idea about the kind of person you were dealing with from the get-go, character-wise?

SE: Well, Vikar is an innocent, if one with disruptive tendencies. The novel begins with his arrival in LA on the day of the Manson murders. There's a rapture about many of the movies he loves that verges on the religious. I was impressed by the fact that some of the people who came out of the New Hollywood in the seventies either had very religious, repressive childhoods, such as Paul Schrader, or early on aspired to be priests or philosophers, such as Scorsese and Malick. Just by virtue of when they appeared in the time line of cinema history, these people were cinematically conscious in a way many of the Old Hollywood directors were not. A lot of the Old Hollywood directors wound up in movies by accident, beginning as artists of other disciplines. It was when I figured out Vikar that the novel fell into place. I guess you would have to say his evolution was slow, in that I had to think about him for a year or so, but then once he came into focus, the novel happened quickly.

AS: Stylistically, you've chosen to experiment with each novel you've written. *Our Ecstatic Days* took an interesting trip with its typography, and in *Zeroville* you've chosen to write in short scenes numbered from 1 to 227 and back down to 0. Did you initially set out to write your novel this way, or did this form evolve as you told this story? Do you find that it's easier to write this way as opposed to a more traditional form, or that writing like this was essential to telling this particular story?

SE: You know, I hear the word *experiment* and reach for my revolver. I don't think of myself as an experimental writer. Experimental writing is about the experiment, and experiments per se usually are for their own sake. My interest is in whatever serves the larger story or characters. The numbers in *Zeroville* were a kind of Godardian conceit and just came to me, in the same way that Kristin "swimming" through *Our Ecstatic Days* came to me at the moment she goes down through the hole at the bottom of the lake that's flooded LA, and that she believes has come to take her small son from her.

AS: How much research goes into writing a novel about Los Angeles and the film industry, and how much of it is just being a part of the artistic landscape? Your book spans over ten years and you've been writing for even longer—so your knowledge of movies, directors, actors, and pop culture in general has to be vast. Being a film critic for *Los Angeles* magazine must have helped the process, but also your experiences as a writer in Southern California too, no?

SE: Well, I'm not sure whether the knowledge of film led to writing film criticism or the other way around. I've definitely always regarded the film criticism as the day job, and was writing novels before I ever wrote criticism. As far as *Zeroville* is concerned, I think at first I resisted the subject of movies precisely because I am a film critic and the idea of writing a novel about movies when I already was knocking out a film piece every month was more uninviting than anything. I think being able to write from Vikar's perspective, or from that of some of the other characters, made a difference. Vikar comes to Hollywood and no one in the movies seems to know anything about movies—rather the people who know about movies are burglars and teenage punkettes and Spanish revolutionaries and call girls in Cannes. I did research as much as I could as I went along. When Vikar sees his first two movies on the same day, *The Sound of Music* and *Blow-Up*, I had gone back and determined that those two movies were in fact released within a few weeks of each other back in 1965, so it was indeed possible for someone to have seen both around the same time. So on that score I tried for as much verisimilitude as I could achieve.

AS: Let's talk about the cover of *Zeroville*. Or more importantly, the tattoos. The character of Vikar has Elizabeth Taylor and Montgomery Clift tattooed on his head. Did the publisher suggest having the picture with the tattoos on it, or was that your idea?

SE: It's the first image in the novel, Vikar with the tattoo on his head of Taylor and Clift from the movie *A Place in the Sun*, and it's as good a visual metaphor for the rest of the book as anything else. I think it's a terrific jacket. Europa got it on the first try, which doesn't usually happen. My only complaint is that if you look closely at the cover image, Vikar has a mustache. I have no idea what possessed the artist to give him one. It's completely out of character and there's nothing about a mustache in the novel and I tried to get them to take it off.

AS: Music seems to play a small yet significant part in your novels. I read that you were, at one time, more influenced by Dylan than, say, Updike or other contemporary authors at that time. Does music still influence you when you sit down to write these days?

SE: Music always has been a huge influence. One afternoon as a seventeen-year-old I heard Dylan's *Highway 61 Revisited* and *Blonde on Blonde* both for the first time back to back, and that was a revelation, a powerful moment. The lesson of that moment was that everything was for grabs: you could write your own ticket artistically if you had the audacity and imagination. Punk had a similar impact for me in the late seventies. The big influences on me, whether musically or cinematically or in literary terms, usually have had to do with *possibility*.

AS: Alan Rifkin said once in an article about those writing about Los Angeles, "All fiction is at some level dreamy, or it wouldn't be fiction. And the recent novels from the bizarro, alternate LA aren't the most masterful fiction in the world. But they're the only American fiction that always looks beyond life's veil—to me the only fiction that's really worth reading." Salvador Plascencia and Joy Nicholson come to mind when I think of current writers that look beyond the norm when we think of the Los Angeles landscape and its inhabitants. Would you agree that the work of today's authors writing about LA (aside from yourself) tends to deal with Los Angeles in a fantastical way that asks the reader to decide "what's really real and what isn't?"

SE: I just think LA lends itself to that and always has, going back to L. Frank Baum, who wrote most of the *Oz* books in LA. The place has encouraged and nurtured the untethered imagination of expatriates like Huxley and Mann, regardless of whether their feelings about LA were overtly hostile, like in the case of Nathanael West, or more ambivalent, like with Fante. I don't know that I'm informed enough to characterize contemporary LA fiction, although I think Rifkin's piece about it in the *Los Angeles Times Magazine* a year or two back was very smart and maybe definitive. But the fact is that twenty years ago, around the time I published my first novel, LA fiction was more of the hard-boiled school—Cain and Chandler up through Nunn and Ellroy—and that has changed with a new generation of writers who don't come by that sensibility authentically.

AS: *Zeroville* seems to be the most straightforward novel you've written thus far. Los Angeles has a way of intoxicating those who write about it by pulling the reality out of its stories and infusing them with a dreamlike quality. John Fante's biographer, Stephen Cooper, called it Southern California Dream Realism. Did you intend for this novel to be a departure in terms of your previous novels and that dream element? Do you ever think you'll tire of Los Angeles as a backdrop for your stories?

SE: Each story tells itself in the way that feels natural. With *Zeroville* I decided from the outset that it should have the pop energy of a movie—linear, always in the present tense, the story told in action and dialogue and movie references, cutting from short scene to short scene. Several people have mentioned how quickly the novel reads, and that's what I wanted, a story that moved like a movie.

AS: You've had female characters that dominate past works, and I wondered if you think Vikar rivals that of Soledad Palladin in this novel. *Zeroville* is littered with excellent female characters, however it seems to me that Vikar and the search for his identity through film as a medium and Los Angeles as a backdrop outweigh anything else (i.e., stronger female characters, landscapes, etc). Would you agree?

SE: In contrast with *The Sea Came in at Midnight* and *Our Ecstatic Days*, which are extremely female books, there's no question Vikar is the central character of the story. He's in virtually every scene until the end. Of course, without saying too much, that's when we find out it really hasn't been Vikar's book at all, but Zazi's.

AS: You're the founder of *Black Clock* magazine, aptly named after one of your works (*Tours of the Black Clock*), at CalArts. Do you feel the opportunities to publish are getting better all the time, or would you say that those who write still deal with the same issues writers did decades ago when it comes to publishing?

SE: To give credit where it's due, if anyone founded *Black Clock* it was Jon Wagner, who was running the CalArts MFA writing program at the time and approached me about editing the magazine. Beyond that and within the established budget I have to work with, I was given autonomy over the magazine and its contents. I think book publishing has gotten worse than ever over the last fifteen years because the established corporate publishers are like the big studios—they only know how to publish blockbusters, trotting out Oscar bait like, say, Denis Johnson, in the fall. The Random Houses and Simon & Schusters don't know how to publish fiction anymore that isn't decidedly commercial. The real bright spot at the moment is that I do believe publishing is in transition, the center is collapsing, you have a vibrant and increasingly literate cyberspace, and the inmates are taking over the ground floor of the asylum, with the asylum bosses trapped upstairs. If serious writers can get over their dreams of six-figure advances—and don't get me wrong, we all have those dreams and there's nothing wrong with them in and of themselves—they can write their future in publishing. In my own case, after being published for twenty years by the big houses I got tired of every book being dumped only so the publisher could come back two years later on the next book and say, "Ah, but you know, the last one didn't do well." I always had this crazy idea that I was supposed to write the books and the publisher was supposed to sell them.

AS: Oftentimes more mainstream fiction is picked up by bigger houses. *Black Clock* is a great outlet for writers who are edgy, experimental in some cases, and even for those who like to blur genre lines and play with form. Tell me about your vision for the publication when you started and where you feel you're at with it now after eight issues.

SE: My idea was that *Black Clock* really would be a writer's magazine, that the only reason a DeLillo or Richard Powers or Joanna Scott or Jonathan Lethem or David Foster Wallace—all of whom have been in *Black Clock*— would be in it was because the magazine offered them the freedom to do anything, to even fuck up if they wanted or needed to. At the same time we would bring in more and more new voices, and I think if you look at how the magazine is evolving you'll see that gradually the stars are giving way more and more to the discoveries. Also, we wanted to be a serious literary magazine coming out of the West rather than just located in the West, and this would be reflected not necessarily in the subject manner or tone but in a kind of constructive anarchy that I think comes to the West naturally.

AS: When we sit down to write, oftentimes the character dictates what will happen in our stories, regardless of any preconceived ideas we may have coming to the table. Were there any interesting character turns that took you by surprise while writing *Zeroville*? Did anything happen to any one character that you feel enhanced the story that you didn't anticipate?

SE: This is a hard question to answer because it's hard to put myself back in whatever head I was in at a given moment while writing the book, back in the middle of whatever conspiracy was made by the conscious with the unconscious. You know, I do believe a novel can have secrets from its own author, and moreover can keep them. I knew Zazi would be important, but I'm not sure I knew how large an impact she would make. I'm not sure I expected Viking Man to be as sympathetic as he became—I came to feel affection for the blowhard, to feel that beneath the bombast he was a better guy than I might have expected. And I think I knew Vikar better than I knew I knew him, if that makes sense.

AS: Having written eight novels now, tell me what you'd like to accomplish as a writer that you have yet to do.

SE: Everything, and nothing.

The Elegant Variation Interview: Steve Erickson

Daniel Olivas / 2008

From *The Elegant Variation*, at https://marksarvas.blogs.com (January 3, 2008).
Reprinted by permission.

Steve Erickson was born in Santa Monica in 1950. Except for the mid-1970s and early 1980s when he sometimes lived in Europe and the New York area, he's spent his life in Los Angeles. Erickson is the author of eight novels: *Days Between Stations* (1985), *Rubicon Beach* (1986), *Tours of the Black Clock* (1989), *Arc d'X* (1993), *Amnesiascope* (1996), *The Sea Came in at Midnight* (1999), *Our Ecstatic Days* (2005), and a new novel, *Zeroville* (2007). He also has written two books about American politics and popular culture, *Leap Year* (1989) and *American Nomad* (1997).

Erickson's writing has been widely anthologized and has appeared in many publications, including *Esquire, Rolling Stone, Spin, Tin House, Salon, LA Weekly, Los Angeles Times Magazine,* and *New York Times Magazine.* Currently he's the film critic for *Los Angeles* magazine and editor of the literary journal *Black Clock,* which is published by CalArts, where he teaches in the MFA writing program. Erickson has received a grant from the National Endowment for the Arts, and in 2007 was awarded a fellowship by the John Simon Guggenheim Foundation. He lives with his wife, artist and director Lori Precious, and their son.

Erickson's new novel, *Zeroville* (Europa Editions, $14.95 paperback), begins in 1969 when a young man named Ike Jerome (who wishes to be called "Vikar") steps off a Greyhound bus in Los Angeles after a six-day bus trip from Philadelphia. To call Vikar a man obsessed by film puts it mildly. Indeed, his reality is completely shaped by movies. We follow Vikar over the next two decades as he evolves into a controversial but renowned film editor. He has also discovered a secret concerning every movie ever made, which becomes part of his obsession. All the while, Hollywood itself undergoes convulsive changes as the studio system crumbles under its own weight. Vikar attempts, in his own way, to make some connections with those who come into his life, including the young daughter of a struggling actress. *Zeroville* is a poignant, disquieting, and brilliant novel.

Zeroville ended up on *Newsweek*'s list of the year's ten best books, on the *Los Angeles Times'* list of the year's twenty-five best books of fiction and poetry, and on year-end lists in the *Washington Post Book World* and the *Toronto Globe and Mail*. It has also been well received by the *NYTBR*, *Philadelphia Inquirer*, *London Times* (despite the fact that it has not, as yet, been published in England), *Seattle Times, Bookforum, El Paso Times*, and *The Believer*.

Despite a very heavy schedule, Erickson kindly agreed to answer a few questions about *Zeroville* for TEV.

Daniel Olivas: In *Zeroville*, you describe Vikar's tattoo on his shaved head as follows: "One lobe is occupied by an extreme close-up of Elizabeth Taylor and the other by Montgomery Clift, their faces barely apart, lips barely apart, in each other's arms on a terrace, the two most beautiful people in the history of the movies, she the female version of him, and he the male version of her." It is ironic that the image of these two film icons makes many people uneasy, even frightened, when they first meet Vikar. Why did you decide to have Vikar's obsession imprinted directly on him?

Steve Erickson: Well, the novel opens with Vikar arriving in LA in the summer of 1969, on what happens to be the day of the Manson murders. So the image tattooed on Vikar's head seems both ominous, a punk and apocalyptic portent, and also a gesture of passion and beauty, just something Vikar would naturally do. His obsession is so strong that he wears it, he makes it part of himself. In his way Vikar is an innocent—he's still living through the wonder of movies that so many of us know as kids. There's a rapture about the movies that Vikar loves that I think is bound to make other people uncomfortable in the way any personal rapture does, whether it's religious or sexual. So the novel couldn't just talk about movies that I happen to like; the movies in the novel had to inform Vikar's character or say something about the story. Vikar is particularly drawn to movies that are deeply irrational—*Vertigo, Humoresque, Written on the Wind*, the Japanese *Blind Beast* and *Branded to Kill*, bonkers westerns like *Johnny Guitar* and *Forty Guns*—and I was struck by how the filmmakers who became part of the New Hollywood in the seventies set out originally to be priests or philosophers, like Malick and Scorsese, or came out of highly religious, repressive childhoods, like Paul Schrader. When Vikar is a young divinity student studying to become an architect, he designs a model that his teachers suppose to be a church, never suspecting that inside the model, in the place where an altar should be, Vikar has put a small movie screen. That close-up of Clift and Elizabeth Taylor on the terrace in *A Place in the Sun* represents the dreaminess of movies, and it's hard to think of a couple who were more dreamlike, so matched as they were in their beauty. I'm not sure movies were ever again as romantic.

DO: Vikar's understanding of life comes almost completely from films. Hypothetically, do you think a person could really function in this world if all he/she knew came from the movies?

SE: I guess it depends on whether you would consider Vikar "functional." A lot of characters in this book would say he's not. He's described by one as not a cineaste but "cineautistic." We're never altogether sure whether Vikar is a savant or socially arrested or just dim. But in another way the movies are Vikar's only connection to something that might resemble a real world to the rest of us, outside the world he was raised in, and I did mean for the novel to get at the way movies are part of the modern consciousness or unconsciousness. You know, we say some experience we've had was "just like in a movie" when what we mean isn't that it felt artificial but that it felt hyper-real, everything moving at twenty-four frames a second and the colors are all saturated, the blacks and whites all stark in their contrasts. In my novel *The Sea Came in at Midnight*, movies are being projected on the city walls—Vikar's world is already like that. Finally he discovers a secret hidden among the frames of every movie ever made.

DO: Your novel begins in 1969, when the film industry was going through dramatic structural and artistic changes. With the collapse of the studio system, how have films improved? How have they suffered?

SE: Well, I should probably say here and now that I don't think of *Zeroville* as a "Hollywood novel." Hollywood novels tend to be about making movies. This novel is about loving movies. So the novel isn't too concerned with the sociology of the business, if you will. On the other hand, the anarchy of the business in the seventies is the backdrop against which Vikar operates. Of course in the end the studios might have collapsed creatively, but not as business enterprises. A film like *The Godfather* was a synthesis of the Old Hollywood and the New, and then with the advent of the summer blockbuster, courtesy of *Jaws* and *Star Wars*, the studios reclaimed their preeminence. To a certain extent the studios reinvented themselves as less movie factories and more distribution houses, largely because the movie business became highly corporatized like other businesses, including, I might add, the book publishing business. A studio like Paramount that made *The Godfather* (and a publishing house like Simon & Schuster, which has published several of my books) winds up owned by Gulf and Western. In short order people were running studios who didn't care about movies or even necessarily like them much, let alone love them. What they cared about was the profitability of movies. Obviously studios always have cared about making money, but in the thirties and forties even Louis B. Mayer knew the difference, as the character in *Zeroville* called Viking Man puts it, "between movies and unleaded." It says something that the closest present-day example of an old-fashioned mogul is someone like Harvey Weinstein, the godfather of independent film. I'm not inclined to romanticize the independent films of the seventies or, for that matter, the nineties. But there's no getting around the fact that the studio pictures of the nineties and zeroes are pretty soulless. It's a rather easy target, but did you see *Transformers*? Thirty years ago, *Star Wars* was inspiring toys. Now it's the other way around.

DO: Vikar develops a parental bond with Zazi, the young daughter of Soledad Palladin, a beautiful but struggling actress. Indeed, his compassion for Zazi far exceeds anything he feels for anyone else. Why did you put at the forefront of Vikar's adult life this relationship, rather than a romantic one with Soledad?

SE: I think the most encouraging thing for me is how readers who don't know much about movies still respond to the book, and I think that's probably because they're caught up in Vikar's story and the relationship with Zazi. Without giving away too much, the father-child relationship that Vikar and Zazi have is at the core of the story: Vikar believes God kills children, and he becomes a kind of protector of Zazi—and makes a promise to Zazi's mother to take care of her. I've realized in retrospect how much the strained or ruptured parental bond exists in all my novels, whether it's a mother losing her son in *Days Between Stations* or a girl in *Rubicon Beach* losing her father, or a father in *Tours of the Black Clock* losing his daughter, or a daughter losing her mother in *Arc d'X*, or daughter and mother not realizing they're related in *The Sea Came in at Midnight*. This theme seemed to culminate in the last novel, *Our Ecstatic Days*, where a lake appears in the middle of LA and the young single mother is convinced it's the chaos of the world come to take her son away. *Zeroville* turns out to be not Vikar's story but Zazi's.

DO: Vikar learns how to edit films at the elbow of Dorothy Langer, a boozy but accomplished editor. As Vikar moves into his own career in film, he follows Dorothy's advice to "fuck continuity." Was this good advice? Can a film succeed in storytelling if continuity is abandoned?

SE: Well, there's continuity and then there's "continuity." If you asked him I imagine Faulkner would have said *The Sound and the Fury* had a continuity, maybe even a rigorous one, just not one anybody had seen before in a novel. On a purely nuts-and-bolts basis, not even getting into it conceptually, continuity is one of those things that filmmakers preoccupy themselves with scene by scene, even as the scenes of a movie are shot entirely out of sequence. You know, is the character wearing the same clothes he was in that scene that was shot three weeks ago but which in the final cut of the film will immediately follow the scene that's being shot today? When the cars chase each other into a tunnel in one scene, do they come out of the same tunnel in the next, or any tunnel at all? If you're familiar with LA or New York, you're constantly seeing a breakdown in continuity in movies shot in those cities—a woman rounds a street corner on Wilshire Boulevard to wind up on Park Avenue. But to Vikar's way of seeing things, a car may disappear into a tunnel and come out someone's garage, in another city or another year, and there's a logic to that all its own. I'm well aware that some might see this as a comment on the continuity—or lack thereof—in my novels, although that wasn't necessarily intended. There can be a continuity in narrative logic without necessarily a linearity in plot, and given its imagistic nature the movies is a medium that just naturally raises questions about these things.

DO: You weave into your plot scores of references to movies, including specific references to particular scenes, history, actors, directors, and editors. In preparation for writing the novel, did you rent films to refresh your memory of movies and the nuances of the performances, directing, and editing?

SE: In only two cases I can think of did I go back and study particular movies—the first, of course, was *A Place in the Sun*. I watched it several times, especially the sequences where Dotty Langer in the novel explains to Vikar how she cuts films and why. The second instance involved a number of Montgomery Clift's other films—*Red River, The Misfits, From Here to Eternity*—because I was trying to catch Clift's speech pattern for the scene between Vikar and Clift's ghost. Clift had a way of speaking that was very distinct: there was a high-pitched Midwestern crackle that's hard to translate into print. Otherwise, now and then I would pull something down off the DVD shelf to, as you say, refresh my memory—I have a pretty decent library, I'm guessing six or seven hundred movies—and I might get drawn in enough to watch the whole picture. But most of the movies in the novel I've seen many times and know pretty well. In a way I didn't understand before, my work in general probably has been leading up to this novel—none of the previous novels are about the movies per se, but there's a silent-film director in *Days Between Stations*, a screenwriter in *Rubicon Beach*, a film critic in *Amnesiascope*, a porn director in *The Sea Came in at Midnight*. So movies clearly have been a preoccupation of the novels, hovering in the background and edging into the foreground, and that preoccupation finally took over this book.

DO: According to Wikipedia, Vikar was "a legendary Norwegian king who found himself and his ships becalmed for a long period." He eventually is sacrificed to the gods to help raise a wind. In your novel, Vikar is befriended by the director who is known as "Viking Man." Your last name is Erickson. So, aside from being a homage to film, is *Zeroville* also a homage to your heritage?

SE: I'm Swedish, if you want to get technical, but if you've seen one Scandinavian you've seen them all, right? There's another Norwegian connection in *Zeroville*, of course, when Vikar's pursuit of a legendary lost silent film leads him to Oslo. And having said this, you know what? I'm not that smart. I forgot about Vikar being a legendary Norwegian king, if I ever knew it to begin with—it's a fantastic insight, though. Congratulations, and thanks, I'm going to steal it. I'll use it on Charlie Rose or *Fresh Air*.

DO: *Zeroville* would make a great film in the right hands. Who would you cast to play Vikar, Soledad, Zazi, Viking Man, and Dorothy Langer? Who would direct? Who would edit?

SE: It's a natural question that I'm getting asked a lot, which puts me in the position of sounding either coy if I don't answer or grandiose if I do. So I would like to establish that this was your idea, not mine. Presumably the director would be somebody very film conscious—the ultimate example is Scorsese. Paul Thomas Anderson, David Cronenberg, Steven Soderbergh, Michel Gondry: each would make a very different and interesting movie. I'm reluctant to speculate on the casting, because everyone who reads the novel is going to have his or her own visual impression of what the characters look like, but Johnny Depp probably would have been the ultimate Vikar before he outgrew such man-child roles—in which case I'll go with Ryan Gosling or Joaquin Phoenix. Neither is anything like I pictured Vikar, but they would capture Vikar's enigma and volatility.

Paz Vega as Soledad, *Spanglish* notwithstanding—we can't really blame her for that one. Frances McDormand as Dorothy Langer. She doesn't look like I pictured Dotty—Langer is older and grayer than her years—but the personality is spot-on and of course it doesn't hurt that McDormand's an awfully good actress and a smart one too, because Dorothy is sharp, even when she's drunk.

Viking Man is confounding because he's almost an archetype and out of his time even in the seventies, let alone the twenty-first century when we're trying to cast him—I can't think of anyone who would be precisely right. The closest I come is Vincent D'Onofrio or Philip Seymour Hoffman. Neither quite has the expansive bravado that comes so authentically to Viking Man—both are more implosive actors—but they have the right physicality, even if Hoffman is a bit too short and D'Onofrio a bit too hulking, and they're both such good actors there's no doubt they would get the character. One has played Lester Bangs and the other Orson Welles, so there you go.

The toughest one is Zazi. She has to be played by four different actresses at different ages between three and fifteen or sixteen, and even allowing for the liberties a movie takes with a novel, I don't think there's a way around it. As I think we've said, she's the second-most important character in the book. At the moment Saoirse Ronan is the hot young actress of that age, and maybe she's too obvious.

As for who would edit, the key reference while writing the novel was a book called *The Conversations*, a series of interviews between Michael Ondaatje and Walter Murch. Murch edited the film version of Ondaatje's *The English Patient* as well as *Apocalypse Now, Julia, The Talented Mister Ripley*, the last *Godfather*, and *The Unbearable Lightness of Being*, which I consider the exemplar of an adaptation of a modern literary novel. Murch couldn't be less like Vikar—he's extraordinarily erudite, a kind of renaissance guy; I thought I knew something about movies until I read these interviews—but while I hardly based Vikar's style of editing on Murch's, reading the interviews gave me a new understanding of editing from which I could invent Vikar's theories of editing, such as they are. Anyway, when Steven or David or Michel or Paul Thomas get around to editing *Zeroville* the movie, they might want to give Walter a call.

Steve Erickson Interviewed by Anthony Miller

Anthony Miller / 2008

From *Lit Park* at www.litpark.com (April 2, 2008). Reprinted by permission.

Steve Erickson's gorgeously discombobulating novels can only truly be mapped against and according to the enigmatic chronological and cartographic coordinates they provide. His writing delves deeply into questions about the permeability of the boundaries between reality and dreams, how history might begin in dreams, and how dreams can constitute their own forms of history. His narratives have incorporated disappearing streets, dying buildings, demolished metropolises, clandestine radio broadcasts, mysterious melody snakes, metaphysical maps and blueprints, and secret rooms that ferry characters across space and time or contain the essence of a character's conscience or fate. Erickson follows not, as he has himself described it, the "clocks of strict chronology" but the "internal clock of memory," venturing through time's slipstreams and sluicing between the viaducts of dreams. In his latest novel, *Zeroville*, Erickson immerses himself in a more communal dream-realm: the movies.

Now in its third printing, *Zeroville* (Europa Editions) is a novel which is not merely inspired by film but one that unravels in a way as if dictated from a cinematic subconscious. *Zeroville* opens with a statement by director Josef von Sternberg: "I believe that cinema was here from the beginning of the world." His epigraph could have been exchanged with—or else coupled with—André Breton's pronouncement (from *L'Âge du cinéma*): "From the instant he takes his seat to the moment he slips into the fiction evolving before his eyes, he passes through a critical point as captivating and imperceptible as that uniting waking and sleeping. . . . It is a way of going to the movies the way others go to church, and I think that, from a certain angle, quite independently of what is playing, it is there that the only *absolutely modern* mystery is celebrated." When Vikar Jerome arrives in Hollywood in 1969 with movies on his mind—literally (with a film-related tattoo on his head) as well as figuratively—he becomes caught up in mysteries that are at once absolutely modern and resonant of ancient stories of belief and sacrifice. In this Big Picture bildungsroman, Vikar is, at various moments, an embryonic Starchild in a contemporary Void and a "cineautis-tic" anchorite in a "Heretic City." Whatever role the reader ultimately elects to assign to Vikar—cinematic medium, madman, martyr, auteur, cipher, collector, crusader—his destiny is inextricably tied to the world of celluloid.

Vikar finds his way into the Hollywood studios and falls in with the most devout of the city's cineastes in Nichols Beach, directors and actors whose films will soon irrevocably alter the landscape. His wanderings through Hollywood also take him on detours to New York City, Madrid, Paris, Cannes, and Oslo, the site of a famous discovery both for Vikar and for cinema. Vikar's journey also provides one version of the history of film culture from the rise of the American independent filmmaker in the seventies through blockbusters and financial boondoggles into the aesthetic indulgences and some "avant-" explorations of the eighties. Those familiar with Erickson's other books will recognize a few recurring characters and locales. The novel also features a few Los Angeles settings outside the requisite Hollywood path. It's worth noting that Vikar's first stop in Los Angeles is Philippe's, possibly the first time the venerable one-hundred-year-old home of the French Dip sandwich has made an appearance in contemporary fiction—even if Vikar ends up being unable to enjoy his sandwich.

Zeroville is inhabited as much by the many figures projected upon the movie screen as by those characters who view, study, debate, and draw their inspiration and even their very identity from what those on the screen speak or reveal to them. The novel is replete with elements of studio lore and irreverent film criticism. Erickson's fascination with and zeal for film erupts on practically every page; reading the novel will likely inspire readers not only to screen or rescreen the movies Vikar watches within the novel but also to rethink the importance of Montgomery Clift and of movies in general. *Zeroville* is an immensely engrossing novel about being enraptured by cinema.

Erickson is the author of seven previous novels, including *Days Between Stations, Tours of the Black Clock, Arc d'X,* and *The Sea Came in at Midnight.* His two unjustly out-of-print but highly recommended books (especially in this election year) about American politics and pop culture, *Leap Year* and

American Nomad, sometimes mistakenly shelved as novels, appear to be the author's personal chronicles of the 1988 and 1996 presidential elections but are in fact nothing less than delirious odysseys across a spectral United States that articulate the voice of the American psyche. (I would campaign for the reissue of these two books—perhaps collected in a single volume.) The recipient of a 2007 Guggenheim fellowship, Erickson is the editor of *Black Clock*, a national literary journal published by the California Institute of the Arts, which has just published its eighth issue. He teaches writing in the MFA program at CalArts and is the film critic for *Los Angeles* magazine. Erickson's website can be found at www.steveerickson.org.

Zeroville was named one of *Newsweek*'s best books of 2007 and one of the year's twenty-five best books of fiction and poetry in the *Los Angeles Times*. It appeared on best-of-2007 lists in the *Washington Post Book World* and the *Toronto Globe and Mail*. The novel has received praise from the *New York Times Book Review*, the *Philadelphia Inquirer*, the *London Times* (even before the book was published in England), the *Seattle Times, Bookforum, The Nation*, and *The Believer*. It has also very recently been selected as one of the five novels in 2008's "Good Reads" by the National Book Critics Circle.

A Place in the Sun

AM: The tattoo on Vikar's head—the first "shot," as it were, in *Zeroville*—captivates and confounds non-cineastes and cineastes, hippies and punks alike throughout the novel. How did you come up with the image of Montgomery Clift and Elizabeth Taylor from *A Place in the Sun* on the fleshy screen of Vikar's cranium? I don't know what you'll think of this, but Clift and Taylor, with their "faces barely apart, lips barely apart," made me think of Vikar's head as something like a silver screen version of the Grecian urn in Keats's "Ode on a Grecian Urn," with its figures frozen forever on the threshold of action. Characters crossing thresholds or remaining fixed—and fixated—at the edges of thresholds of various kinds, it seems to me, have always been an integral part of your stories. Could you elaborate on this mark that Vikar bears?

SE: Well, you've been reading my novels long enough to know that they operate on a pretty intuitive level, even—at the risk of sounding completely mystical or pretentious about it—on a level that's unconscious. And with the movies, after all, you're talking about a collective dream language, and with Clift and Taylor you have what the novel describes as "the two most beautiful people in the history of the movies, she the female version of him, and he the male version of her"—and in that particular moment from *A Place in the Sun*, Clift and Taylor are on a terrace away from the eyes of others, a party is going on inside the house, and they're on the verge of something. The seed of their fate already is planted in the womb of the factory girl that Clift has impregnated back in town. The two lovers are on the verge—and it's already too late. In a way, it may have been the end of cinematic romanticism, then and there—it's hard to think of any couple or image after that as purely, deathlessly romantic. So that scene from *A Place in the Sun* represents something Vikar himself doesn't understand, and that romanticism stands juxtaposed against the moment we first see Vikar, who arrives in LA in the summer of 1969 on the day of the Manson murders. The image tattooed on his head is portentous, ominous—Vikar is a punk angel bearing the sign of the apocalypse, so obsessed with movies it just seems natural he would engrave the sign of that obsession on his skull.

The Passion of Joan of Arc

AM: Vikar comes out of the same kind of sheltered upbringing and seminarian education as Paul Schrader, where being forbidden to watch films as a child created a lust for them as obscure objects of philosophical-theological desire. The very first film Vikar sees upon his arrival in Hollywood is *The Passion of Joan of Arc*. You also describe Michel Sarre in your first novel, *Days Between Stations* (who sits down with Vikar briefly in *Zeroville*), watching *The Passion of Joan of Arc*. You even make Vikar responsible for the 1981 discovery of the lost Oslo print of the film. What is it about that film and Mademoiselle Falconetti's Joan that haunts Vikar and Sarre—and you?

SE: Not unlike Vikar, I first saw *The Passion of Joan of Arc* in 1969, not in a small revival house like Vikar but at UCLA—and what I saw of course was the outtake version, the version that Carl Dreyer put together when he believed the original to have been destroyed in a fire. It was one of the greatest movies I ever saw, I never had seen anything like it, and this was the version comprised of Dreyer's *leftovers*! Everything about *Passion of Joan of Arc* is mythic, including that half century when the film was believed to be lost . . . Falconetti's performance—the only one she ever gave on film, which by all accounts deeply unhinged her . . . and just the intensity of the Joan of Arc story itself.

You're one of the first interviewers to have caught on to the Schrader allusion—I've always been struck by how the new directors of the seventies, the most film-conscious generation of filmmakers, started out aspiring to be priests or theologians or moralists, or came out of seriously repressed families. Schrader, Scorsese, Malick. A young architecture student in divinity school, Vikar designs a model of a church with a small movie screen inside, in place of an altar, and along with *A Place in the Sun*, for him *The Passion of Joan of Arc* is the ultimate example of the movie as epiphany, a kind of hinge between the cinematic and the religious.

2001: A Space Odyssey

AM: After *The Passion of Joan of Arc*, the next film that Vikar goes to see in Hollywood in 1969 is *2001*. Vikar, like all those who confronted Kubrick's film in the darkness of the theater, has an encounter with that film's Starchild and sees himself as "a kind of starchild as well." (Vikar's last name, Jerome, also makes me think of another extraterrestrial visitor from the movies, Thomas Jerome Newton in *The Man Who Fell to Earth*.) Can you talk about how Vikar is a sort of "embryonic, perhaps divine Starchild" in a land of very different "stars"?

SE: Well, I liked the juxtaposition of *2001* and *The Passion of Joan of Arc*—as I said, it parallels to a certain extent my own understanding of movies, although in 1969 I was about five years younger than Vikar is at that point in the story. *2001* and *Joan* share a kind of anarchic spiritualism, even as they tell their stories from opposite ends of both modern history and the modern imagination. On an endless bus trip from the East Coast, Vikar comes to LA feeling like he's hurtled through the cosmos until he's gone as far as anyone can go—LA was at the end of everything in those days. It was at the end of time; it was the future geographically and metaphorically. Tokyo and Hong Kong hadn't become *Blade Runner* cities at that point. Vikar has cut himself loose of not only his past but, most importantly, his parents, particularly his father. He's an orphan the way the Starchild in *2001* is the ultimate orphan, the way Joan became an orphan.

The Conversation

AM: Vikar's obliviousness to everything except movies prompts one character to dub him a "cineautistic." It's as if he's some kind of forerunner

of new species of man: Homo *cinematicus*. His naïve deployment of various
utterances he hears spoken by those around him could be read in such a
way as to make Vikar a cipher, but it could also suggest a weird talent Vikar
possesses to "splice" together what he hears at certain moments into new
and different contexts.

SE: *Homo cinematicus*—that's fabulous. I'm going to pretend I really
am that smart and that's exactly what I was thinking. It probably doesn't
matter whether Vikar's editing is a form of his cineautism, or whether his
cineautism is a kind of psychic editing.

Môjuu

AM: You have Vikar utter a line from the weird sculptor in the strange,
psychosexual Japanese cult film *Môjuu* (*Blind Beast*): "I have eyes in my
fingers." Some of your central characters are voyeur-artists who create works
that, like those of the sculptor in *Blind Beast*, are essentially reflections of
fevered psyches, like the pulp-turned-pornographic writer Banning Jainlight
in *Tours of the Black Clock*, or the Occupant, that doomstruck menologist
from your novel *The Sea Came in at Midnight*, who obsesses over all the
collected endtime increments (the bangs *and* the whimpers) that comprise
his room-sized apocalyptic calendar of the twentieth century. How would
you say Vikar is like or unlike your other obsessive characters from previous
works?

SE: What's the cliché about dreams, that everyone in your dreams,
including those who seem to be someone else, represents a facet of you? I
admit that many of my favorite characters in literature are the obsessives—
Ahab, Heathcliff, Joe Christmas in *Light in August*. Vikar certainly is an
obsessive, inscrutable in the manner of the Occupant, and he has in him
a violence like Jainlight's, and the childlike, questing nature of Michel in
Days Between Stations and Etcher in *Arc d'X*. He was as key to the novel as
you would expect—I thought about the book for a couple of years, and only
when Vikar came into focus did the rest of the novel fall into place quickly.
He defined the tone and perspective of the novel. Once I understood him—
and though I love movies and always have, I'm just not obsessed the way
Vikar is, there are too many other things I care about—it was easy to see
the novel through his eyes, it was easy to know what he would think or do,
and that dictated a lot of choices, even as the novel deliberately declines to
dissect his thinking or explain it.

The Death of Marat

AM: Among the films Vikar watches in the novel, there is the great lost silent film by Adolphe Sarre, a film which appears only in your novels *Days Between Stations* and *Amnesiascope*, where it is reviewed in a weekly newspaper despite the fact that it exists (at least initially) only in the mind of a beleaguered film critic. You have included a forgotten silent-film director, a screenwriter, and a film critic in your previous novels. Why did you choose to make Vikar a film editor? How is *Zeroville* an extension of or a departure from your ideas about film in your other novels?

SE: Well, as you point out, the movies have been in the background of many of the novels. I'm not sure why it took this long to write a book where film was front and center, a novel where people actually would sit around and talk about movies—real movies—the way people who love movies do in real life. It made sense for Vikar to be an editor because, as such, he's a conduit, a medium. When Vikar first gets to Hollywood he finds a town where no one seems to know or care about movies—later when he's actually working on a movie, after sitting in on a preproduction meeting he wonders how he can love movies so much and not understand anything anyone else is saying.

In many ways the scene that led me into the rest of the novel was one where a Black militant burglar—this is in 1970—breaks into Vikar's apartment and Vikar captures him and ties him to a chair, and then they spend the rest of the night watching movies on TV. On the one hand the incongruity of this burglar knowing all about Bette Davis and Joan Crawford movies was absurd, and on the other hand something about it captured perfectly for me how we all live secret lives through the movies. The scene seemed to distill the appeal and power of movies.

Belle de Jour

AM: At least as she appears to Vikar, Soledad Palladin is a figure who belongs more to cinema than to reality. She is rumored to be the daughter of Luis Buñuel, the lover of Jim Morrison and Frank Zappa, and, as befits the elusive nature of her character, the first actress meant to portray the vanishing woman in *L'Avventura*. Where did this figure come from?

SE: In her own way Soledad is probably the only character in the novel who's as mysterious as Vikar. Her personality seems to change with the light—one moment she's virtually stripping on a New York sidewalk in order to clothe a homeless woman, the next she's displaying a feral, ruthless sexuality. It's hard to tell from one moment to the next whether she's sacrificing everything for her daughter, Zazi, or doesn't care about her at all. She's very loosely based on a true European actress of that period named Soledad Miranda, who has a cult following that considers her to have been one of the world's most beautiful women—she made a lot of soft-core Eurotrash vampire pictures like *Vampyros Lesbos* and *She Killed in Ecstasy*, and died very young in a car crash. She was from Seville, and I took that part of Miranda's life and created the rest, turning her into an über-Siren of the era, the kind of fantasy figure who exists for anyone who loves movies.

Vertigo

AM: As grounded in reality as her mother Soledad is evanescent, Zazi is the character in the novel who establishes the most authentic human connection with Vikar. Under Vikar's peculiar tutelage, Zazi becomes the one most willing to debate her take on movies with the cineastes in the novel with all the tenacity of an adolescent Pauline Kael. Yet, by the end, she seems to inherit something of Vikar's vertiginous cinematic delirium. How would you characterize Zazi's influence on Vikar and on the novel?

SE: At first Zazi is like a lot of the people Vikar has met in LA: she doesn't really respond to the movies at all. But as you noted, in some ways she turns out to be the best critic in the novel, with iconoclastic insights into sacrosanct pictures like *Casablanca* and *Rio Bravo*. By the end she's dreaming movies she's never seen, and in some ways *Zeroville* turns out to be more Zazi's story than Vikar's. When readers who don't know much about movies tell me they like the book, I think it's because they've been caught up in the relationship between Vikar and Zazi.

Kiss Me Deadly

AM: Vikar, whose given name is Isaac, also wrestles throughout the novel with various reverberations of the old biblical tale of the father sacrificing the son in Abraham's divine sacrifice of Isaac. I think it's telling that Vikar's exclamation of choice, which might not be an expletive at all, is "Oh, mother."

SE: Well, there's a story about "Oh, mother!" that I haven't told. Ten years ago when I was the film critic for *Spin*—the nadir of my professional life— the editors set up a date between me and Jenna Jameson to go see *Boogie Nights*, which was just out. Difficult as I know some will find this to believe, at the time I had no idea who Jameson was, but she was at the peak of her porn superstardom. Jenna showed up in a tight baby-blue jumpsuit zipped down to her belly, with stupefying breasts bigger than she was, and we saw *Boogie Nights* together—I know you think I'm making this up—and the startling thing was how shocked she was by it. During the screening she kept exclaiming, "Oh, mother!" and then, a decade later, it popped out of Vikar's mouth when I was writing the novel, and I couldn't remember where I had heard it except that it came to him—or me—very naturally and, as you point out, it completely expressed the relationship Vikar has with his father. About halfway through writing the novel, the penny dropped and I remembered about Jenna. So the creative process can work in odd ways, you know?

The Godfather

AM: Vikar compares the death of Fredo in *The Godfather* to the Abraham-Isaac story, but there might be a number of cinematic variations on the Abraham and Isaac story throughout the novel, in such films like *Pat Garrett and Billy the Kid* or even *Blade Runner*.

SE: It's difficult to say too much here without giving away the novel's core. But Vikar believes God kills children, and he has a father-daughter relationship with Zazi that's unlike any other relationship that either of them has. He makes a promise to Soledad and becomes Zazi's protector. Only in retrospect have I realized how much this is a theme in a lot of my novels, from *Days Between Stations* to *Rubicon Beach* to *Tours of the Black Clock* to *Arc d'X*. It reached sort of a culmination in the two previous books, *The Sea Came in at Midnight* and particularly *Our Ecstatic Days*, where a lake appears in the middle of LA and the young single mother is convinced it's the chaos of the world come to take her son from her. Writing *Zeroville*, I realized early on that the movies in the novel had to be selected rigorously— they couldn't just be personal favorites or the canon, whatever the canon is these days. There's not that much in *Zeroville* about *Lawrence of Arabia* or *The Third Man*, after all, two of my favorite movies ever. The movies Vikar responds to, he responds to for a reason. They mean something to him along the lines you've mentioned or illuminate something about him or somehow inform his reaction to the world around him.

The Long Goodbye

AM: *Zeroville* is inhabited as much by screen characters as by the actors and directors in Hollywood who create them. Your novel made me think of "secret histories" of cinema in books like David Thomson's *Suspects* or Geoffrey O'Brien's *The Phantom Empire* more than so-called Hollywood novels. At one point in the novel, describing private eye Philip Marlowe in Robert Altman's *The Long Goodbye*, you surmise, "Three years later Marlowe will move to New York, change his name to Bickle and drive cabs for a living."

SE: I admit that this may be a difference that matters only to me, but I've never thought of *Zeroville* as a "Hollywood novel." Hollywood novels tend to be about making movies, and this novel is about loving movies. It's about how movies have become so much a part of contemporary consciousness, or the common unconsciousness, that when we say something that's happened in our lives was "just like in a movie," we're alluding to a kind of hyper-reality rather than the way movies are illusory.

Vikar drifts in and out of theaters like other people drift in and out of hotel lobbies or train stations—what's projected on the walls blends in with life outside. In my novel *The Sea Came in at Midnight*, movies are projected on the city walls. For Vikar the world already is like that, until finally he discovers a secret hidden among the frames of every movie ever made.

The Parallax View

AM: Your novels have included historical characters, some with names like Thomas Jefferson and Sally Hemings, others who are unnamed but recognizable just the same. Did you watch or read anything in particular to help you shape any of the real-life figures from cinema that ricochet through *Zeroville*? The character Viking Man is an absolutely inspired version of John Milius, and you give him so many of the great lines in the novel. Have you heard anything about the novel from your characters' real-life counterparts?

SE: No, the lawsuits haven't started rolling in yet. Here's a very strange thing: Just as I was finishing the novel, my wife [Lori Precious] and sister-in-law were working on a Korean War documentary, in which there's been some possible feature interest, and who should become involved but . . . Milius. Maybe he'll have second thoughts after reading the novel, though I have a lot of affection for him as a character. He may be a blowhard but his heart's in the right place. I've never met Milius, so it's more precise to say that Viking Man is my version of Milius, drawing on some select facts of Milius's life that anyone who knows anything about movies would know. I admit that at first Viking Man seemed almost too broad a characterization, so much an archetype, but he was a perfect counterpart to the impenetrable Vikar, and both are out of their time, as though Vikar is from the future and Viking Man is from the past.

Most of the movie references for the novel, whether they're characters or movies themselves, were pulled from memory. I can only think of a couple of instances where I went back and studied something in particular. I watched *A Place in the Sun* again for the passage in the novel where Dorothy Langer, the veteran editor, shows Vikar how and why she cuts films. For the scene later in the book between Vikar and the ghost of Montgomery Clift, I went back and watched *Red River, From Here to Eternity, The Misfits*, in order to catch his Midwestern speech pattern with its high-pitched sort of crackle, which was as difficult to translate into print as it is distinct to hear.

Other than the movies, the crucial text was a book called *The Conversations*, an ongoing discussion between Walter Murch and Michael Ondaatje, who of course wrote *The English Patient*, which Murch edited in its film version. Murch also cut *Apocalypse Now, Julia, The Unbearable Lightness of Being, The Talented Mister Ripley*, the third *Godfather*. Murch is like a Renaissance man, with a vast, worldly intelligence about everything—he's not Vikar, in other words. It was a revelatory book.

The Sound of Music

AM: Vikar arrives in the capital of film only to find its denizens much more smitten by pop music than by cinema. Only a character in one of your novels could describe the von Trapp family from *The Sound of Music* as "a family of sirens living in snowy mountains, pursued by police and leaving a trail of malevolent music" and liken them to another family, the Manson Family. You leave Vikar at the side of the road as he hears a song exhorting him to board the "Marrakesh Express": "It's horrible; they've forgotten *A Place in the Sun* for this?" Yet, songs and allusions to songs by Iggy Pop, Roxy

Music, David Bowie, and others appear in the novel. When punk—what Vikar calls "the Sound"—arrives on the scene, Vikar becomes something of a punk icon at CBGB and Madame Wong's, and he reflects upon the fact that he has "come to care more about the Sound than the Movies." As a fan and a critic who has surveyed both Los Angeles songs ("L.A.'s Top 100," *Los Angeles*, November 2001) and films ("The 25 Greatest Films about Los Angeles," *Los Angeles*, March 2003), how do you grapple with your own personal feelings about these respective mediums of sound and vision?

SE: Music was just the tenor of everything in 1969 and 1970, particularly in LA. American movies were still catching up with the cultural explosion of Bob Dylan and the Beatles, just as Dylan and the Beatles were running out of steam. Crosby, Stills & Nash was the hot act of the moment, being touted as the "American Beatles," but you know, "Marrakesh Express" wasn't exactly "Strawberry Fields Forever." It wasn't even "Ob-La-Di, Ob-La-Da." When he gets to LA, Vikar finds music has displaced movies as the cultural currency and feels betrayed—and six or seven years later, when he's distracted by punk, it's like a married man having an affair before coming to his senses and returning to the home of the movies, even as he never entirely loses his attraction to the lover.

Even as a film student at UCLA who wanted to be a novelist, I went through periods where music meant more to me than anything, and I guess if there's anything remotely autobiographical about *Zeroville* it has to do with when I lived in Echo Park in the early seventies and the air was full of James Taylor and Carole King and the Eagles, none of whom meant much to me. I was the only person I knew in LA who had a Roxy Music record, the only person I knew in LA who had a Stooges record, the only person I knew in LA who had a New York Dolls record or a Mott the Hoople record or a Velvet Underground record. I wasn't the only person I knew who had a Bowie record, but I was the *first* person I knew who had a Bowie record. It was at once strange and alienating to be living in this heavily Latino section of LA on the top floor of an old Victorian house right out of *Chinatown* and trekking down to the corner newsstand to find *Creem* among all the Spanish-language magazines so I could read Robert Christgau while washing my clothes at the laundromat, and at the same time it was a distinctly LA kind of experience, living a Frankenstein life sewn together from discarded fragments of more coherent lives. And that music that seemed antithetical to LA in some ways, at complete odds with the Eagles, in fact was cinematic, vivid, dangerous in a glamorous way that was true to LA, even as it was coming out of London or New York. It was music that grew more out of the anarchic Seeds/Love/Doors/Beefheart tradition of LA music rather than the utopian tradition of the Beach Boys or the Byrds or the Mamas and Papas.

Now, Voyager

AM: The extensive conversation about the movies you mentioned earlier between Vikar and the Black militant burglar who breaks into his house is undoubtedly one of the funniest scenes in any of your novels. Among other topics, they discuss Max Steiner's Oscar-winning soundtrack to *Now, Voyager*, a soundtrack that marked, as the burglar (who is bound to a chair) says, "the only time one of the biggest stars of all time lost a creative power struggle to the composer."

SE: The story is that Bette Davis tried to get Max Steiner fired from *Now, Voyager* because she thought his score upstaged her—a myopic view on her part to say the least, because *Now, Voyager* isn't the same movie without Steiner's music and, consequently, whether she understood it or not, Davis's wouldn't have been the same performance. His score didn't upstage her, it flattered her. I've since heard she tried to get Steiner kicked off other movies too, like *Dark Victory*—don't know if it's true but, if so, she obviously had it in for Max Steiner.

"The Unheard Music"

AM: What are your favorite movie soundtracks?

SE: Notwithstanding the imagistic nature of movies, it's striking how many great movies just wouldn't be great if not for the music. *Chinatown* originally had a honky-tonk kind of soundtrack, which would have been a terrible mistake—fortunately it was replaced in the last couple weeks of postproduction by Jerry Goldsmith's score, which he knocked off very quickly, given how it's his most inspired work. *Casablanca* isn't the same movie without the music, and probably *Gone with the Wind*—not a movie I'm especially fond of, so I'm hard-pressed to say for sure—isn't either, and those are Steiner's most famous and obvious scores. *Now, Voyager* is more otherworldly and so is *The Fountainhead*, an insane film that verges on the hallucinatory by way of Steiner's music. Those are Steiner's best. They shimmer; they sound like they're floating above the clouds.

From Steiner to Franz Waxman, who did the score for *A Place in the Sun*, most of these guys came out of Europe, were classically trained, aspired to be classical composers, but fled Hitler and wound up in Hollywood the way a lot of European novelists from Mann to Huxley wound up in Hollywood, wondering what the hell they were doing there. Even Bernard Herrmann, who was a New York kid, came out of a European tradition—*Vertigo's* soundtrack is a noir version of Wagner's *Tristan and Isolde*, which makes sense, of course.

David Raksin is one of the rare American-influenced composers of that period who can stand with the Europeans. He wrote only two really great scores, *Laura* and *The Bad and the Beautiful*, but the films are unimaginable without them, particularly the former. Then there were all of Randy Newman's various uncles. John Barry and Ennio Morricone are the two great film composers of the last fifty years who can easily stand with Steiner, Waxman, Herrmann.

"Shadowplay"

AM: Late in the novel, a delirious Vikar hears Joy Division's "Shadowplay," a song about searching and longing and getting lost and longing to get lost, but which also has a title that could certainly serve as a definition of motion pictures. Have you heard this new cover version currently playing on the radio by the Killers?

SE: Haven't heard the Killers' version, but I think it's in the same collection as an interesting cut they do with Lou Reed. Along with "Atmosphere," "Shadowplay" probably is my favorite Joy Division song—it certainly evokes a displacement that's as liberating as it is terrifying, and images of a secret city, with wandering streets that spiral down to some forbidden center.

"When the Music's Over"

AM: Have you seen Anton Corbijn's film *Control*? How did it compare in your view with *24 Hour Party People*? How do you think Joy Division should best be remembered?

SE: I've seen part of *Control* and found it pretty interesting—but you know where it's going, right? And you know it's not going to end well, and that the story is just going to get sadder and sadder, whereas *24 Hour Party*

People had about it a feeling of palpable celebration, even in Joy Division's music which, albeit in a tangential fashion, had its own LA connection—there's a Jim Morrison poster hanging on Ian Curtis's wall. I know some folks hate the Doors, a band that certainly had its silly moments, but without them, Iggy and Patti Smith and X and Joy Division wouldn't have been who they were.

"The Right Profile"

AM: You quote the song by the Clash in which Joe Strummer sings, "Monty's face broken on a wheel / Is he alive? Can he still feel?" One thing that plagues Vikar is that the Montgomery Clift on his head is continually mistaken for James Dean (and Elizabeth Taylor for Natalie Wood) in *Rebel Without A Cause*. What do you think would have happened if Clift had perished in his car accident in '56? What role did Montgomery Clift play in the Hollywood of the fifties and early sixties?

SE: Clift was John the Baptist to Brando's Jesus. I don't know what exactly that makes Dean—St. Peter? At several points in *Zeroville* one character or another makes mention that Clift surviving his car crash wasn't the best career move, particularly given the price he paid. The next ten years until his death were extraordinarily difficult ones of pain, disfigurement, psychic torment. Because Clift was a better actor than Dean and his range was greater, his persona isn't as defined—in Dean's three movies, he more or less played three incarnations of the same anguished adolescence, with which anguished adolescents across the country identified. On the other hand Clift didn't have the ferocity of a Brando; he wasn't the force of nature that Brando was. So I think he's been a bit lost to the winds of time except for those who know about him, and for those who know about him, something about him is special, subtler, more shaded and certainly more haunted than either Brando or Dean. I think he gave himself emotionally to roles in a way Brando's or Dean's egos wouldn't have allowed.

In a Lonely Place

AM: Could you talk about why you decided to check yourself into the Roosevelt Hotel in Hollywood to work on this novel? Did you subscribe to any personal rules regarding how you would handle the allusions to films, or have specific concepts you kept in mind in order to lend this novel a pace and energy more appropriate to, say, a screenplay?

SE: Well, you've put your finger on the matter. I wrote a short story called "Zeroville" for a *McSweeney's* anthology in 2004 edited by Michael Chabon. It had some of the elements of the later novel, but the central character was far more conventional than Vikar and there wasn't the pop momentum that it seemed a novel about the movies should have. It didn't seem like a novel about the movies should follow the Faulknerian chronology of memory that's characterized other books of mine. So I did subscribe to some narrative laws, as you put it, that I never thought about in other novels I've written—keep it linear, always in the present tense, telling the story in action and dialogue along with movie references, in short scenes that cut from one to the next. Not to be like a screenplay, but certainly to approximate the rush of a movie.

Everyone mentions how fast the book reads, and a serious writer distrusts that a bit, a serious writer wants the reader to settle into the book. I hope it's not speaking out of school to report that Don DeLillo phoned me and said, "It reads fast, but it's a very fine work." Note the "but." I checked into the Roosevelt for four nights, in a room down the hall from the one where Montgomery Clift lived in between filming *A Place in the Sun* and *From Here to Eternity*, and knocked out the first fifty pages, up through the burglar scene.

Written on the Wind

AM: Around 1980, Vikar attempts to adapt J. K. Huysmans's *Là-Bas* for the screen, a punk-influenced version of the nineteenth-century novel called *God's Worst Nightmare*, to star Harvey Keitel and to be shot by Robby Müller. You have written about the problems of literary adaptation in various articles, and you contributed a list of what you regard as some of the most successful cinematic adaptations for last year's "Fiction into Film" issue of *Bookforum*. What are your current thoughts on how your own novels might be adapted to the screen?

SE: When Anthony Minghella made *The English Patient*, he famously told Ondaatje, "You realize we're going to fuck up your book." Over the years, to the point of tedium I've cited Philip Kaufman's version of Milan Kundera's *Unbearable Lightness of Being* as the best modern adaptation of a contemporary literary novel—it's as good a movie as the book is a novel, maybe better, because while Kaufman was faithful to the spirit and the themes of Kundera's story, he knew he had to break it down and build his own version. I've always said if anyone can make a great movie of Kundera and an interesting movie of Ondaatje, not to mention *The Remains of the Day* or *The Hours*, about which I have varying degrees of enthusiasm as movies but all of which, I think, warrant respect, my own novels are probably pretty easy in comparison.

Some Came Running

AM: Any particular advice for the future screenwriters and directors who would adapt your books?

SE: In a way I think *Our Ecstatic Days* is the most filmable. Paradoxically this is considered my most "experimental" novel, a term I detest but which I'll use here to make a point. For all the unconventional departures of the novel, at its core are some very traditional conflicts—it's the story of a mother trying to protect her kid, which is about as basic a narrative as there is. I imagine a female director making it—Jane Campion, Sofia Coppola if she wanted to take on something of that scale. I think *Days Between Stations* could make a good movie. I think *Tours of the Black Clock* could make a good movie, though a very dark one. At the center of those novels are very archetypal narratives or strong characters, and more than novels, movies deal in archetype. *Zeroville* would lend itself relatively easily to a film, though I doubt it's anything a studio would initiate, because I'm not sure many executives or producers understand that *Zeroville* is less *The Player* than a punk *Cinema Paradiso*. If it ever happens at all, I imagine a particularly film-conscious director doing it—a Soderbergh, a Cronenberg, P. T. Anderson, the Coens, even a Tarantino—or an actor like Ryan Gosling, Joaquin Phoenix, or Tobey Maguire who sees a good role in Vikar, or someone like Frances McDormand as Dotty Langer.

La Planète sauvage

AM: "Comic-book characters!" Viking Man bemoans to Vikar sometime in the early eighties. "That's the movies now in a scrotum sac—glorified afternoon-serials and cute little robots. Who's to say it's right or wrong? Maybe this is the age we need new myths." As you have written about comics (the introduction to Neil Gaiman's *The Sandman: Dream Country* trade paperback, a 2001 *Bookforum* interview with Alan Moore, an appreciation of *American Flagg!* in the 2004 writers on comics collection *Give Our Regards to the Atomsmashers!*) and worked in a comic-book store twenty years ago, I wondered if I could ask you to reflect on comic books and their current place in the cinema. What are your thoughts about the many recent comic-book adaptations, from films with iconic superheroes (Spider Man, Batman, the X-Men, the Hulk, Hellboy, Iron Man) to those adapted from more aesthetically and politically complex and ambiguous graphic novels (*Ghost World*, *V for Vendetta*, *Sin City*, *A History of Violence*, *Persepolis*, the forthcoming *Watchmen*). How do you explain the rise in bringing these stories to the screen and their respective successes and failures? Has anyone approached you about adapting your novels into graphic novels? Which of your books do you think might make the best graphic novels? What about *Zeroville* as a graphic novel?

SE: The most telling thing is that the best comics or graphic novels are so much more sophisticated, both visually and narratively, than even the best movie versions of those novels and comics. None of these movies is written on the level of Alan Moore's work, though *V for Vendetta*—Moore's perennial disgruntlement aside—gave it a fair shot. I'm just not sure which directors respect comics enough to do right by them. Sam Raimi does. Maybe Bryan Singer does—his *Superman* had some lyrical, even moving moments. I think Tim Burton does, though I'm not sure he ever really cared about the Batman story per se. Christopher Nolan's *Batman* has some good things, Christian Bale in particular, but I thought the 2005 film was so worried about getting off to a fast start, which is to say conforming to an action-picture formula, that it never took the time to give itself over to the myth in a way that would fully have involved us. Some years ago I met a comic-book artist in Japan who supposedly turned *Rubicon Beach* into a graphic novel. He did it pretty much renegade style, which is to say he didn't bother to acquire the rights for it, but that was okay—it was so cool I didn't care. I can see *Tours* as a graphic novel. So much of *Zeroville* is about the dialogue, I'm not sure a graphic novel could accommodate it.

Nightdreams

AM: Vikar discovers the same mysterious image he glimpses in a frame of the 1928 *Passion of Joan of Arc* in a far less well-known 1982 "avant-porn" film called *Nightdreams*. You have written about *Nightdreams* here and there, in many places as one instance of a group of films you dubbed, in *Amnesiascope* and in some of your film columns, the "Cinema of Hysteria." What is the Cinema of Hysteria? Could Vikar Jerome be considered a kind of Cinema of Hysteria "made flesh"?

SE: That's a great question. Yeah, like Robert Johnson's "blues walking like a man," or whatever the line is, Vikar is film-rapture walking like a man, and like we were saying before when we talked about the religious backgrounds of so many filmmakers of the seventies, Vikar feels a special connection to movies that transcend any kind of earthbound logic. The Cinema of Hysteria is a clandestine cinema that's been forming throughout the twentieth and twenty-first centuries, movies that make no "sense" but that we instinctively understand anyway—not only *A Place in the Sun, Vertigo, The Passion of Joan of Arc,* and *Now, Voyager,* but *Môjuu, Humoresque, Written on the Wind, Branded to Kill, Pretty Poison, Black Narcissus, In a Lonely Place, One-Eyed Jacks, Point Blank, Cutter's Way, The Last Temptation of Christ, Lost Highway.*

Because sex is the most rapturous and irrational of acts, porn would seem to naturally lend itself to Cinema of Hysteria, except of course that for the great majority of its audience porn is so fundamentally *functional*. That audience isn't interested in hysteria; it's not interested in Jenna Jameson as a guide into the recesses of the psyche. *Nightdreams* was the first of the modern avant-porn, though some of Russ Meyer's pictures—*Up!, Beneath the Valley of the Ultra-Vixens, Faster, Pussycat! Kill! Kill!*—qualify as Cinema of Hysteria. Every now and then a porn film comes along that has Cinema of Hysteria aspects to it. Some of Michael Ninn's stuff like *Shock* and *Catherine*. The trick is just watching them as silent films, with the sound off, because as soon as these actors have to deliver lines, the spell is broken.

Alphaville

AM: The title of your novel derives from the line of futuristic private eye Lemmy Caution in Godard's *Alphaville*: "This isn't Alphaville, it's Zeroville." Hollywood is characterized as a land of "zero-reset." *Zeroville* could be regarded as a kind of historical novel not only in that it takes place in a now-heralded age where the influence of the studios was waning but also in that its characters are part of a vanishing—if not completely vanished— celluloid age of frequenting movie theaters and engaging in disappearing rituals like double features and midnight screenings. Vikar Jerome is an inveterate moviegoer and you catalog, either with titles or with short synoptic descriptions, the many films he sees. He comes to be a collector, or at least a coveter, of film prints (St. Jerome being the patron saint of translators, librarians, and encyclopedists). Are we fast approaching a kind of Year Zero of a type of movie viewing? How do you think the age of home viewing has altered the experience of watching films and talking about the nature of films?

SE: You know, I remember when I began collecting movies—I would tape them off the now legendary Z Channel in LA. Then I began buying videos and then DVDs, and at first a lot of people thought it was strange: Collecting movies? Movies *you've already seen*? Now almost everyone I know buys and collects DVDs to at least some extent. They may not have the six or seven hundred movies I have or may not fetishize them the way I do or pore over the archive diligently agonizing whether to keep *Poison Ivy: The New Seduction* just because Jaime Pressly is naked in it, but for better or worse movies, like books, have become *artifacts* as well as *experiences*, and that replaces the social ritual of seeing movies with other people, except in the case of spectacles, because spectacles call for crowds and always have and probably always will.

There's one scene in the novel where Zazi sees *A Place in the Sun* on television after having seen it in a theater with an audience that laughed at it, and she tries to explain to Vikar how seeing the movie by herself was very different from being part of a collective response, in which suspending not just disbelief but rationality and giving oneself over to the dreaminess of the movie was impossible. Though Zazi never uses the term *Cinema of Hysteria*, that's what she's talking about—these are movies that work best when seen alone. I'm convinced that one of the reasons *Vertigo* rose in the pantheon of great films since its original failure when it was released in the late fifties is that a whole generation of budding young film lovers saw it on TV around 1962 as I did, at the age of twelve, alone in my living room when my parents were down the street at a party, and everything about it blew me away and unsettled me—the surrealism of it, the eroticism, which I understood only as well as twelve-year-olds in my day understood eroticism. And as with Zazi and *A Place in the Sun*, I've never seen *Vertigo* "work" with an audience in a theater, and I've seen it with an audience at least four times. Kubrick's *Eyes Wide Shut* is the most recent example I can think of—a movie that seems absurd in the collective dark, shared with other people, but watched alone on DVD has the force of a private dream.

So as we near that Year Zero that you're speaking of, and as movie watching becomes more a solitary experience, I can't help believing it will have some impact on the movies themselves. That social ritual will be lost and it will be a shame, but some more private ritual—maybe like reading—will replace it, in the same way fewer of us listen to albums anymore but rather build the individualized soundtracks of our lives, song by song.

Establishing Shot: An Interview with Steve Erickson

Joshua Cohen / 2008

From *KGB Bar Lit* at www.kgbbar.com. Reprinted by permission.

Steve Erickson's many novels (*Days Between Stations, Rubicon Beach, Tours of the Black Clock, Arc d'X, Amnesiascope, The Sea Came in at Midnight, Our Ecstatic Days*) read as if written for the readership of other worlds— worlds not different from ours so much as parallel, the real turned upside down, inside out, and yet centered, inevitably, around Los Angeles; an alternate cityscape, purged of cloying commerciality, populated by dreamers, and informed not by mundane and compromised reality, but by a rarefied innocence that, transposed through metaphor to describe our own condition, offers our reading and dreaming lives, here and now, a modicum of hope, and even redemption. The perceptual skew of his new book, *Zeroville*, turns Hollywood into Babylon, or an Eden redux. Here, Erickson gives us his tightest establishing shot yet: an image of film as the scripture of a secular age. Its hero, Vikar Jerome, is a film editor who, in the rise and fall of his career, uncovers the secret history of our time—call it a celluloid Apocrypha—through a madcap, and maddening, resplicing of film frames. What results—what is framed—is nothing less than a new creation myth. What is created is nothing less than us.

Erickson, movie critic for *Los Angeles* magazine and editor of *Black Clock*, published by CalArts, where he teaches, responded to questions about his *Zeroville* via email.

KGB: First off, is this book any sort of *roman à clef*? Factual characters are fictionalized everywhere: Charles Manson, Martin Scorsese, Robert De Niro; Vikar, your film editor hero, has Montgomery Clift and Elizabeth Taylor tattooed on his skull. Your character Viking Man is, fairly obviously,

John Milius, most famous for having written the script for *Apocalypse Now*, and, also, as being lampooned by John Goodman for his character in the Coen Brothers' *Big Lebowski*. With all this background, is Vikar himself based on anyone real?

SE: No *roman à clef*, other than that the story is set in the context of those real events, as you indicated, with references to those real people. When a novelist creates a character there may be a model, but if the book comes to life at all, the character becomes his or her own person. You're right that Viking Man clearly is inspired by Milius, but I don't know Milius and have never met him—so it's more precise to say that Viking Man is my version of a Milius, trying to stay clear of the Lebowski portrait, at least in my own head, while acknowledging at the same time that I drew on select facts of Milius's life that are identifiable to anyone who knows anything about movies. Vikar is more a full creation, with a little bit from this source and a little bit from that. It was when he came together for me as a character that the book came together too.

KGB: A follow-up. Vikar is Vikar Jerome: Does his name have anything to do with St. Jerome, himself a vicar of sorts, the fifth-century translator of the Bible to Greek [*sic*]? Are you trying to say that film editing, Vikar's eventual profession, is, itself, a form of translation?

SE: Well, my calculation wasn't that erudite or smart. But I was aware that the name *Jerome* conveyed a kind of churchly quality, if you will, and I certainly did see Vikar's natural creative role as a mediator rather than as, if you will, an originator—more the prism than the light, through whom we see fifteen years of cultural upheaval in movies and music, in the LA of the seventies and early eighties. We never really understand Vikar, of course, whether he's a savant or just sort of socially retarded, but Viking Man's characterization of him as not a cineaste but "cineautistic" captures him better than anything.

KGB: Vikar begins as an excommunicated theology student and ends as a famous film editor (winning the only editing prize ever given at Cannes) who unwittingly uncovers a secret history of the world, dispersed in the frames of various films. Is film, to you, a holy medium—"holy" as in the archaic sense of "magical"? Do you think art is a replacement, or usurpation of sorts, of scripture, or of the authority of religion?

SE: I think of art and scripture as coming from the same place, which is an effort to interpret what is beyond interpretation. For true film obsessives— which is to say more obsessive than I—there almost is no higher truth than film. When Godard concluded one of his films with the words "End of cinema," by which he meant not just the end of his particular movie or his particular work but the end of an art form, it was intended to have the same impact as those who declare the "end of history" or that God is dead. I love movies and always have, but I'm not someone who's truly consumed the way that Vikar is or some of the filmmakers who came out of the seventies— Scorsese, Schrader, Spielberg, De Palma, Bogdanovich. There are too many other things I care about. There have been large periods of my life when I was just as consumed by music or fiction or politics. But all of those things aspire to the transcendent.

KGB: All of your books tend to propose stories that teeter between metaphor and realism, or, better, actuality—Vikar's discovery of this secret history is a perfect example of this technique. Do you believe in an objective reality outside of your books? Or—is "everything possible"?

SE: I don't know. This is one of those questions where even our definitions of "objective" are up for grabs—which may answer your question right there. I accept "objective reality" but I leave open the possibility that there's something bigger.

KGB: "Zeroville"—read: Hollywood—is shown here in its dissolution. The studio system is bankrupt. Angry young filmmakers appear and begin doing things their own way. Charles Manson and family kill people. Drugs are everywhere. The music changes, cranks louder. How did you yourself experience this shift in the early 1970s? And does the counterculture of those years and the years just prior have any relevance to today's mass culture?

SE: I was a teenager in the sixties and in my twenties in the seventies, so I came of age during that time and it had enormous impact on me. Even then the moment was special, crystalline—there was a sense of possibility, and I keep feeling the current era trying to find its way back to that same sense, though that might be noxious boomerism talking. At the same time there also was a way in which, living in LA, I was at odds with the more immediate culture, and while generally Vikar isn't very autobiographical, some of his experiences brush up against mine. Living in Echo Park in the early seventies, I was the only person I knew in LA who owned a Roxy Music record. I was the only person I knew who owned a Stooges record or a New York Dolls record or a Mott the Hoople record or an Eno record. I didn't listen much to the Eagles or Carole King or James Taylor. So I felt at one with the culture and at odds with it.

KGB: Film editing is the subject of remarkable little essays scattered throughout the book. Have you picked up anything from film editing applicable to your own work? The form of *Zeroville*—small chapters, arranged symmetrically, climaxing at middle only to rewind numerically back to zero—seems as if influenced by the form, or only the appearance of the form, of a screenplay. How influential have cinematic techniques been on your writing?

SE: Well, I was a film student at UCLA before resigning myself to the fact that whatever talent I had—and certainly my temperament—was better suited to writing novels. That said, the movies had an enormous impact on me and on my fiction. There was a conscious decision to tell *Zeroville*'s story according to the narrative laws of a movie, in action and dialogue and movie references, in a linear structure that didn't feel compelled to motivate everything, short scenes cutting to other scenes, and the Godardian numbers. I read a book called *The Conversations*, a series of interviews between Michael Ondaatje and film editor Walter Murch, which was a revelation—after the third reading I had to make myself stop, because I worried it would influence me too much. Murch is an amazingly smart guy, something verging on a Renaissance man—I thought I knew something about movies and editing, and reading the book, I was daunted by how much I didn't know, and still don't. But the striking thing was how often the editing decisions Murch makes resemble some of the decisions a novelist makes. Minute decisions that come down to a few frames or a few words, that no viewer or reader can possibly register except subliminally—but all those subliminal decisions have a cumulative impact.

KGB: Montgomery Clift, besides being the subject of Vikar's tattoo, makes a cameo appearance. You seem to have chosen him due to his outsider status (homosexuality, drug abuse), his brooding aspect, and his survival of that terrible auto accident. Who is the literary equivalent of Montgomery Clift?

SE: Wow, great question. You've got me. I have no idea. Somehow I don't think it's Philip Roth. I chose Clift for all the reasons you mention, and also because I really did begin with that image tattooed on Vikar's head—the close-up of Clift and Elizabeth Taylor on the terrace in *A Place in the Sun*—because it's such an emblematic image of the movies in all their dreaminess, and it's hard to think of two better looking people so perfectly matched in their beauty, two people who had more cinematic chemistry, a chemistry that clearly was bigger than sex. After that moment, I'm not sure the movies were ever again as persuasively romantic.

KGB: Hoping not to give too much away for free—but Vikar's discovery of the scattered film frames is wonderfully frightening. His discovery seems to flirt with the idea that we haven't created film, film's created us. Is film the ultimate medium? Or is it, itself, replaceable with future technologies? How do you deal with film-as-ultimate-medium, or with a technological replacement to film (the internet, the interactive), as a novelist, as a writer—as someone working in one of the oldest mediums, in the medium least conducive to such change in format or technology?

SE: I was seventeen or something when I saw a Claude Lelouch movie called *Live for Life* and had an epiphany exactly along the lines you've mentioned: "Movies are the Ultimate Art Form!" It shows how you can be influenced by something as bad or cheesy as a Claude Lelouch movie, something that, even as you're seeing it, you know isn't very good, and paradoxically the very thing about it that is cheesy or not very good is the thing that's revelatory—in this case, the overwrought use of cinematography, music, editing. This is why I don't get too hung up on "good taste"—you learn a lot from the things that constitute "bad taste," which of course raises the question of just how bad the bad is, or just how good the good is. At the time, it seemed clear that art couldn't go farther than movies, probably because we had no notion of virtual art or cyberculture—at least I didn't. That was when I became a film student, watching movies all day and supplementing it with classes in literature and political philosophy. But in the end, like most creative people I didn't choose my medium, it chose me, and I make the best of it. It doesn't matter if fiction is a dying art—and it may be—it's what I'm cut out to do, for better or worse, either well or not, which is for others to decide, obviously. Obsolescence may be my destiny. But it doesn't matter.

An Interview with Steve Erickson

Daniel Duffy / 2009

From *Word Riot*. Reprinted by permission.

Steve Erickson is the editor of *Black Clock,* one of America's leading literary journals. He has written for *Esquire, Rolling Stone, Spin, Details, Elle, San Francisco, Bookforum, Frieze, Conjunctions, Tin House, Salon,* the *LA Weekly,* the *Los Angeles Reader,* the *Los Angeles Times Magazine,* and the *New York Times Magazine,* as well as several other literary journals and magazines, and his work has been widely anthologized. He is the author of eight novels: *Days Between Stations* (1985), *Rubicon Beach* (1986), *Tours of the Black Clock* (1989), *Arc d'X* (1993), *Amnesiascope* (1996), *The Sea Came in at Midnight* (1999), *Our Ecstatic Days* (2005), and *Zeroville* (2007). He has also written two books about American politics and popular culture, *Leap Year* (1989) and *American Nomad* (1997). He's received a grant from the National Endowment for the Arts, and in 2007 was awarded a fellowship by the John Simon Guggenheim Foundation. He's a teacher at CalArts and the film critic for *Los Angeles,* and he lives with his wife, artist and director Lori Precious, and their children.

Daniel Duffy: In a great interview with Angela Stubbs of *Bookslut* back in 2007, you said, "I do believe publishing is in transition, the center is collapsing, you have a vibrant and increasingly literate cyberspace, and the inmates are taking over the ground floor of the asylum, with the asylum bosses trapped upstairs." How is life on the ground floor treating you nowadays? It's getting a little crowded, I'm sure, but everyone seems to be getting along well enough, right? Are the bosses still upstairs? Is there still running water? Has anyone been shanked?

Steve Erickson: The water seems to be rationed out, and I think the bosses are hiding—I don't hear much through the vents. It doesn't matter anyway. The trend pretty much is irrevocable—it's generational. Cyberpublishing is what the next wave of writers and editors understands, in a way I can't pretend to. The larger question is whether this is just a new delivery system for the same old literature or whether it opens up as well the creative possibilities that mainstream publishing has squelched over the last quarter century as it's become more like the movie business, with a taste (if that's the word) for blockbusters and an incomprehension of anything else.

DD: Your editorial statement says that *Black Clock* "revels in the kind of constructive anarchy that follows from allowing writers the chance to publish free of editorial impositions." What does that mean, exactly? What is the editorial process at *Black Clock*, and what impositions do you, as the editor of the magazine, strive to avoid?

SE: I realize my "statement" runs the risk of sounding grandiose. Actually, for six years I've tried to avoid "mission [or] editorial statements," to the despair of both my staff and those who put up the money for the magazine and place stock in such things. *Black Clock*'s editorial process is either serendipitous or ad hoc, depending on what pejorative you want to use, except for the fact that from the beginning the plan has been to build the magazine around writers.

DD: You consistently publish work from some really heavy hitters—in the past you've featured work from Don DeLillo, David Foster Wallace, Richard Powers, Jonathan Lethem, Rick Moody, Samuel Delany, Joanna Scott, Miranda July, Aimee Bender, Brian Evenson, Michael Ventura . . . The list goes on and on. How many authors do you solicit per issue? Is there a certain criteria involved with you soliciting an author, or is it just a matter of personal taste?

SE: I approach about fifteen writers per issue, maybe more, allowing for a few who will decline for one reason or another. It kind of astonishes me how many say yes, given that we pay virtually nothing and the circulation isn't huge—that speaks to some regard for the magazine, I think, as well as just the natural generosity of so many of these people. In issue 11, for instance, there's Richard Powers, who I assume has opportunities to publish elsewhere. I operate on the assumption that I don't know everything and that I don't even necessarily have to love everything the magazine publishes (we might not publish much if I did), and that sometimes it's enough if I'm convinced there are smart readers with interesting taste who will love it. If there's a piece that the rest of the staff loves that I don't, I'm open to the possibility I might just not be getting it and should publish it anyway. On the other hand, if there's something I love that the rest of the staff doesn't, I'm still going to publish it.

DD: *Black Clock* publishes a lot of experimental fiction—your editorial statement describes the work featured as "audacious rather than safe, visceral rather than academic, intellectually engaging rather than antiseptically cerebral, and not above fun." A lot of editors say that they can tell they are going to publish a story from simply reading the first line, but that's got to be a lot harder with more experimental work. Still, I just flipped through several issues of *Black Clock*, reading only first lines, and they were all pretty solid. Are you a first-line guy? Have you ever had any specific instances where you've accepted or rejected a story after reading the first line?

SE: You know, I hear the word *experimental*—which has been used about my own work now and then—and I reach for my revolver. To me, experimental work is about the experiment—it's by definition about the form—and that's not interesting to me. I'm enough of a traditionalist to believe that the form, however radical it may be, still must serve the old verities (as that old experimentalist, Faulkner, called them) of character and story. So I hope that's what I was saying, or trying to, in my dreaded editorial statement. I don't know that I've ever known a story was going to work from the first sentence, but if I'm reading a new writer, it's usually true that from, say, the first paragraph, I can tell whether someone has a voice or a vision.

DD: I imagine that emerging writers submitting to *Black Clock* have usually done their research, and that you don't get many lackluster, first-person narratives about "my stupid ex-boyfriend" or "my parents' divorce" or "my life is so horrible because I'm eighteen and I'm living in a dorm room." Still, as an editor of a literary magazine, I'm sure you have some story themes that instantly turn you off. What are some examples of stories that you never want to see again?

SE: Well, the plight of living in a dorm room does sound like a nonstarter. But I would like to think I'm still open to a really brilliant stupid-ex-boyfriend story. I mean, *Wuthering Heights* and *The Great Gatsby* are basically stupid-ex-girlfriend stories, right?

DD: You are a prolific novelist, essayist, and critic, as well as a columnist and a teacher at CalArts. *Black Clock* is obviously very important to you, as you have so much more going on, and yet you still find the time for it. How do you balance the workload of the magazine, a project that doesn't draw income, with the rest of your life? What is an average day in the life of Steve Erickson like? Do you still find time to write a little every day, even when school is in session?

SE: It's hard and not getting easier, and you haven't even mentioned parenthood, which sucks the oxygen out of the schedule like nothing else. Thirty minutes out of bed, I'm literally behind in my day, and the disheartening thing is that it's the writing—or the writing I care most about, anyway—that gets pushed aside, because it isn't something I can just squeeze in a half hour here and a half hour there.

DD: A recurring theme in several of your books is the underestimated artist striving for recognition. Was this a prime motivation in your getting involved with *Black Clock*? Do you revel in the opportunity that you have as an editor to find some underestimated emerging writer and give him his first chance to see his work printed in a national publication?

SE: Oh sure. If we're not discovering new writers, then the magazine is a failure as far as I'm concerned. Purely tactically, we started with lots of famous "star" writers and are generally evolving to more and more newly discovered voices. Now we seem to publish every issue at least one or two things that come to us unsolicited—I think about a third of the writers in the new issue haven't published anywhere else to speak of. I suppose I've become sensitive to charges that we're some sort of elitist cabal dismissive of outsiders. In the beginning, when there literally were four of us putting out the magazine, it was strictly a manpower/workload issue.

DD: In an interview with the *Los Angeles Times* regarding *Black Clock* back in 2004, you said: "As the publishing business gets more like Hollywood, I want more good writers to have a place to go." In today's recessionary Hollywood, studio executives are becoming increasingly hesitant to cast actors who will demand upward of $15 million and a hefty portion of the film's revenue to appear in a movie. Instead, they're favoring big concepts with low-paid actors. Does that translate in some way to the publishing business? In other words, do you foresee a time in the future when some of the emerging writers whose work you've featured in *Black Clock* will be offered deals from the big publishing houses who simply can't afford the J. K. Rowlings and the Dan Browns of the world anymore? Is the recession going to make publishing houses take more chances on emerging writers?

SE: Well, the interesting thing about Hollywood is that at some point it began to view a $25 million movie as more of a risk than an $250 million movie, and that's what's happened with publishing. A $25,000 advance is considered riskier than a book getting a $250,000 advance, because publishers feel they know how to market the second and have no idea how to market the first. The result is that, unlike a couple of decades ago when my first novels were being published, not even the best and savviest and most powerful editors have the autonomy to buy a book. The paperback department has to sign off on it, the marketing department has to sign off on it, the publicity department. The system now is constructed to give itself as many chances as possible to say no, because no is always safer than yes. I don't know whether any of the new writers we've published will command such advances or not. I should add that, while I'm not a big fan of the *Harry Potter* books—my kid wound up a bit bored by them—I don't begrudge Rowling her advances. Her books earn them in sales, and she got a whole new generation to read, so more power to her.

DD: You studied film at UCLA and have written about film for *Los Angeles* magazine since 2001. How fun was it for you to devote issue 10 of *Black Clock* to the topic of noir? Was that your idea? And do you get to pick the topic of each issue of the magazine, or is it a more democratic process, shared among the editorial staff?

SE: When *Black Clock* started, I vowed to avoid themes, as such, and you still never see one announced on the cover of the magazine, unless the illustration—such as in the case of the issue you're talking about—somehow conveys it. The new issue barely has a theme at all, and when we do have one, as much as anything it's just because it provides an organizing principle editorially. The noir issue is a good example of how things sometimes happen with this magazine. Robert Polito had submitted a piece for the previous issue (9) about politics and the election, and it didn't seem to me to have as much to do with politics as Robert thought it did. And I might well have published it anyway, because it might have been one of those examples of publishing something that was only very tangentially connected to whatever our unstated theme was, except that in his story there was a line about "the birth of noir," or something like that, and there and then in my head the noir issue was born. Like I said before: serendipitous or ad hoc. Usually the ideas are mine but not always. The underlying theme of issue 8, travel, was editor-at-large Anthony Miller's idea. The twelfth issue, sports, is the brainstorm of our senior editor, Bruce Bauman, with a lot of help from our other editor-at-large, David Ulin. Sometimes I have to be mindful of how things might look. A couple years ago I wanted to do an issue about movies but I had a novel about the movies coming out around that time and I didn't want my decisions about the magazine to look self-promotional. So I put off a movie issue. Maybe in another year.

DD: Fifteen works that were first published in *Black Clock* have gone on to win awards. Probably more by now. Additionally, you yourself have won fifteen awards or so for your own writing, as well as a Guggenheim fellowship. I don't really have a question here—I guess I'm just saying congratulations. It's really refreshing and encouraging to see someone who has always been devoted to a sort of cutting edge experimental freedom in writing getting so much recognition.

SE: You know, here's the thing about awards: It's nice to get them and you accept them graciously when you do and make the most of them—but you don't get too hung up on the "validation" that they offer or don't. Most of the time, awards go to everyone's second choice, because the first choices cancel each other out. Except on the rare occasion that someone gives me one, of course. Then it's a bold gesture of uncommon perception.

DD: The tenth issue of *Black Clock* was the first one I laid my hands on, and I instantly felt like I was showing up late to a really great party. Did I show up at ten o'clock to a party that's only going until midnight, or is this thing going to be raging until dawn, and maybe even into the following day? As we approach 2010, what do you foresee in the future for your magazine?

SE: Well, I hope the party goes on all weekend, of course, not just into tomorrow. But I accept, maybe more than anyone else working for the magazine, that this thing is existential and probably will end sometime. For the California Institute of the Arts that publishes *Black Clock* and, more to the point, invests in it, the payoff is unquantifiable—the magazine certainly isn't earning its way in terms of hard dollars and cents. But I don't think there's too much question that *Black Clock* has raised the profile of the institute and its writing program, and the publishers must see it that way too, at least so far. I think I've been clear from the beginning that at the point they believe the magazine is no longer worth it, that's their call and I'll understand and accept it whether I agree with it or not.

DD: Any final thoughts or advice for emerging writers looking to submit not only to *Black Clock*, but to any other literary journal, magazine, or press out there right now?

SE: I don't think my advice to any writer interested in *Black Clock* is different from that to any other aspiring writer, which is that you've got to be in it for the long haul. It took me years to get published, and since then it's taken me years to get to this point—whatever or wherever this point is. Write write write, submit submit submit, get-rejected get-rejected get-rejected. Tenacity will make its own luck. Plan on conquering the world one reader at a time.

Every Moment I'm Awake the Further I'm Away: Dream Analysis with Steve Erickson

Joshua Chaplinsky / 2012

From *LitReactor*, at www.litreactor.com (January 31, 2012). Reprinted by permission.

This marks an anniversary of sorts for me. It was a little over four years ago that I hatched a scheme to score myself an ARC of the latest novel from one of my favorite authors. Said scheme involved pretensions to journalism and pretty much launched my dubious career as an internet writer. The author was American surrealist Steve Erickson, and the book was a love letter to cinema entitled *Zeroville*. Erickson was my first ever interview, and the experience was everything a first time should be—exciting, memorable, and with someone (whose work) you love.

So naturally a new novel demanded a new interview. Erickson's latest, *These Dreams of You*, continues in the vein of *Zeroville*, presenting a more accessible story without dulling the author's "postmodern" edge. It takes place at the crossroads of race and politics and revolves around a family in crisis as they search for the birth mother of their adopted daughter, a four-year-old African girl whose body is a radio. The book is as funny, inventive, and emotionally complex as Erickson fans have come to expect.

I'm not sure how well he remembered the first, but Erickson was kind enough to submit to a second round of my probing. It's a good thing this interview wasn't conducted over a meal, because as relevant as they are, the subjects of race, religion, and politics are not considered polite dinner conversation.

Joshua Chaplinsky: *These Dreams of You* takes place against the backdrop of President Obama's election. You've written about politics before (*Leap*

Year, American Nomad), but to my knowledge you've never been this candid or topical about it in your fiction. What was it about that political time period that inspired you?

Steve Erickson: I realize this may seem like a distinction without a difference, but I don't think of this as a political novel. If anything it's a historical novel, where our present-day history—that we already know to be history—unfolds as a backdrop to a family's struggle to survive. It's history that's personal and outpaces our imaginations. The story opens on the election of a Black president in what is for the family as well as the country a moment of crisis. These people don't think of themselves as living political or historical lives: they're just trying to get by and figure out who their adopted Ethiopian daughter is, and not lose faith in the country or each other even when they find themselves in exile, scattered across Europe and lost in the place where time began. You know, Ethiopia used to be called Abyssinia. As in, the abyss.

JC: How closely do the character Zan's political views mirror your own?

SE: I guess they mirror mine in the sense that Zan was raised a conservative and became disillusioned early on in no small part because his ideology failed the great moral question of the time, which was racial justice. He remains skeptical of ideology and dogma in general.

JC: Does that mean you are a free agent, politically? Or do you toe any particular line?

SE: It means that I'm not registered with any party and am not comfortable associating myself with any party, even as I usually vote with one but have occasionally voted for the other.

JC: On his radio broadcast the day after the election, Zan dedicates Sam Cooke's "A Change Is Gonna Come" to Obama's victory. Toward the end of the novel Zan says of the president, "His music that once so mesmerized . . . seems to have gone silent." How do you feel now about the amount of change promised versus the amount we have seen?

SE: Well, as that particular passage in the novel suggests, the silence is as much about our failure to hear the music anymore—and how the moment no longer seems to allow for it—as it is about anyone's failure to make it. The music exists not just by virtue of the singing but also the listening. One guy isn't going to transform what won't be transformed. One guy isn't going to unify or reconcile what isn't willing to be unified or reconciled, especially when people are openly rooting for his failure before he's walked in the front door. If my friends to the left of me think Obama is a corporate sellout, while the same corporations despise him and my relatives to the right of me thinks he's Leon Trotsky, is he completely responsible for that disconnect? At what point are the rest of us complicit?

JC: Has Obama been a disappointment?

SE: Oh, probably, but then he was bound to be. We set him up for that. Before he ever got into office, his presidency had a mythic dimension that no one was going to live up to—150 years ago this guy would have been on an auction block in chains somewhere along the Mississippi. The real question is, Has Obama disappointed us or have we disappointed ourselves? If a gap remains between the promise and its fulfillment, that's the story of the country and always has been. On the other hand, the very event of Obama's election was unfathomable five years before it came to pass, or maybe I mean five minutes, and there's just too much on the slate for that election to wipe clean all by itself. Along with what happened to the Indians, slavery remains the country's irredeemable transgression, and though we may be doomed in any effort to make it right, we're obligated to try anyway. The futility doesn't mitigate the obligation. The obligation doesn't alter the fact that no white person like myself is in any position to assess just how fulfilled the promise is.

JC: *These Dreams of You* feels very personal to me, and has a lot of auto-biographical touches. From living in the canyon to Viv being an artist to the adoption of an African child, how much of what wound up in the novel was actually taken from real life?

SE: Well, I suspect you're smart enough to know I'm not going to answer that. It's not a matter of privacy, which I give up to some extent by writing such a novel, but because any answer would be misleading. Beside the fact that this novel involves integrating and orchestrating and structuring a lot of moving parts, fiction in general aspires to a conspiracy, not a collision, between experience and imagination—which means the experienced stuff always is more transformed by imagination than the reader or even the writer knows, and the imagined stuff always is more informed by experience. The details of Zan's biography certainly don't entirely conform to mine. The choices of what information to include or exclude inevitably push characters away from their models, and at some point in the writing, very literally the characters start looking different in my head. They don't completely resemble their real-life counterparts anymore—they're not quite the same height, or quite the same age, or quite the same temperament. They're more like the real-life models' distant cousins.

JC: Please tell me your adopted child is as precocious and single-minded as Sheba.

SE: My editor's only criticism of the novel when he first read it was that there were things in it that he didn't believe a four-year-old could say or do. Because the only thing that matters is what works on the page, and it's the last refuge of a bad writer to insist that he knows for a fact a four-year-old not only could say such things but did, ultimately I decided I had to delete some of Sheba's most precocious statements. My daughter can be unbelievable, but my character can't.

I'M HUNGRY YOUNG MAN! [Sheba] bellows at her father when she wants something to eat. She calls Viv "young lady" and Parker "baby," which incites the boy into answering, "You're the baby, you're the baby!" Eventually Sheba expands defiance's repertoire, the tenor of insult becoming more nuanced until finally, some months later in London when she, Parker and Zan wait to board a double-decker bus, she snarls to the father, "Out of my way, *old* man." Drawing her finger across her throat at him, she stuffs her thumb back in her mouth like Churchill corking his face with a cigar. "I'm a professional!" is her latest rallying cry and coup de grâce, learned from her brother or television and employed to end any contentious conversation. "Eat your carrots, Sheba," says Viv.

"Leave me alone!" says Sheba. "I'm a professional!"

"Clean up your room."

"I don't need you telling me, I'm a professional!"

JC: Was your wife's stained glass butterfly artwork ripped off in real life like Viv's was?

SE: Yes.

JC: Is that the end of that situation? Do you ever regret not going after him [Hirst]?

SE: Sure. But it's never been a realistic prospect financially, and the theft of intellectual property—or plagiarism, to put it more directly—is difficult to prove legally, even when the evidence is manifest to common sense. As I think you know, in my wife's case the matter has been written up a lot. There have been full-page articles in British newspapers like *The Guardian* with side-by-side pictures of her work and the other artist's so that anyone looking at it can judge for himself. A couple of years ago there was a chapter about the controversy in a book called *The Dangerous World of Butterflies*, by Peter Laufer, and at the other artist's exhibits, protesters outside the galleries have carried signs reading LORI PRECIOUS DID IT FIRST. It's been on YouTube. In other words, it's well documented and everyone knows it happened, and you would think translating it into legal action would be easy, especially since this is an artist who's notorious for not only stealing people's work but brazenly making a modus operandi of it.

JC: *Dreams* also deals with the recession and the mortgage crisis. Flash forward to 2011: What are your feelings on the Occupy movement?

SE: Well, again, this novel isn't about economics any more than it's about politics, because I don't understand much more about economics than most people and neither do my characters. The family in *Dreams* is just out-flanked by one bad turn after another, like a lot of people in the country right now. There was a major national poll a couple of months ago which reported a statistic I've never seen. Three out of four people in the country now believe the vaunted capitalist system is rigged against them in favor of the wealthy. In the past, even in troubled times there was a bedrock faith in not just the effectiveness but the ethos of capitalism, but now there's the sense of a stacked deck, and if this is true then it's potentially revolutionary and explains why the Occupy movement struck a chord not just with the chronically pissed-off but the broad middle class. The challenge for the movement now is not to become Woodstock. About a month and a half ago I was discussing it with Jonathan Lethem, who's been fairly involved in Occupy, and we were noting how the dispersion of the crowds in the streets this past fall was a gift, that it came just when the demonstrations threatened to get goofy and turn into sex, drugs, and rock 'n' roll. Now the movement is compelled to be less theatrical, find leaders, consider concrete strategies.

JC: To me, *Dreams* feels like a stylistic continuation of your last novel, *Zeroville*. But whereas that novel was an ode to film, *Dreams* is an ode to music (at least in part). What is it about these other mediums that informs your writing?

SE: I came of age when not only Kubrick and Arthur Penn meant more to me than Bellow and Updike (though not necessarily Pynchon and Dick), but Dylan and Ray Charles and the Doors and the Beatles meant more than any of them. The zeitgeist was defined by music in a way I'm not sure it has been by any art form before or since. Music didn't just reflect the zeitgeist but was the zeitgeist in ways that, for better and worse, were social and cultural and philosophical and political in the broadest sense. There's a key moment in *These Dreams* when Zan as an eighteen-year-old is pulled by a young Black woman from a crowd that's about to trample him. Though Zan and the woman will never see each other again, their lives will go on to intersect in a profound way that neither knows. The scene takes place at a campaign rally, but the crowd from which Zan has been rescued is gripped by the same kind of hysteria that we associate with a concert, and even at the time there was something very rock 'n' roll about Robert Kennedy's campaign that never was duplicated until the Obama campaign. There's always music in the background. Zan plays records on a pirate radio station in the canyon where he lives, and when Sheba comes to live with them, the family realizes her body is a transmitter, broadcasting from unknown places the music of the future. Zan calls her Radio Ethiopia.

JC: You deal a lot with race in *Dreams*. At one point Zan says, "There are things about race that no white person can understand." Regarding the new novel he is working on, he says, "Isn't any white person who writes about race asking for trouble?" Is this something you are asking yourself?

SE: Oh, sure. This was something I was aware of from the beginning, and this will sound strange but the only answer, assuming it is an answer, was to never forget—and for the reader to never forget—that a white person is telling this story, that even when part of the story is told from the perspective of the young English Black woman Jasmine, there's never a presumption on my part of having an insight or wisdom that's beyond a white person. The African experience in this country is singular. No other instance of bigotry or repression is comparable because Africans remain the only people who didn't choose to come here, who chose to be part of the country in spite of having been brought against their will and institutionally enslaved in a way no one else has been. So I always had to remember that there are things about this story that are and remain beyond me. I've always believed a novel has secrets from its author, but this was a case where I knew the secrets were there—I knew they existed and what they were secrets about even as I never knew what the secrets are.

JC: Are you breaking down the fourth wall on race in the novel and working out your own issues?

SE: That's a good way to put it. How successfully the novel accomplishes this, or how many times I blow myself up trying to tiptoe across its minefield, is for other people to say.

JC: In a conversation with J. Willkie Brown, Zan says he believes in God fifty-one days out of one hundred. How many days out of one hundred do you believe in God?

SE: Fifty.

JC: Is that just sort of a noncommittal answer, or do you battle back and forth?

SE: I mean that belief battles doubt and comes out just enough ahead, then I can't quite call myself an agnostic, even though it's the only rational response to the question of God. As I think may be clear from Zan's riff on the Gospels as experimental fiction, my skepticism of religion is pretty deep. Religion is just spiritual rather than secular ideology. But I also believe that the atheist is as blindly committed to his nonbelief as the faithful is to belief, and in the novel Zan points out to J. Willkie Brown that the other man needs his atheism no less than the devout needs his faith, and for reasons that are just as emotional and psychological and no more based on "reason." Smugness is the atheist's sanctimony.

JC: In the novel Zan is invited to give a lecture on "The Novel as Literary Form Facing Obsolescence in the Twenty-First Century." What with the current state of the publishing industry, do you actually feel that the novel is in danger?

SE: I'm not sure it's as much about the current state of the publishing industry as it is the current state of the imagination. As long as there are writers they'll find a way to be published, assuming they can be disabused of their romanticism about New York publishers. Everyone knows the major New York publishers are extinct as a delivery system for interesting fiction. About a year ago a well-known novelist, one of his generation's best and universally considered successful, openly confided to me that he's been losing his publisher money for years and is well aware it can't go on. As in the film business, the indie publishers increasingly are taking creative control, and on top of that, the digital age has opened all the asylum doors and out have streamed the lunatics. So if you're willing to accept that you're unlikely to ever make any money, the odds of finding someone to publish you may be a little better than they've been—which isn't to suggest for a moment it's easy. The question of the novel's obsolescence has more to do with how much the form has to say to the twenty-first-century imagination, when more and more kids, including my own, no longer imagine verbally. It's a generation of congenital imagists, and we can decry video games all we want, but this is the evolution at hand. As it always was bound to be, the imagination is just different from what it was before World War II, when the novel was the preeminent art form, before it gave way to a mass media age and mass media forms like music and cinema. So the novel has to go where none of those other things can, which often is toward a breakdown of linearity and the literally visualized.

JC: In 2010 you wrote the introduction to Grace Krilanovich's debut novel, *The Orange Eats Creeps*, excerpts of which had previously been published in the literary journal you edit, *Black Clock*. What was it about Grace and her writing that led you to become such an advocate?

SE: Well, I had read bits and pieces of Grace's novel as she wrote it, and it reminded me of earlier sensibilities that had been passé for so long they're new again—Céline, Huysmans, Miller, Burroughs. Her novel was an onslaught of sense and language without a restrained or ironic syllable in it. I don't know Grace that well—I couldn't tell you a thing about her family or past—so it's hard to say how much this was calculated and self-knowing and how much was instinctual.

JC: Does an author like Grace give you hope for the future of the novel?

SE: Sure. When I said in the introduction that *The Orange Eats Creeps* was a response to what seems to have become literary inertia, it was the passion that drives the work I was talking about. The same with those *Velvet* guys—for good or ill or sometimes both, these are all writers hellbent on sticking their heads into the void and trying to make out whatever's moving in the dark.

JC: I'm assuming by the *Velvet* you're talking about Chris Baer, Craig Clevenger and Stephen Graham Jones? Are you familiar with their work at all? I know for a fact Craig is a huge fan of yours.

SE: I wrote an introduction to their *Warmed and Bound* anthology. Clevenger always has been very generous in his advocacy on my behalf. I'd like to get him and some of the others into *Black Clock*.

JC: Ah, I should have known that. Clevenger is the reason I started reading your stuff. It'd be great to get those guys into *Black Clock*.

A while back it was announced that James Franco had secured the option to *Zeroville* with an eye to direct. Has there been any movement on that?

SE: I know for a fact that a script has been written. I also can say pretty certainly that the movie is not going to shoot in early 2012, as was planned at one point. Hearsay has it that Franco has pushed it off to next year. On the other hand, next year the option will have run out—so unless he decides to exercise it before then and buy the book outright, any film remains to be seen, both literally and figuratively. There have been a couple other indications of interest since.

JC: Have you read the script? Will you have any involvement with the production?

SE: I haven't read the script. The writer is Matthew Specktor. I know some of his work and he's very good. He has a very good novel coming out in the next year called *American Dream Machine*. I made it clear to him and to Franco that I understand this is their movie, not my novel, and that I think I know enough about novels and movies to grasp the difference. If at any point they want to know what I think, I'd be happy to tell them.

JC: In our previous interview, you said that someone like Scorsese or Tarantino or Soderbergh or P. T. Anderson would be ideal to direct *Zeroville*. How do you feel about someone as inexperienced as Franco taking a shot? I personally think he is the wrong man for the job.

SE: Well, he's the right man for the job in the sense that he likes the book a lot and wants to do it and has an enthusiasm for it that I haven't heard from any of those other people, though a reliable source has it that Anderson is at the least aware of the novel and perhaps has read it. I'm not always convinced experience is more important than going where the passion is, whether it has to do with choosing a publisher or agent or the guy who wants to make a movie of your book. If Franco never makes the movie, then he wasn't the right man for it—which is to say that sometimes these things have a way of answering themselves. I admit that for a long time my assumption was he was going to play the novel's main character.

JC: Continuing with film, you said issue 15 of *Black Clock* is going to be about movies that never happened. Can you tell us any more about that?

SE: Seven years ago we did an issue we informally called "the lost music of the imagination," about music that never happened—the album Hendrix recorded with Miles, the record Zappa produced for Dylan, the release by the Beatles in the summer of '68 of the twelve-minute "Revolution" instead of "Hey Jude." We first considered a movie issue back around the time *Zeroville* was published and held off because I worried that, given the novel, it might look too self-promotional. Maybe I overthought it, but after some time went by and we came back to the idea, one of our editors-at-large, Anthony Miller, suggested the angle of movies that never happened. Anthony has written a brilliant time line of alternate cinema history that opens the issue, and we have work by Lethem, David Thomson, Lynne Tillman, Rick Moody, Michael Ventura, Claire Phillips, Mark Z. Danielewski . . . Well, if I start naming people, I'm going to get in trouble. A lot of very good writers. When Geoff Nicholson proposed a story called "Buster Keaton: The Warhol Years," I would have published the title alone. I didn't tell Geoff that.

JC: Sounds great. Since you are also a film critic at *LA* magazine, I'd like to ask: What were some of your favorite films of 2011?

SE: There are films by Lars von Trier I find unwatchable, but *Melancholia* is his masterpiece by a long shot and the best movie of the year. Together *The Tree of Life*, *Take Shelter*, and *Melancholia* are a three-part biopic of existence. Before the backlash completely sets in on *The Artist*, I hope people remember that a year ago anyone making a black-and-white silent movie would have been considered out of his mind. I also like *Tinker Tailor*

Soldier Spy, Margin Call, and Michelle Williams in *My Week with Marilyn.* The James Bond producers would kill for a movie as good as the new *Mission: Impossible.*

JC: Anything else on the horizon? What do you have planned for 2012?

SE: I plan to make a million dollars and pay off the fucking house. I plan to never fly coach again. I plan to see if I can find that one extra day of God. I plan to not write a word. That last one already has gone awry.

JC: That's good to hear.

Swinging Modern Sounds #78: Conceived as a Playlist

Rick Moody / 2017

From *The Rumpus*, at www.therumpus.net (March 7, 2017). Reprinted by permission.

Steve Erickson is one of the most imaginative, most original, most surprising, and most enduring writers working in fiction today. He is in the league of Pynchon, DeLillo, Atwood, Rushdie, Okri, Pamuk, Ondaatje, Lethem—a maximal visionary, with a restless historical consciousness that devours epochs and artistic phenomena the way a shredder lattices up your secret documents into recyclable collages. Erickson has never repeated himself, not even once, in a literary career that now spans several decades. He fits as easily in speculative fiction as he does in literary writing, and he could just as happily burst the confines of either. His subjects are the West, America, film, music, history, desire—excepting that he exceeds all of these. He is never less than innovative, but never less than heartfelt either. Political rage and human longing are just as liable to be motivating forces in the work. And the writing, in every single novel (there are now ten of them, including the just-published *Shadowbahn*), is inspiring and singular, with lancing moments of intensity. I can think of few novelists writing today whose vision I admire more, whose new work I look forward to with more enthusiasm.

Shadowbahn, released on February 14 from Blue Rider Press, is among the most unusual, and most extreme, in a literary career that has often been marked by its unpredictability. As Erickson notes below, *Shadowbahn* begins with the sudden appearance in the Badlands of the Great Plains of a replica of the Twin Towers of the World Trade Center, and it goes on from there, tying up loose threads of popular culture and calibrating them against eruptions of national insecurity. Somehow, moreover, the playlist of the twenty-first century, that mock turtle soup of curatorial routine, becomes the de facto way that *Shadowbahn* gets told, in little bursts of curated recorded music, and I will leave it to you to see how this is the case. The counternarrative of *Shadowbahn* is, in this journalistic context below, the occasion for me to ask Steve Erickson a few questions, as I have often done in person (he frequently edited my work when he was editor in chief of the late, lamented CalArts literary magazine *Black Clock*, and we have therefore been friendly for some ten years), further to the project of bringing your attention again to this incredibly important American writer. We talked primarily by email (but with the intention to render email functionally indistinct from a human face-to-face conversation), over the end of January and beginning of February.

The Rumpus: How long after *These Dreams of You* did you conceive of *Shadowbahn*, and what was its point of origin?

Steve Erickson: It was one night in March 2013, about a year after the publication of *These Dreams of You*. My head had been completely blank since finishing *Dreams* at the end of 2010—I felt completely tapped out. Often in the past, a new novel has picked up on something that, I would realize in retrospect, didn't get fully resolved in the previous book—but while there *was* a connection between *Dreams* and *Shadowbahn*, it wasn't in that way.

I was home by myself, my wife and kids were elsewhere, and I was thinking about a workshop I had taught that day, where I had been trying to make a point about the role that research plays or doesn't play in writing fiction, and how one may research for the sake of verisimilitude without necessarily becoming a prisoner of that research. In the workshop I had done something I don't usually do, which was give an example from my own work, a scene in *Dreams* where a father and son take a train from Paris to Berlin, and the train pulls into Berlin at night and the son is wonderstruck by the flashing neon futurism of the Berlin Hauptbahnhof. There's only one problem, and that is the train from Paris doesn't arrive in Berlin at night. It arrives in the early morning. I know because I've taken that train. I researched train schedules to find out if the schedule for the Paris train had changed in the years since, but it hadn't. And then I decided I didn't care. I told my students, "It's my novel, and my story, and my train, and if, for the sake of advancing my story, and maybe revealing something about my characters, I want my train to arrive at night, it will arrive at night. For that matter, it's my Berlin, and if I want to put it in the middle of Iowa, I will."

Exactly what synapse morphed Berlin in the middle of Iowa into the Twin Towers in the middle of the Badlands, I'm not sure, and I'm not sure how I thought to put Elvis Presley's stillborn twin Jesse in one of the Towers. Both ideas pretty much came at the same time, though, and suddenly that image of the Towers also became informed by everything I had been thinking about the country over the previous twenty years. It became informed by this idea of where the country was heading, and even then, I wasn't feeling very optimistic. I do remember mulling for an hour or so whether someone should be in the second tower before realizing that, as I wound up writing, "the whole point of the other Tower [was] its emptiness"—that the other Tower was, in a sense, the twin who was missing. So I carried that around in my head for the rest of the year before I began writing the first week of 2014.

Rumpus: I admire the point about research, and also the idea that the world can be altered imaginatively. I often think about the impossible Malta of *Catch-22*, and the way it becomes a character in that book. That particular perturbation of reality has empowered me many times of the years, along with, of course, models like Philip K. Dick and the London of *Gravity's Rainbow*. When you conceived of the Twin Towers image, were you already thinking about the political ramifications of it? Or was it more intuitive and emotionally conceived? How important is the political substratum to you generally?

Erickson: Oh, it was as close to a completely out-of-the-blue idea as I've had. Entirely intuitive. But that's typical. Ideas are mysteries to me—I get them and have no idea where they came from, which I assume is true for a lot of novelists, and have no idea what they mean. When I start writing the story, I don't necessarily even want to know what they mean. Having said that, the metaphorical implications of the Twin Towers in the Badlands weren't exactly coy. I wasn't looking for a metaphor—as a novelist yourself, you know the metaphors you go looking for usually aren't any good. But it didn't take long to figure out that one had been presented to me. Politics seem to naturally find their way into my fiction anyhow. I never envisioned myself a political novelist and still don't—was it Stendhal who said politics in art is like a gunshot in church, unseemly but impossible to ignore?—but there's usually been a subtext if not something more overt, and these days in particular it seems not only unavoidable but even irresponsible to not acknowledge politics in some way.

That's a great point, by the way, about Pynchon's London. The audacity was that it wasn't a future London or even an alternative London but a historical London, a London very fixed in the historical memory and historical imagination, and he still made it his own, and did so even as that particular London in that particular recent history was no farther from him at the time than Berlin right before the fall of the Wall is now to us. If not so flamboyantly, I always felt Durrell's Alexandria seemed reimagined, but not having been to Alexandria, I'll never know.

Rumpus: How does the image feel to you now? Presumably entirely unimaginable to the Steve Erickson who came up with this idea in 2013 was the political drama of the present moment. It would have been unimaginable to me, too. (As you know, when I started my diary of presidential politics in 2015, and covered Donald J. Trump's announcement of his candidacy, I said: "This clown will never be elected.") Does the image seem to have more imaginative and emblematic contour in this present instance?

Erickson: Well, the Erickson who had the vision of the Towers may be the only Erickson among however many of us there are who could have imagined the present moment, which isn't to say I would have imagined a Trump presidency in 2013, or 2014, or 2015, though by the spring of last year I was getting an uneasy feeling about all of it. I never *really* thought he would get elected, but by last April I wasn't entirely discounting it either. Had you told me he would carry white women—that I wouldn't have believed. I thought that was the firewall, that there just weren't enough old white men to put him in office. It wouldn't have occurred to me that while this old white man, which is to say me, was voting for Clinton, white women were choosing an overt misogynist over the first woman president. Someone will have to explain that one to me someday.

What I did foresee those four years ago was the country slipping past any prospect of unifying over what the country means, and that this last election, whoever won it, wasn't going to be the end of it. That scene on the new novel's second page with the truck driver who has the bumper sticker that reads SAVE AMERICA FROM ITSELF—I wrote that at the beginning of 2014, and if not as a novelist then at least as a human being and an American and a father, I would have hoped that scene would be less relevant now rather than more. In retrospect any resurrection of the Towers in the Badlands almost feels . . . optimistic. In all the ways it's ominous, it offers some redemptive possibility in my own mind that now I worry is behind or beyond us. Now I think the only way of saving the country is for one side to win and one side to lose. I think for the foreseeable future we have to disabuse ourselves of any ideas of unifying, or coming together, or all getting along. I don't think we're going to reconcile the America that elected the first African American president with the America that just elected a president avidly endorsed by the Ku Klux Klan—I'm not sure I even want to reconcile the two. I have members of my immediate family, and my wife's immediate family, who voted for the guy, and now there's this gulf that I have no interest in bridging however much I love those people. It's almost like the Civil War.

Rumpus: I know this is a personal question, but part of why I have always felt you had a uniquely pertinent and important sense of how politics play out, and how they are liminal in literature and in culture, is because of your own political journey from your youth to your adulthood. Would you mind sketching out that journey here?

Erickson: I was raised a right-wing Republican and was about eighteen when I had to admit to myself that in regard to the great domestic crucible of the day, civil rights and racial justice, conservatives were on the wrong side historically and morally, and that it took too much intellectual and psychological jujitsu to pretend otherwise. I didn't want to pretend anymore; I wanted to be on the right side. This led to the realization that one of the basic philosophical tenets of conservatism—which says that the more power devolves from the federal government to the states, the greater individual freedom grows—is just flatly contradicted by crucial junctures in the country's life, most conspicuously in the 1860s and 1960s, when it's been the federal government that's interceded against the states to secure individual freedom.

Then in my early twenties the nature of conservatism itself changed. When I identified as a fourteen-year-old conservative, it was closer to what we today think of as libertarianism—conservatism, at least for me, had been defined by Jeffersonian credos like "the best governed are the least governed" and "I have sworn eternal hostility against every form of tyranny over the mind of man" that were very idealistic and romantic to a kid. By the late seventies, however, conservatism was becoming more corporate on the one hand, more theocratic on the other. In reaction to the sixties, conservatism was more about order than freedom, more about conformity than singularity. It became inescapable that as conservatives were wrong about people of color, they were also wrong about women. They were wrong about gay people. The only individual freedoms they seemed to get exercised about were the freedom to make a profit and the freedom to own a gun.

And then just as important, maybe more important, is that I didn't just change the way I thought, I changed the way I was. Out of the house and on my own, I faced the fact I didn't much like who I was. I didn't like my judgmentalism; I didn't like my absolutism. I didn't like my repression of natural empathy, my pinched lack of emotional generosity. How I had been thinking politically had less to do with what was wrong with the world and more to do with what was wrong with me, with my fears and insecurities, failings, weaknesses. Moreover, all those things were at odds with the things about myself that made me want to be a writer. So I decided I would change myself, be the person I wanted to be, be the person that I hoped I really had been all along. I would rip out my wiring and rewire myself. Plus, I was listening to *Electric Ladyland* a lot [*laughs*].

Rumpus: Well, that's sort of where I wanted to go next. Can you chart your listening through the crucial period of early seventies, etc.? Music is so utterly central to *Shadowbahn*, is written into its very form, that I'm curious to hear how music has played a part in your life and work up until this novel.

Erickson: Yeah, that's a really long story. I hope I can be just a *little* succinct, but feel free to turn off the tape recorder figuratively or literally [*laughs*].

There's just no overstating the role that music played. The truth is it played at least as great a role in my life and writing as literature and maybe more. In the contemporary literature of the time, the only thing that was having a comparable impact was Márquez and Pynchon, Dick, Borges, maybe DeLillo a little later. Music shows up in most of my novels, maybe all of them, which obviously isn't unique—it's in your novels and Lethem's and Dana Spiotta's and Richard Powers's, Bruce Bauman's *Broken Sleep* from last year. Colson Whitehead has talked about the impact of music on his work.

The two defining events of my musical education were hearing Ray Charles and then, one epic afternoon, *Highway 61 Revisited* and *Blonde on Blonde* back to back, both for the first time. Charles was a shock because I was a white boy living a white-bread existence, an only child in a house whose parents had no use for rock 'n' roll or Elvis Presley. I was raised on Sinatra and Nat King Cole, and please let me hasten to add it's no disrespect to Cole, who I still love, when I simply note he didn't exactly represent Black music at its grittiest and most soulful. Rhythm and blues purists may disdain Charles's country albums of that time, but they were the Trojan horse that smuggled into my white sensibility an unmistakably Black voice—I hadn't heard anyone sing like that. Ray Charles was the gateway drug. Once you've heard "Born to Lose," sooner or later you're going to get around to "Lonely Avenue" and "I Don't Need No Doctor," and then Aretha and Otis, and Sam Cooke and Bobby Bland and Wilson Pickett.

As for Dylan, I never much cared about his folk era and still don't—other than "A Hard Rain Is Gonna Fall," one of his half dozen greatest songs, little of it made the impact of "Visions of Johanna" or "I Want You." "Like a Rolling Stone." "Just Like Tom Thumb's Blues." "Absolutely Sweet Marie" and "One of Us Must Know" and "Sad Eyed Lady of the Lowlands." Those records changed my ideas about writing, about *art*—not just the words but also their *sound*. For better or worse I'm the writer I am today because of hearing those Dylan records. For better and most certainly *not* for worse, I'm the person I am today because of hearing Charles.

As for the early seventies, having moved out of my folks' and living in Echo Park, which was then and remains heavily Hispanic, I was living a non sequitur life musically speaking. The surrounding airwaves were filled with the Eagles and Linda Ronstadt, who I didn't care about. I don't want to misrepresent here any nonexistent cool-factor on my part. It's hardly like I was too hip for that stuff, and if "Hotel California" came on the radio right now, I'd turn up the Joe Walsh guitar at the end. I think Joni Mitchell and Jackson Browne each made at least one really good album. I did listen to quite a bit of Randy Newman and Neil Young at the time, Van Morrison who was in his California phase, and my brain tells me that Steely Dan were probably better than I liked them. And there was a lot of LA music from just a few years before that I loved and still do. But none of that early-seventies LA music that was the currency of the time was anything I obsessed about, and I didn't know anyone else who obsessed about what I obsessed about— so my taste sort of isolated me, in the way it felt ten years later like my early novels isolated me from the rest of what was going on in fiction. I was the only person I knew in LA who had a Roxy Music record. I was the only person I knew in LA who had a Mott the Hoople record, or a Velvet Underground record. I was the only person I knew who had a New York Dolls record. For that matter I was the only person I knew who had a Bruce Springsteen record—his second one, before the breakthrough. I wasn't the only person I knew who had a Bowie record but I was the *first* person I knew who had one. Those records had drama that I missed from the other stuff—audacity, danger; they were bigger than life when James Taylor quite deliberately meant to be smaller than life.

Same with punk—at the beginning there were about six and a half of us in LA listening to it, and I remember the owner of the Music Odyssey on Wilshire Boulevard openly and loudly berating me to the rest of the customers for buying the early import of the Sex Pistols' first album, standing behind the register *taking my money* while announcing, "Hey everyone, check out the asshole buying this shitty record!" A month later the American version of the album came out with a song added to it so of course I had to get it and submit myself to the indignity all over again [*laughs*].

That was the peak of my musical life in terms of following it obsessively. Because as you know, being a man of taste and sophistication, the eighties were objectively, quantifiably, empirically, diagram-it-on-a-blackboard the worst decade in the history of recorded music, and more and more of it just started passing me by, maybe not Prince or Run-DMC or the Jesus and Mary Chain, but a lot of it. And these days, while there are artists I keep up with—I suspect PJ Harvey is one for the pantheon—I have, as my friend [film critic] John Powers once put it, "reconciled myself to my taste," which is to stay that instead of checking out Twenty One Pilots, I'm afraid I'm likelier to listen to my Eno playlist or James Brown. It's taken me nearly twenty years to figure out that the Drive-By Truckers are pretty good [*laughs*]. Mostly over the last thirty years I found myself exploring things that preceded me: Miles Davis, Duke Ellington. I went back to Sinatra—not the Rat Pack, ring-a-ding-ding shtick but the bluesy torch stuff of the late fifties. And that sense of context, that connection between the music and whatever was going on socially and historically when the music was made, found its way into this new novel. That's about as succinct as I can get. And I don't think I even mentioned the Beatles.

Rumpus: The engagement with music, however present in the earlier work (which, as you say, it certainly is), takes a dramatic turn in *Shadowbahn*. The novel is suffused with music. There is very nearly music on every page. Perhaps this even understates it. There *is* music on every page, to varying degrees, and there are entire sections devoted to it. What changed this time out? And in what way does music become the best vehicle to perform the elegy that the novel seems to perform?

Erickson: The focus on music wasn't initially part of the plan. That probably sounds ridiculous when one of the novel's major characters is Elvis's twin—how could such a book not be about music? And I certainly didn't mean to write an Elvis Presley novel. I guess unconsciously I knew more than I knew consciously, because when I got to those Towers early in the story, they began singing, like the ground in *Rubicon Beach* or the lake in *Our Ecstatic Days* full of melody snakes. Then I may have, if anything, overly steeped myself in music—since I usually can't read other fiction when working on a novel, I gravitated to Marcus, Guralnick, Christgau, Mikal Gilmore, Ralph Ellison's jazz essays, and Geoff Dyer's *But Beautiful,* Lethem's music pieces in *Ecstasy of Influence,* and David Toop's work on ambient music, Bangs's gazillion-word piece on the Troggs, and in particular a book called

On Celestial Music by one R. Moody that was probably the best example of sustained writing about music in a manner that feels unabashedly personal without abandoning its critical faculties.

So as you say, music became hardwired into this book like none other, and as the novel progressed, if anything I had to not let it take over. There are a lot of moving parts to the narrative, and I spent months focusing on the balance of those parts, and as you know, having read an earlier version, about a fourth of the song entries wound up being cut, and what remained wound up collapsed or cut in half. I've just seen a fairly prominent review in which the reviewer [Fiona Maazel], who calls herself a "dilettante" about American music, got caught up in the story anyway and ran down each musical lead, which I take as an encouraging sign that—unlike *Zeroville*, which fully intended to be a novel about movies—*Shadowbahn* is a novel about America and therefore, inevitably if tangentially, about music too. Western music is arguably America's greatest contribution to the twentieth century, cultural or otherwise. With a few exceptions like Kraftwerk, most great twentieth-century Western music is in some way American-based. And the great paradox of America, the paradox that distills America, is that this greatest of American contributions to humanity, this American contribution that probably has influenced more people around the world for the good, that probably has brought more people around the world unqualified joy, was born of America's greatest evil, slavery. Or one of the two great evils anyway, counting the European extinction of those who were on the continent first. That's your elegy.

Rumpus: I am very honored to be on a list of writers I really admire. Bangs's *Psychotic Reactions* was a book that significantly influenced my development, and the same is true of *Lipstick Traces* by Greil Marcus. And *But Beautiful* is also lasting, and important, and remarkable. I have found Geoff Dyer to be a really reliable source for music tips. He turned me onto the Necks, for example, whom you would love if you don't know about them already.

I admire what you say about American music and its origin in slavery. If you listen to West African music and then listen to the early blues, that leap doesn't even seem like a leap at all. At least this is the case when the early blues are played by African American musicians (before the syncopations and extra measures got streamlined into the twelve-bar thing, when white musicians got hold of the idiom, or at least in many cases); their reliance on the West African model is easy to hear. And I agree that the indigenous music of America is so central to how it conceives of itself, how it identifies itself.

In *Shadowbahn*, along similar lines, on page 111, Elvis's twin (J. G. Presley) develops a bona fide music critical voice and attitude himself, and it's a voice that is significantly challenging and intense, as far as the book goes (those imagining a wooly, imaginative speculative fiction, for example, will be asked to engage with a significant jump cut, as far as style goes). At what point did that become part of the plan, and how did you come to inhabit that voice? And is it influenced by your readings in music criticism?

Erickson: Well, the specific section you're asking about has to do with a record review that Jesse writes for a music magazine in the late 1960s, or rather I should say *a* late 1960s, since they're not the late 1960s you or I or the reader knows, in large part because Jesse has replaced his brother. With the section's sudden transitional lurch, which is hardly the first or last in the book, I was trying to have my cake and eat it, in that I wanted to disorient readers but not so much or so soon as to lose them entirely, even as I know it's undoubtedly bound to lose some.

Whatever else the book's virtues or flaws may be, if you're the kind of reader who likes to know where a story is going before it gets there, this is *not* your book. To some extent Jesse is the difference between an idea—the Twin Towers resurrected in the Badlands—and a novel, so I spent close to a year thinking about him before I began writing. As the stillborn twin of the most famous and influential singer of all time—however reasonable or unreasonable anyone might consider that distinction—who would Jesse be? I did some research into identical twins, talked to people I know who have identical twin children, and was struck by how much the subject of twins is still a mystery to biological and psychological science. In a very real embryonic sense, of course, twins literally are two halves of the same person, and yet, once born, they're not the same. And in this story Jesse is haunted not only by the twin who didn't make it—as in real life Elvis was haunted by Jesse—but also by a knowledge of who that twin would have been and how he would have changed everything.

The result was the section on page 111 that wound up cut down considerably from its original length. It was one of the earliest things I wrote in trying to find a character who was a contradiction, a yahoo who, nonetheless, has these incongruously cerebral outbursts, whose language is mostly hayseed interrupted by impenetrably intellectual allusions, and this section is the most conspicuous display of that. And again, as somebody who read a somewhat earlier version of this novel, you know that just as it was a challenge to balance all the various elements of the book, it was a challenge to balance all the various elements of Jesse, particularly when Jesse himself has no real idea who he is. I was hoping to find some sweet spot between the archetype on the one hand and the not-utterly-abstract on the other, especially in contrast to the other two main characters in the story, white and Black siblings who I wanted to be as real-life as possible. And because of whose shadow he lives in, Jesse's relationship with music in general is estranged, to say the least, and becomes increasingly violent, since he comes to believe that just the very existence of music threatens his own existence, in the same way that the very existence of music provides a shadow history of America and how it went wrong from the outset.

Rumpus: I want to pause for a moment over your "transitional lurch" here, because it's such a beautiful way to describe a gesture that is quintessentially Ericksonian. In *Arc d'X*, for example, there is moment when Sally Hemings hops disconsolately over some centuries, and moves out of her subjugation at the hands of a great founding father of our nation, into a much more speculative novel. I'm wondering whether this "transitional lurch" itself has a musical footing. It reminds me, for example, of some of the really abrupt changes in form in the Miles Davis of the electric period, when he was thinking about Stockhausen. Or: it reminds me of the Mothers of Invention, when the players were waiting for Frank Zappa to cue them from his baton. Or: you hear such things in that great five-year period of Sun Ra from the mid to late sixties. Is it a musical figuration for you?

Another point of origin, it seems to me, is filmic. You have written a lot about film, and film is as essential to what you do, I think, as music is. Would the "transitional lurch" have to do with the jump cut in experimental film of the sixties and seventies? As someone who has occasionally visited one upon a reader now and again myself, I feel great excitement and admiration when I come upon one of these Ericksonian "lurches," because they are merciless, and unapologetic, and they require great interpretive leaps, arabesques even. How do you think about this tendency in your work?

Erickson: Wow, what an observation. I'm not sure I've ever put my finger on it but you're obviously right. In terms of film, the whole last ten or fifteen minutes of *2001*, say, is one such lurch after another, in a way that had nothing to do with then-conventional notions of science fiction but in the process invented a whole new science fiction. In retrospect we can see that *Miles in the Sky* and *Filles de Kilimanjaro* were really just inspired warm-ups for *In a Silent Way*, and beyond that beckoned *Bitches Brew*, *Pangaea* and all the rest. Brian Wilson's *Pet Sounds* is a quantum lurch from "California Girls" and *Beach Boys Party* that came just months before. The Beatles may be the best example with "Tomorrow Never Knows" concluding *Revolver* and taking it off into something no other pop music had done, Zappa being one of the possible exceptions with *Freak Out!*, I suppose. What's interesting, of course, is that in fact "Tomorrow Never Knows" was the first track, not the last, recorded for *Revolver*, in the same way that "Strawberry Fields," "Penny Lane," and "Day in the Life" were the first tracks recorded for *Sgt. Pepper* before the band decided, in one of the most consequential mistakes in pop music history, to leave two of them off the album—the main point being that, after making those lurches, the band had to keep retrenching in order to catch up with itself. The *White Album* turns these abruptions and juxtapositions into a worldview—the chaos of 1968 as organizing principle.

It doesn't seem irrelevant that all this was happening in a two- or three-year period, and I assume acid had something to do with it, though I'm not aware of Miles doing acid and I'm certainly not aware of Kubrick doing acid. I never did acid, unless listening to *Revolver* and watching *2001* counts [*laughs*], but this was a period when I was coming of age and absorbing the influences of an emerging aesthetic that incorporated Einsteinian notions of space and time, even if you didn't know anything about Einstein, which I certainly didn't. Transitions per se were superfluous. There was no reason for a transition if all it was doing was performing a transitional function, if it wasn't doing something else as well. Of course you can argue that Pynchon's *V.* anticipated all of them.

Rumpus: All of your work, or the majority of it that I have read (which is almost all), traffics in really dynamic ideas about form. In *Shadowbahn* it's the little short-take chapters, each with its chapter title, in a nearly square size that I sort of thought of (when I first beheld them) as CD (box set) liner notes. In *Zeroville* the story is told inside of film grammar, in the mise-en-scène in which the protagonist labors as a film editor. (I'm trying to come up with a good way to describe the effect of the shape of that novel, and this is it for this morning!)

I wonder whether these forms are in the imagination phase of composition, are preliminary, or are more a thing that you discover along the way. Are they always integral to the expression of the theme? Or do they represent an ambition with respect to form, i.e., something that you want to make literature do?

Erickson: The form is always integral to the expression of the theme, as you put it, or to the sheer telling of the story, and sometimes the right form is apparent to me from the outset and sometimes it isn't. One of the reasons I'm not so keen on people calling me an "experimental" writer is that it suggests the work is about the experiment, when it's always the opposite— any "experimentation" is dictated by the material.

About twelve years ago I published a novel called *Our Ecstatic Days* about a single mother trying to protect her small son from the chaos of the world as represented by a lake that has suddenly sprung up to flood Los Angeles. Her son vanishes and the mother gets it in her head that if she swims down to the bottom of the center of the lake and down through the hole where the lake has sprung, she'll surface in another lake in another Los Angeles where her son will be waiting for her. So about a quarter of the way into the novel she swims down this hole . . . and then I got this idea to have her swim through the rest of the novel in a single line that would cut through the rest of the text over the next 230 pages—one line that would represent one narrative reality while, back in that reality where our story began, that other narrative would continue to unfold over years and decades as the woman grew older and lived out the rest of her life, never getting her son back. Until I got to that point of the story, I had no idea I was going to do this. This idea of the woman swimming through the other story came to me only when I reached the moment when it happened—and I knew it was a fork in the writing process, that there was no going back from this idea and that it would, in turn, dictate many other decisions as to the form of the rest of the text and the rest of the book.

On the other hand, in the case of *Zeroville* I decided from the outset that the storytelling should follow the dramatic laws of a movie, as you imply. Everything is externalized in the present tense in terms of action and dialogue, there's not a lot of backstory, there's a minimum of motivation, which renders as an enigma the lead character, who's in every scene, and it's the only truly linear novel I've written. *These Dreams of You* took the fractured form of a mosaic, which it made sense to push further in *Shadowbahn* only once I had written half of it, when I found myself drawn more and more into Calvino-crossed-with-the-*White-Album* territory, by which of course I don't mean Didion. Then, in the revision process, I pulled back a bit from all that kaleidoscopia, asking myself at each juncture how much I wanted to challenge the reader and how much I wanted to help him or her over the cracks of my landscape. A constant process of putting in and taking out, of cohering and coming apart, of gravity and entropy. Those choices are always about what best serves the story I want to tell, not the other way around. In essence I'm really a very traditional writer. I subscribe to the notion that, ultimately, characters do drive everything else.

Rumpus: *Our Ecstatic Days*, as you describe it, brings us around again to the issue of twinning, which is so central to *Shadowbahn*. There's not only J. G. Presley therein, and the antimatter Beatles described in the book (they are sort of a preoccupation of Presley's), and there are also the Twin Towers themselves. (As a footnote, let me say that as someone who lived in the city of the Twin Towers, I hated those buildings architecturally, for my whole youth, until, at a certain point, I became really interested in Donald Judd and minimalist sculpture. Then I began to think about them *as twins*, as identical objects, whose most interesting feature was how they related to each other in space, and how that fraternal relationship changed as you moved about them in downtown NYC. I came to love their strange diagonal orientation to one another, and to the plaza where they sat, and that relationship continues to be luminous, spooky, and very powerful, in the memorial spaces that, with a continuous rushing of Hudson River water, now occupy the footprints of the former twins.)

The twinning seems like a Steve Erickson gesture, as though there are *always* possible worlds, with their slightly perturbed realities hovering just beside the story, whatever the story is. We know that this kind of counternarrative activity has a strong analogue in the mainstream of speculative fiction, in, for example, *The Man in the High Castle* (by which I mean the novel, not the television series), but also in slightly more conventional works like Roth's *The Plot Against America*. What does the twinning mean to you? I'm taken by your remarks about Einstein, above. Now that we are in the twenty-first century, not the late sixties, the scientific support for a much more flexible and nuanced theory of how time and space work is everywhere around us: there is string theory (with its ten dimensions), the theory of everything, and all the manifold discussions of subatomic physics and spooky action at a distance, and so on. Your holes in Los Angeles, conceived of by extension as holes in space-time, seem to be springing up all around us.

Erickson: That's a great observation about the Twin Towers, one I could never have come up with because I never lived with them the way you did, though I did go to the top once and—even as it was seemingly safe—it was terrifying in some elemental or even primal way.

As for my preoccupation with twins, that's something for a psychiatrist to decode, because it's been a recurring motif since my first published novel thirty-two years ago [*Days Between Stations*], where there are not only twin brothers separated at birth but another character who wears an eye patch and changes his identity depending on which eye he covers. Maybe there's something I don't know about my own birth [*laughs*].

That said, when I started writing novels I was less conscious of twins as such than of a sense of *something other*, the sense that there's always another possibility or, as you imply, maybe many. A Cartesian argument—and let's be clear that I'm no less out of my depth discussing Descartes than I am Einstein—might hold that if we can imagine other possibilities, they must exist. That the human imagination couldn't conceive of other possibilities if we hadn't somehow glimpsed their shadows cast across our imaginations in the first place. That we actually *remember* these other possibilities as much as we imagine them. And if the Original Moment that first shadow was cast, however long ago it was, split into twin possibilities, and if each of those twins split themselves into twins, then the number of possibilities is way, way, way beyond exponential, way, way, way beyond billions or trillions or quadrillions or whatever higher measure there is.

In terms of America, I think any profound consideration is bound to return us to the notion of twins because, though you certainly can contend there are many Americas, our history has been binary from the beginning, with its hairline fracture down the country's center between what America has wanted to be and what America has been. That fracture is slavery, of course. To some extent it's still slavery, in that collectively we refuse to come to grips with the American fact of slavery. There are millions of white Americans today who still can barely bring themselves to acknowledge that the Civil War, with its twin Americas locked in a death match, was about slavery. They'll argue it was about economics, and they're right only because one of those economies was a slave economy. They'll argue it was about culture, and they're right only because one of those cultures was a slave culture. Half the country seceded from the other half when Abraham Lincoln was elected because half the country couldn't abide his position on slavery. You would think 150 years later this had all become pretty historically incontestable. Yet millions continue to contest it in the face of history. Rather the denial of slavery and all its monstrous repercussions defines to one twin America what the country is and means, and therein is the DNA of those "alternative facts" that people believe when they can't stand to believe the truth. It's the American version of Holocaust denial and no less an intellectual obscenity. It's a kind of treason. And I don't think the twins can get along anymore. I don't think they can transcend their division anymore. And I think this will be a hard lesson for those of us who make an effort to be tolerant and empathetic. One twin is good and one is evil. One is going to have to win and the other is going to have to lose, as happened in the 1860s. Out of that will emerge yet another American Possibility, for better or worse.

Rumpus: One last question, about human emotions. Your work, it seems to me, for all the spectacular prose (which I deeply admire) and the highly imaginative fields of story in which you plow, is always first and foremost about human emotions. According to this logic the work doesn't, to me, seem conventionally postmodern, but, rather, much closer to how some people conceive of "post-postmodern," a kind of writing that is both formally inventive and aware, but not at all antithetical to humanism and its truths. This is in stark contrast to the writers of the "experimental" period of the sixties and seventies, whose modality was often comic (I'm thinking of Gaddis, Barthelme, Gass, Elkin), but who would otherwise not be mistaken for sentimentalists. Is your humanism baked in? A first cause, or a fact of the matter?

Erickson: I think it may have been Sarah Vowell who once wrote that, for all the crazy things that happen in my novels, I'm basically an old-fashioned guy [*laughs*]. Strip away the morphing landscapes and rips in the space-time continuum, and my stories are about things that novels have always been about: love and sex and identity and memory and history and redemption. To the extent that I've ever understood postmodernism—and I'm sure there are people out there who do, but I'm not one of them—one of its distinguishing traits is the story's awareness of its own artifice, and how that awareness becomes part of the story. And if that's right, then I have no idea how I ever got lumped into postmodernism except that I believe, since I was first published, people just haven't quite known where else to put me.

To some extent this has accounted for the, uh, vagaries of my so-called career. The last thing I want is that sense of artifice—rather I want the reader drawn into the story and lost in it and vested in it. So the emotional connection is everything, albeit a connection on my terms. Obviously cheap sentimentality isn't something any good novelist wants to traffic in, but I think it's a problem if you consider it to be the most egregious of all creative sins. I think it's a problem if you consider it the thing to be avoided at all cost. I think it's a problem of you're not willing to risk the consequences of that kind of emotionalism under any circumstances. Then you wind up in the cul-de-sac of irony, and while a particularly deft sense of irony may be one of the tools of great storytellers, I think it's also true that if irony serves as a retreat from an emotional engagement that you're overly concerned is uncool, that's a failure of nerve.

So in answer to your question, "Is the humanism intuitive or labored over?" the answer is yes. It begins intuitively, it becomes the reason for writing the thing, and then it's to be considered and fine-tuned and even calculated, if you have a good editor like Katie Zaborsky was for me at Blue

Rider who might try to reel you in now and then, let you know you've taken it too far. If you're a smart writer, you listen. But I'd rather first risk taking it too far than not far enough. I'd rather first risk taking it far enough that there's nowhere else to go—which probably accounts for why every novel lately feels like the last. One of these days, I'll be right.

"America Happened to America": A Conversation with Steve Erickson

Joe Milazzo / 2017

From *Entropy*, at www.entropymag.org (August 10, 2017). Reprinted by permission.

It would be wise, I think, to keep these introductory comments brief. Steve Erickson's innovative, eloquent, and downright visionary fiction has been inspiring other storytellers[1] for over thirty years. His last several novels, starting with 2005's *Our Ecstatic Days*, have been especially noteworthy, and it should come as no surprise that his latest, *Shadowbahn*, is one of the best-reviewed books of 2017.

"A book like *Shadowbahn* serves as a bulwark against numbness and the dangerous belief that the only response to incomprehensibility is inaction," writes David Leo Rice in *The Believer*. In *Granta*, Jonathan Lethem describes the novel as "jaw-dropping" and singles out its "radical audacity," "intensely personal self-reckoning," and "lucid-dreaming prose." And the *New York Times*'s Fiona Maazel calls it "sad . . . droll . . . gorgeous . . . compassionate, weird, unpredictable, jaunty," and "alarmingly prescient." In short, *Shadowbahn* is one of those rare books that truly demands to be read.

Perhaps all that's left to say is that I was fortunate enough to study with Steve while pursuing my MFA in writing at the California Institute of the Arts and that my good fortune extended for several years afterward, as I continued to work with him on the staff of the literary journal *Black Clock*. Talking with Steve about his artistic practice these past few months represents a kind of homecoming for me. I'm glad to be able to crack open the door to that experience here. Now, reader, I'll stand aside; this threshold is yours to cross.

When the Twin Towers suddenly reappear in the Dakota Badlands two decades after their fall, they broadcast music to the tens of thousands that gather, including siblings Parker and Zema from LA. On the ninety-third floor of the South Tower, Jesse Presley—the stillborn twin of the most famous singer who ever lived—suddenly awakes. Over the hours and days and years to come, he is driven mad by a voice in his head that sounds like his but isn't, and by the memory of a country where he survived in his brother's place.

Joe Milazzo: *Shadowbahn* would seem to be an extension or a continuation of—if not a sequel to—your last novel, *These Dreams of You.* At least, this book holds open a space in which central characters from *These Dreams of You* might yet act. What about these characters compelled you to continue writing through (and alongside) Parker and Zema?

Steve Erickson: As you probably know, having done it yourself, writing a novel can be an evolutionary process. Some novelists plot out everything before they begin writing, but in my case I'll start with a story that then sometimes develops along unexpected lines. I didn't foresee this new novel as any sequel to the last, and in my original conception Parker and Zema played a smaller part. But the characters, a dozen years older than we last saw them in the previous book, asserted themselves. They staked a bigger claim to the book, and after you've written enough books and enough characters you learn to pay attention to that. I think ultimately the bigger connection between the two novels—inevitably, in retrospect—is America. Thematically this novel picked up where the last off, with a growing unease that something about the country was coming apart philosophically.

JM: Although it was composed before Trump's political ascendance, *Shadowbahn* may be the first novel to confront, in an explicit sense, the new norms (or normalizations) of Trump's America. To that extent, it feels like a reckoning with the notion that the American experiment is over, has been over, and that the manner of its conclusion augurs something beyond catastrophe. Which is to say: some set of conditions that, while ruinous, fall far short of the high eschatological drama we expect from the calamitous. In your role as novelist, how would you describe your relationship to History with a capital H?

SE: The Marxist view is that everything's a product of history, everything's a result of historical forces as surely as two chemical compounds produce a third. My view is the other way around: that history is a product of everything else. History doesn't make for the irrationalities of existence, the irrationalities make for history. So the novels are less about human lives in a historical context as they are about history in the context of the story I'm telling about my characters. We all live in historical times, but in terms of this country in particular, the decade and a half between 9/11 and the last election is the most existentially crucial and dangerous of our lifetime—you may have to go back to the 1850s and 1860s for anything comparable. When I wrote the second page of *Shadowbahn*—where a truck driver has on his rear fender a bumper sticker that reads SAVE AMERICA FROM ITSELF— it was the first week of 2014, and less a matter of prophecy than paying attention, because what happened this last November has been coming awhile. Let's not let ourselves off the hook by supposing Donald Trump is something that happened to America. Rather, America happened to America, and Trump is the result. Unless you're a novelist who's completely disengaged, I don't know how you any longer avoid the subject of America. Stendhal said something to the effect that politics in fiction is like a gunshot in church—rude but unavoidable.

JM: This is one of my favorite passages in *Shadowbahn*: "In the thirteen years since Zema came to America, she has never had any idea that having no idea who she is and having no idea where she belongs makes her more American than anyone." What was once Edenic (or at least pastoral) about America—that sense of limitless possibility—has curdled into something else: at worst a sense of profound terror, and at best the internalizing of a failure that is anything but individual. How much are the characters in *Shadowbahn* "condemned to be free?" Or are they merely condemned?

SE: Almost definitionally this is a nomadic country. All our ideas about "freedom" and "independence" are bound up in a kind of psychic if not literal nomadism. The guy who writes the nation's founding declaratory document about life, liberty and, most subversively, the pursuit of happiness—note the aggression inherent in the word "pursuit"—becomes our third president and the most important thing he does is buy up a mass of wild-ass real estate from the French and send a couple of explorers westward however far it was that Far went. But along with the nomadism is a duality that's been there from the beginning—Free America and Slave America—and that American duality itself has a dual nature, a division between dialectic order and conflicted disorder. When they decided in the early 1960s to build the world's tallest building in America's biggest city, what did they do? They built two, twins. So you have 300-plus million people in the country with little sense of history, who have two competing ideas of what the past is, who regard the past as either a place to live and never leave or as a place to flee and never think about again, but in either case not as something that informs the present or the future. It's a country of constant identity crisis, a country that names itself after its dreams and then clings to that branding as a way of trying to remember who it is. If the country is condemned as you say, then it has condemned itself. You're not going to easily reconcile a country that elected the first African American president with a country that voted for the first president in modern times to be openly and avidly endorsed by the Ku Klux Klan.

JM: Perhaps because the book itself is saturated with *détourned* familiarities, while reading *Shadowbahn* I felt I was given more occasion than usual to reflect upon other (if not exactly comparable) narratives. Poe's *A. Gordon Pym* being one. But I also found myself coming back, again and again, to those "disaster movies" so characteristic of American cinema in the 1970s. I think there are complicated reasons for why this last echo called loudly to me, but I won't pursue those repercussions at length here beyond noting that, like a good disaster movie, *Shadowbahn* impressed me as simultaneously suspenseful and inexorable. Regardless, all these echoes inspired me to reappraise what I've long believed to be an overlooked aspect of your writing: its power to move the reader. I mean that your books are eventful in a rather intimate sense. I think of how *Our Ecstatic Days* is constantly being driven forward by sorrow, or the various tragedies inflicted upon Banning Jainlight in *Tours of the Black Clock*. Assuming you feel one, how do you cope with the emotional toll that comes with having to live with your novels, both in their making and once they've been "finished"?

SE: Well, this may be as profound a question as I've been asked about the work, and it's hard for me to answer without sounding vague. It requires me to somehow contrast my intentions as a writer with perceptions of the work by readers, and I don't know that I can or even should speak to the way those two things might be at odds. *Our Ecstatic Days* was the most emotional book I've written; it was the book where I pushed myself the farthest both emotionally and creatively, until the two fused. Years ago there was a point writing *Tours of the Black Clock* when I had to walk away from the book for a length of time, my story had become so intense for me. The writing of these novels is sometimes traumatic in the most precise sense of the word, followed by a kind of post-traumatic stress. And as time goes by and the books go by, I would say this becomes more difficult rather than less.

JM: John Hawkes once famously stated that, as a novelist, he felt he had to dispense with "plot, character, setting and theme" in order to focus on what was of chief concern to him: "totality of vision or structure." *Shadowbahn* is transparently, concretely a text. The book's pages have been designed and laid out in such a way that the reader is required to give some consideration to their constructedness. Why these short entries, many no longer than one or two paragraphs? Are the headings on each page chapter titles, or something else? Is this somehow a metrical novel? However, contra Hawkes, those accustomed and hypothetically accessible elements of fiction ("plot, character, setting and theme") matter very much in your work. What does "totality of vision or structure" mean to you? In a general sense, how do you perceive form and content meaningfully interacting in your own oeuvre?

SE: Someone recently used the word *immersive* to describe this new book and my work in general, and I was surprised it hadn't occurred to me before, because it's such a good characterization of my intentions. I think that, earlier on, I was sometimes called a postmodernist because it was simply the handiest word at the moment for people who didn't have a better one, and if I resist the term it's because postmodernism calls attention to its own artifice, which is the opposite of the immersion that my work aspires to. So even if now and then I wander into some quasi-discreet semiotexte, it's no less for the purpose of creating something immersive—the typographic landscape functions as no less immersive as do story and character and everything else. I hate to sound so conventional, but character still drives stories, whether those stories have the more straightforward linearity of something like *Zeroville* or something more fractured like *Shadowbahn*, and the functions of story and character still dictate the form. In the case of *Shadowbahn*, that form didn't manifest itself until I had written half the book, at which point, for reasons I'm not sure bear articulating, some kind of Calvino-crossed-with-the-*White-Album* schematic asserted itself.

JM: Lately, I've been listening to a lot of Oval. They were a midnineties German "band" most known for making truly digital pop music. Members Markus Popp, Sebastian Oschatz, and Frank Metzler would physically alter and otherwise glitch out prerecorded compact discs, sample them, and then assemble the results. Who or what figures most prominently on your current playlist, and why?

SE: Music took over the novel in a way I didn't anticipate. It's hijacked more than one or two of my novels. The music choices were initially intuitive—I didn't know the Towers were going to start singing "Shenandoah" until I got to that part of the story, and then suddenly all kinds of music started coming out. Later, in revisions, I tried to seize back the book from the music, deleting about a quarter of the music entries and cutting those that remained to about half their original length. These were the last major changes I made to the novel at a point when I had a fuller perspective on what I wanted the novel to be—then I gave more conscious consideration to which entries to keep and why. I became struck by the paradox that America's most fully joyful contribution to the world, the one thing America has given to the world that everyone loves unabashedly and without qualification, is music, and that this music was born from the most incontestably evil thing about America, which was slavery. You can make a pretty good argument that in the Western world, anyway, the popular music of the twentieth century was invented by African Americans—list the twelve or fifteen or twenty greatest musical artists of the twentieth century between Berlin and LA and the vast majority are going to be Americans, and the vast majority of those are going to be Black. The white American exceptions you can count on one hand: Sinatra, Presley, Dylan. So ultimately I made musical choices that told a story about America, allowing that sometimes that meant songs by Europeans like Bowie or the Beatles, who have been called "honorary Americans" down through the years by . . . I can't remember who now. Trilling or Fiedler, I think, or Greil Marcus.

JM: The song "Oh Shenandoah" haunts *Shadowbahn*. But "Oh Shenandoah," as the novel is painfully aware, is not a stable or singular entity. The more the song disappears, the more it resonates. The song is everywhere and nowhere, an unacknowledged, unfathomable presence that, like instinct, vibrates within and couples contingency to consequence. And so there are as many versions of "Oh Shenandoah" as there are Americas (all Americas, like the presets on a car stereo, being alternate realities). What version of this song do you first remember hearing, and what effect did it have on you?

SE: The first time I remember hearing "Shenandoah" may have been in an early sixties Cinerama movie called *How the West Was Won*, one of those cast-of-thousands epics that studios were trying to fight off TV with. I was a kid and can't say for sure. "Shenandoah" has always been around, in the way you say, and in terms of this novel its American ever-presence is the point of it. As Marcus noted to me and as you've noted, it's a song that's everywhere—you hear it in the music of Warren Zevon, Randy Newman, Tom Waits. Dylan has recorded it, Springsteen has recorded it, it's been recorded by everyone from Paul Robeson to Judy Garland. The version I heard in my head when I was writing the book is a relatively recent one, by Dave Alvin, who used to be in LA punk bands the Blasters and X.

JM: Do you consider your dreams a kind of autobiography, or, for you, is dreaming more a form of research?

SE: Yes.

JM: *Shadowbahn* is a book of strange resurrections. The World Trade Center Towers reappear in the South Dakota Badlands. Jesse Presley usurps his twin brother's place in the American unconscious, and, instead of transforming the world via his singing, warps his guilt and envy until his existential condition itself becomes a form of demagoguery. Is the counterfactual the new postapocalyptic? What advice would you give the younger generation of literary artists who hope to "save America from itself"?

This is a country where tens of millions of white people still don't want to admit, 150 years after the fact, that the Civil War was about slavery. That's the American version of Holocaust denial, and I admit this new hostility to fact gives me pause about what I do. The idea behind the sort of fiction I write has always been that there's an emotional truth bigger than fact that lies in dream, imagination, and the unconscious—the idea has been that reality is what we make it, that we can reimagine reality and that fact can confine or even exist at odds with some truth that's "bigger" than fact. The problem these days, however, is that America has become a nation of surrealists. We now have what Jelani Cobb of the *New Yorker* calls an "à la carte" approach to reality, where and when fact is subject to whatever revisions make it more palatable. In a country where the powers that be have declared war on truth, writers who sojourn into the imagination without a moral compass or a sense of the real risk rendering themselves irrelevant, not to even mention irresponsible. If you're a novelist these days and you have any awareness of what's going on around you, if you have any capacity left for smashing your own delusions, then you're bound to try and make sense of your self-indulgence. I don't know if frolicking on the playground of the imagination cuts it anymore.

Note

1. Yes, even you, fellow Dallasite Rhett Miller . . . some of us remember how you used to style yourself as some ex-member of the Cleaners From Venus.

Steve Erickson Saw Trumpism Coming

Alec Baldwin / 2017

From *Here's the Thing*, WNYC-FM (November 6, 2017). Copyright © 2017 by WNYC-FM. Reprinted by permission.

Alec Baldwin: This is Alec Baldwin, and you're listening to *Here's the Thing*. People who know me well know that I keep a folder of writing that has changed my life in some way. Among these personal gospels is Eisenhower's farewell address, "Vacillation" by Yeats, and a 1995 essay called "American Weimar" by novelist Steve Erickson. Reading it for the first time twenty-one years ago was a bolt of lucid fear: fear for this country, and fear for the values at its foundation. The piece is an indictment not of America but of modern Americans: a people in denial of our past, still exhausted and divided by Vietnam, and too angry at each other to harness any goodwill. "America wearies of democracy," it begins, "and the result is a hysteria of which we're barely conscious, a hysteria in which democracy appears as a spectacle of impotence and corruption." Since writing these words, Erickson has become one of America's foremost novelists. He's got ten books, countless awards, and a Guggenheim fellowship to prove it. But in 1995, all I knew was that someone had finally put his finger on what felt sick about this country. "The nation gets meaner and more petty," he writes, "until rage is the only national passion left." Twenty-one years later, the national sickness Steve Erickson diagnosed has only progressed.

Steve Erickson: The rage has evolved beyond what I even anticipated then. I've become more aware over the years that have passed of this profound division in the country that I realize now has always been there. If people ask, "How did we get to where we are now?" my answer would be, "We've actually always been here." We've always been these twin Americas— the one that made a promise, and the one that broke the promise the moment it was made. And we've never really reconciled the two, and I think it's going to be difficult to reconcile the two. I'm not sure that the America that elected the first African American president can be reconciled with an America that voted for the first president in modern memory to be openly endorsed by the Ku Klux Klan.

AB: You reference something here—I'm going to read this—"as one historical phenomenon after another—from the assassination of John F. Kennedy to the Vietnam war, to Watergate . . . to O. J. Simpson hurtling down the LA freeways—is offered as the moment when the country 'lost' its innocence. . . . We have not grown up enough to accept that America has never been innocent at all . . . that such an idealist and romantic country was created out of such profound transgressions is a more complicated paradox than we can entertain." Now I want you to articulate for our—they can read other things written by you—you know, what happened to us in the wake of Vietnam.

SE: You know, I think we had to reconcile ourselves with what could not be reconciled with, which was fifty thousand Americans, not to mention the countless—

AB: Hundreds of thousands of Vietnamese.

SE: —of Vietnamese who died for what exactly?

AB: Right.

SE: We don't have an answer to that. Nobody believed anymore at that point that the collapse—

AB: It was in the national interest.

SE: Right, that the collapse of Southeast Asia was somehow—

AB: Could mean anything to us.

SE: Meant anything to the national interest.

AB: Right.

SE: In the same way that, a hundred years later, we still don't know what World War I was really about.

AB: You were old enough to go to Vietnam; did you go?

SE: No, I was in Nixon's lottery, which matched you up with your birthdate, and you got a number. And if your number was below 200, you were probably going to go. I got number 345. Your life was hanging in the balance depending on this random chance of this lottery, and I think that when that can't be reconciled, a national people have to create some psychic rationalization for it because the meaninglessness is too overwhelming to live with.

AB: Someone like Cruz, who says that Vietnam wasn't the problem, the countercultural reaction to it and the lawlessness of what happened to it— nothing infuriates me more than that.

SE: Right.

AB: You can take the excesses, the drugs, the silliness, the ephemera of the representations of the countercultural movement in our society and strip those away and say, "This was when people cared." And people who belittle and blame the countercultural protests of that period, I don't know why it is that nothing infuriates me more than that when I read that.

SE: Well, because they're blaming the wrong thing. But I will make this distinction: the first time somebody burned an American flag, I think we lost the next fifty years. There were bad tactics in the service of good causes that the Right was then able to—

AB: Pounce on.

SE: Seize upon.

AB: Right.

SE: But to go back even further, talking about what we've choked down, and the loss of American innocence: 150 years after the fact, there are still millions of white people who will not admit the Civil War was about slavery. That is the American version of Holocaust denial. It keeps us from becoming what we want to become. It's a lack of acknowledgement that keeps us from fulfilling the American idea. I think Americans, whether they're trying to rationalize the meaninglessness of Vietnam, or 250 years of slavery, it may be in the American DNA to always think that everything is Year Zero. It might be in the American DNA to have cut ourselves loose from history and therefore not ever have to answer for it or to it. Trump is not something that happened to America. America happened to America. And Trump is the result of that. Trumpism was born out of claims, in the face of all evidence, that the first African American president was not a real American and not a real president, to which the Republican Party at the time said almost nothing. And the Republican Party deserved what it got. Unfortunately we got it too.

AB: What is your political process and what's your political rearing with your parents when you were young?

SE: Young?

AB: You grew up in Southern California your whole life?

SE: That's correct, and I was raised a conservative Republican by my parents.

AB: Really?

SE: Who were—

AB: Artists.

SE: Who were artists and who had started out when they were very young as FDR Democrats but like a lot of people at that point, were starting to drift rightward.

AB: Why?

SE: Well, I think that—

AB: Cold War?

SE: Cold War, and then later on in the sixties, a reaction to the counterculture—

AB: Right.

SE: —which I think has defined our politics over half a century more than we know. I think a lot of the reason, for instance, that working-class people are persuaded to not vote their economic interest is because of these values that came out of this conflict between—

AB: Yeah.

SE: —the culture or the mainstream, and the counterculture—

AB: Reagan wanting to take on students in this state in particular.

SE: Exactly. So I was raised a Republican conservative, and to make a long story short, a number of things happened. First of all, by the time I came of age or was seventeen or eighteen, I realized that on the great domestic crucible of the day, which was civil rights and racial justice, conservatives were on the wrong side morally and historically. That in turn undercut a basic tenet of conservatism which says that the more that power devolves away from the federal government down to the state down to the locality, the greater individual freedom grows. The problem with that is that is contradicted by history on any number of occasions. It's taken the federal government intervening against the states to secure the individual freedoms of African Americans, women, gay people. And then as my ideas about the role of government in life changed, as I accepted that sometimes it takes the federal government to preserve the social contract, conservatism changed. It became—when I was identifying as a conservative as a teenager, it was closer to what we now think of as libertarianism. And in the late seventies and early eighties, it starts to become, on the one hand, more corporate, and on the other hand, more theocratic. And it felt like, you know, that for all the lip service that conservatives give individual freedom, what they really cared about was order. And the only individual freedoms that I ever heard conservatives get exercised about were the freedom to make a profit and the freedom to own a gun.

AB: Right.

SE: And so generally my politics shifted while I think, arguably, the center of gravity shifted. Because if you go back and look at, for instance, Barry Goldwater's views now, I mean, Goldwater was an environmentalist, he was pro–gay rights, he was pro-choice, he supported the Voting Rights

Act. Goldwater rightly identified as the most extreme nominee of a party in the twentieth century.

AB: Do you believe that?

SE: Well, I mean his vote against the '64 Civil Rights Act was a bad vote.

AB: Sure.

SE: Nonetheless, I think that his views, which were so extreme in 1964, are now significantly to the left of the current Republican Party. So I shifted one way; the center of our country's political gravity shifted another way. And that's why I wound up where I wound up.

AB: To me, at the same time, philosophically it's been this friction between capitalism and democracy.

SE: Right.

AB: Like how much we're on a boat, and which containers do we throw over the side of the boat to keep the boat from capsizing.

SE: Yeah, and I think the last ten to twenty years have just confirmed that or validated it. Unfettered capitalism nearly drove this country over a cliff ten years ago.

AB: Right. Sure.

SE: I think there's a lot to the argument, the current argument, that we're pretty close to an oligarchy at this point.

AB: We're there. It's very demoralizing and it's very depressing.

SE: Fifty years ago, you could use the word *capitalism* and the expression *free enterprise* in the same sentence. Now it's laughable to think that capitalism is free enterprise, and the conservatives who are distressed by centralized state power never seem to feel the same distress over centralized corporate power.

AB: What was writing in your life? I mean, I'm not just saying this, you are such an amazing writer.

SE: Thank you.

AB: And you've been reviewed with some of the most, I mean, just glowing—I mean, that's a cliché—and what was the writing process for you as a child? When did you realize, this is what I'm going to do?

SE: I realized pretty early. When I was young, let's say five years old, I stuttered very badly, to the point that teachers thought I couldn't read. And this is actually fairly typical of writers: you have a verbal facility, but it's being obstructed—

AB: Shuttered.

SE: Shuttered in your speech, so you retreat inside your head. The verbal facility manifests itself in written words. You're living inside your imagination. It doesn't make you more sociable, but by the time I got to college, I liked college a lot.

AB: Where'd you go?

SE: I went to UCLA.

AB: And why so—for someone as open-minded as you, why so California-centric? Was there any thoughts of "I want to go to Berlin, I want to go to London? I want to go—"

SE: Yes, but it was far enough, and I remember a sense of liberation.

AB: What town were you in in the Valley again?

SE: Granada Hills.

AB: So, for those of you who don't know Los Angeles, he's right. The gap between Granada Hills and Westwood: Westwood really is like Paris compared to Granada Hills.

SE: Absolutely. It was another world. And I thought Westwood was the big city, you know?

AB: It was.

SE: And after that, I actually did go to Europe, and I lived there off and on for a while. So UCLA was the next step away.

AB: This is Alec Baldwin and you're listening to *Here's the Thing*. Steve Erickson's most recent book is *Shadowbahn*, a funny, heartbreaking roadtrip through our divided country. The writing is intensely visual, which reflects Erickson's own alternate life path.

SE: I majored in film.

AB: Why?

SE: Well, I started out a political science major, and I was taking a lot of literature courses, and I wanted to take some film courses. But the bureaucracy at the time, and it may still be the case, was such that I could still take the political courses and literature courses if I was a film major, but I couldn't take the film courses if I was a poli-sci major. So it was a completely tactical choice. It was a way—since I knew I wanted to be a writer, and since what I majored in really didn't matter much to me—

AB: That's a very wise insight. It doesn't matter what you major in.

SE: Right, because I was going to go off and do what I was going to do. And so I made a strategic choice that allowed me to do all that things I wanted to do.

AB: What was film school like? I mean, UCLA is a top film school. What was that like for you?

SE: It was great.

AB: But you didn't pursue that.

SE: I didn't pursue being a filmmaker.

AB: Why? Do you think you were capable? The guy, the stuttering boy from Granada Hills who goes inward, was he able to express what he wanted to in film as well as writing?

SE: I think you nailed it with the question. I realized at some point that I probably should make a choice, that both of these things would be really hard. It would be impossible to try to do both. And the thing that you're right on about is that film, as you would know better than I, is a more collaborative endeavor.

AB: Highly so. You nailed it.

SE: Being a writer, you lock yourself in a room and you have as little interaction with humanity as you can get away with, and you know what? That suited me. That's who I was.

AB: What's the first time you sold a piece, and you became a professional writer?

SE: I sold a piece, actually, to the *Los Angeles Times Calendar*. The gist of it was that the line between reality and fiction was blurring. This was the early seventies.

AB: How did you sell a piece back then? How does that work?

SE: Well, you know it works the way it still works, which is that I knew somebody who knew somebody who could get the piece into the hands of the editor of what was then the *LA Times Calendar* and give it a real read, because that's what it takes. I teach writing, and as I tell my students, without trying to depress them unduly, editors look for a reason to say no. They're not looking for a reason to say yes, so you have to be sure you don't give them any reasons to say no.

AB: How do you do that?

SE: When I submit a novel, for instance, it's pristine. It's so clean you can eat off the thing. It's laid out to look the way the book is going to look so they can visualize how it's going to look. And when I get papers from students where there are typos, and that kind of thing, I just explain to them you can't do that.

AB: Right. How can you expect people to care if you don't care?

SE: Exactly, and every little flaw becomes cumulative. It builds up and it reinforces this impulse to turn the thing down.

AB: So you wrote this piece. Now did you have books you'd written in your pocket?

SE: I was writing novels all the time. I was writing since I was in high school. I wrote five novels before I published one.

AB: Your first book that's published is what?

SE: The first book is published in 1985; that's twelve years after I had published the first piece, and if you had told me at that time that it was going to be—I'm glad there was nobody to tell me that it was going to be another twelve years. Because they felt like twelve years in the wilderness. And by the time I sold the book, I remember the feeling was more relief than anything else, because it just seemed like it was never going to happen.

AB: And was it the same thing? Somebody who knows somebody?

SE: The thing that was instrumental was finding the right agent.

AB: During that twelve years, how do you support yourself? You weren't doing the teaching thing then, were you?

SE: No, I wasn't.

AB: What does the writer do those twelve years?

SE: I was working for the PR department of the Auto Club.

AB: So you had a job job.

SE: I had a job job. I was also writing freelance pieces for the *LA Times*, the *LA Weekly*, which had just launched in the late seventies. The *Los Angeles Reader* was another.

AB: I remember that.

SE: So I was cobbling together a living, but it was always clear in my mind that success for me meant becoming a published novelist.

AB: And when you got the book published in '85—because you got a literary agent.

SE: Right.

AB: And are you still with that literary agent?

SE: Yes.

AB: You are?

SE: I am, and I had had several agents before her; none of them could sell my work. I had gone to New York to find an agent. I had interviewed with four agents. They had all read this novel that wound up being my first published novel. They all said, "It's a really interesting book but I don't think I can sell it." And then I finally found somebody who said "I don't know if I can sell it, but it's a really interesting book." And she wound up selling it to somebody who had turned it down.

AB: What's her name?

SE: Melanie Jackson.

AB: What company is she with? Her own?

SE: Her own, yeah.

AB: Why have you stayed with her all this time? What does she do for you?

SE: So here's a quick story that revolves around that first novel and how the first novel sold. She had submitted it to somebody at Simon & Schuster who had turned it down, and a couple months pass by and it's gone to some other people. And then one afternoon she gets a phone call from this editor at Simon & Schuster who had turned the book down. And the editor was bemoaning the fact that another book that she had turned down had gone on to be published and had gotten attention, and was doing well, and she was thinking "I shouldn't have turned that down." And my agent said, "Yeah, and you're going to feel the same way when somebody publishes Erickson." And the next day, *the next day*, Simon & Schuster bought the book. That's what a good agent does.

AB: You're pretty tough on Bill Clinton in some of your writing. Was it because, on the simplest level, he let you down?

SE: Yeah, I wound up voting for him twice. I still believe that he might have done the country a favor if he had resigned during Monica.

AB: You do?

SE: It would have put Al Gore in, who probably would have won in 2000.

AB: Right.

SE: You know, once the issue became less about his affair and became more about impeachment, I switched. I did not think what he had done was a constitutionally impeachable offense.

AB: No, no, no.

SE: And it was clear to me that the Constitution was being molested by Republicans.

AB: Ken Starr has more on his conscience for what he did to this country.

SE: But Bill Clinton sure helped them out, giving them a target.

AB: And as my friend said to me, he said to me—I had this horrible incident—I'll mention this because I'll throw my own thing on the table. I had this horrible incident where I left this blistering voicemail for my daughter that my then-ex-wife put on the internet. She released it to a tabloid organization that played it on the internet. And as my therapist said back then, he said, "Well, you know, that was wrong and that made things worse, and that was terrible, but none of this would have happened if you hadn't left the voicemail." None of this would have happened if he had not done what he did. In the time we have left, I want to talk to you about your books. How does that process—again for our six listeners who are writers out there—you must be a rabid reader.

SE: I used to be a rabid reader. I don't always have the time to read, and when I'm working on a novel, I don't read other fiction. I'll read history, or I may read poetry even, but I don't want to go into someone else's world.

AB: Who are writers that you admire?

SE: Pynchon, Márquez, Faulkner, Henry Miller, the Brontës. Those were writers who influenced me in some way.

AB: Do you have a reading list you give to your students in the writing class?

SE: I do.

AB: Send it to me [*laughs*]. I want that! If I get one thing out of this—

SE: I mean, they tend to form object lessons. So if I want, for instance, to show students how landscape can be a character in a story: *The Sheltering Sky* by Paul Bowles. Or how voice can drive a narrative: Miller's *Tropic of Cancer*. So that's the function of the reading list.

AB: Are you still teaching now?

SE: Yeah, I am.

AB: And you teach at?

SE: I teach at UC Riverside.

AB: At UC Riverside. And so that's—how far of a drive is that for you from the mountains there?

SE: It's seventy-five miles.

AB: Oh my God.

SE: I know.

AB: And you teach—the class meets how often?

SE: Once a week.

AB: Once a week. For three or four hours?

SE: Right, and if I have two classes that quarter, I'll put them both on the same day and I'll have one monster day.

AB: Just getting it out there.

SE: Getting it out there, yeah.

AB: And the class is entitled what?

SE: Well, I have the luxury of creating my own classes. Sometimes I'm teaching workshops, so we're critiquing the work of the students. This coming quarter—this would probably be interesting to you—I'm teaching a course of fiction into film. That is, I give them a list of novels and we watch the adaptations.

AB: You're doing that when?

SE: This coming quarter. September, October, November. This airs—

AB: I'm sad I'm not going to be out here. I could come visit your class. I could sit in on your class.

SE: That's right. They would be thrilled.

AB: If you teach it again, I'll come sit in on your class.

SE: They would be thrilled if you were just sitting there.

AB: If I sit in the room and listen to you talk.

SE: Yeah.

AB: So you do that, and how many years have you been at UC Riverside now?

SE: I've been at UC Riverside now, this is going into my fourth year.

AB: And what is that impulse in you to teach?

SE: Well, it pays my bills, for starters.

AB: Right.

SE: And I learn things about writing when I'm teaching things about writing.

AB: You enjoy it.

SE: I do enjoy it, and I think I'm getting better at it.

AB: What's hard about it for you? What do you wish you were better at?

SE: You know, the hardest thing about it is negotiating the fact that you really can't teach it. That writing is not—*talent* is not a teachable thing. Skill is a teachable thing, but talent or vision or even voice are things that the students have to bring.

AB: Right.

SE: And the other thing about workshops and writing programs in general—which I think are generally really valuable, but—they do, by their nature, tend to socialize what is really antisocial behavior. You're sitting around with other people talking about your writing, and that's okay up to a point. There's also a point where you need to have the solitude to grapple with your—

AB: You need to go to Morocco.

SE: That's right.

AB: Your most recent book is?

SE: *Shadowbahn.*

AB: Talk to me a little bit about how that came about.

SE: You know, I just, one night I remember the family was gone, I was alone, and—this will sound more mystical than I mean—but I had this vision, if I can use such a grand word.

AB: You can. You're allowed to use that word.

SE: Of the Twin Towers suddenly reappearing in the Dakota Badlands twenty years after their fall. And people start to gather. And they become like this American Stonehenge. And people then start hearing music coming out of the towers. And living in the southern tower is Jesse Presley, who was the real-life stillborn twin of Elvis. And he's going mad hearing a voice in his head that sounds like him but he knows isn't his, and imagining an America where he survived in his brother's place.

AB and SE: [*laughter*]

AB: That's how it works?

SE: Yes.

AB: It just comes to you?

SE: That's how it works, yeah. I will write something, especially when I'm starting, and it starts slow, and it's intermittent, and—

AB: The writing is intermittent?

SE: Yes, which is not great. One of the things that I try to talk to the kids about is, the more of a routine you can make it, the better. But if I can't make it a routine, I'll write it, I'll be excited about it, and then as time goes by, I start to worry it to death. But you know, one of those unteachable things along with voice and talent that we were talking about is instinct, and after you've been doing it a long time, you start to develop an instinct for what's working or what's not working, which isn't to say that after a year and a half you're not so sure. You've been living with the material for that long. You've started to lose perspective. Six publishers turned it down, as was the case with this novel.

AB: You get demoralized.

SE: And you go, "Are they right," you know? "Am I wrong? Am I not seeing it?" All those doubts. I don't think you ever stop grappling with those doubts.

AB: And are you working on another book?

SE: At the moment I don't have an idea in my head.

AB: Writer Steve Erickson. "American Weimar," which we linked to at HeresTheThing.org, stands as one of the sharpest essays ever written about the country's past and present. The current political crisis has only made its warning more urgent. But here's something to cheer you up: Erickson's Hollywood farce *Zeroville* is returning to its spiritual home. James Franco picked up the rights. He and Seth Rogen star. That's coming next year at a theater near you. This is Alec Baldwin, and you're listening to *Here's the Thing* from WNYC Studios.

An Interview with Steve Erickson

Bruce Bauman / 2017

From *The Slice*, issue 20 (Spring/Summer 2017). Reprinted by permission.

In his ten novels and two nonfiction books since the debut of *Days Be-tween Stations* in 1985, Steve Erickson has created a world unlike that of any author working today. When people ask me to describe Erickson's work—as they often do, knowing I was senior editor for thirteen years on the national literary journal *Black Clock*, of which Erickson was cofounder and editor in chief—I quote the Lovin' Spoonful: "It's like tryin' to tell a stranger about rock 'n' roll." Erickson is a literary magician. His work is a unique North American magical realism: Faulkner meets García Márquez meets the Dylan of *Highway 61 Revisited*. In the last thirty years he has imagined a reality both completely recognizable and what only can be called "Ericksonian."

Writers from Jonathan Lethem to Rick Moody to Mark Z. Danielewski have credited his influence. While working with him on *Black Clock*, I saw the respect and admiration he received from David Foster Wallace, Richard Powers, Joanna Scott, Susan Straight, Samuel Delany, T. C. Boyle, Aimee Bender, Greil Marcus, Janet Fitch, Geoff Nicholson, and Don DeLillo. Erickson has received a Guggenheim fellowship, a Lannan Foundation Lifetime Achievement Award, and an American Academy of Arts and Letters Award in Literature. Recently Steve and I talked over Mexican food and via email about literature, politics, being and becoming a writer in these times, and his new mindblower, *Shadowbahn*.

Bruce Bauman: Years ago your novel *Arc d'X* [1993] included a section about "Steve Erickson, an obscure novelist who died," to which a couple of your other novels have since made reference. Also, the character Banning Jainlight from *Tours of the Black Clock* [1989] makes frequent cameos in other novels. This adds to my feeling that all your books are one long novel.

Steve Erickson: People have mentioned this over the years. It isn't part of any epic intent other than that sometimes one book bleeds into another. A couple of decades back I realized that each novel tends to pick up on something that doesn't get fully resolved in the previous one. *Shadowbahn* is a bit unique in that it wasn't born that way, though it has characters from the earlier book [*These Dreams of You*, 2012]. I just had this brainstorm of the Twin Towers appearing out of nowhere in the Dakota Badlands twenty years after their fall, and in the South Tower is trapped Elvis Presley's stillborn twin, while the North Tower, where Elvis should be, stands empty. If all the books *are* a single thing, it's circular—you can enter the orbiting system at any point, and the whole suddenly becomes something else. I'll let readers decide what it adds up to.

BB: Where do you think that image of the Towers came from?

SE: Whatever kind of flashback someone who's never taken acid has [*laughs*].

BB: Consider yourself lucky. This was after *These Dreams* was published?

SE: Yeah.

BB: Did you start writing right away?

SE: Being a novelist, you know that an idea is one thing and a novel is another. For years I had this idea of a secret movie hidden by God, frame by frame, in all the movies ever made—but I couldn't write *Zeroville* [2007] until I had picked the lock of the story's main character, which took years. Similarly, *Shadowbahn* still needed a couple of tourist guides to get us cross-country while the rest of the story unfolded, and they turned out to be *These Dreams*'s siblings twelve years older. I pondered for a year or so before beginning work the first week of 2014.

BB: You know I'm a big fan of, and have been influenced by, D. H. Lawrence's *Studies in Classic American Literature* and Leslie Fiedler, who expanded on the theory of the American novel as a road novel. *Shadowbahn* is most definitely a road novel. Did you think of it in that classic tradition?

SE: Is *Moby-Dick* a road novel?

BB: You get seasick instead of carsick.

SE: I guess all American wanderers are in search of their white whales. Someone—it may have been Sarah Vowell in the *Believer*—once called my novels "restless" because, for better or worse, they cover a lot of ground. Whether that's just the nature of my storytelling or because I have a kind of narrative ADD, I don't know. Obviously this new book adheres most classically, to use your term, to the road-novel trope, with Parker and Zema driving from Los Angeles to the Great Lakes to see their mother. Coincidentally, in the last few months I went back to the Lawrence, which I last read forty years ago, and was reminded how great he is, particularly on Poe and Melville. I'm not sure he'll ever convince me about James Fenimore Cooper.

BB: Fiedler tried to convince me about Cooper too, and I didn't buy it.

SE: What do those guys know? [*laughs*]

BB: Other books of yours are time-travel/spec-fiction road novels, as opposed to classic time-travel sci-fi.

SE: If we're going to psychoanalyze this—which, as you fully realize, is a dangerous thing to do—most immediately striking is the untethered nature of the stories. The sense of things coming apart. Others should draw their own conclusions on what this says about me.

BB: Can you talk about going back and forth in time in your books?

SE: I grew up in a Los Angeles where time was a ball of tangled yarn rather than something stretched end to end. Out in the Valley hinterlands that later became the porn capital of the world, you had old Western frontier sets under a sky streaked by purple jet trails from rocket tests in the Santa Susana Mountains—past, present, and future jammed into a single moment. My childhood landscapes routinely changed not in years or months but in weeks or days. So even relatively stationary novels with geographical or temporal centers like *Amnesiascope* [1996] and *Our Ecstatic Days* [2005] are interrupted by detours. There's the sense of a center that grows more entropic than gravitational.

BB: In *Shadowbahn*, past and future are the antagonists, represented by the Towers. Unlike many novelists, you rarely have a human antagonist— your protagonists are often flawed, and their battles are with the forces of history and nature. This seems quite Faulknerian. Melville did the same in "Bartleby," and Fitzgerald in *Tender Is the Night*, in which Dick Diver is his own worst enemy, as the future is his enemy—unlike in *Gatsby*, where Tom Buchanan is certainly the antagonist.

SE: I'm not sure that's occurred to me before, but you're obviously right. Antagonists in my books are all relatively supporting characters, no one on the level of Buchanan—maybe I don't have what it takes to create a great villain. I'm more captivated by characters of contradiction, even monstrous characters of monstrous contradiction. Ahab. Joe Christmas in Faulkner's *Light in August*.

BB: The Towers and their music seem to represent an America that doesn't understand itself and Americans who can't understand each other. That they're never as close or as far as they appear echoes the final page of *Gatsby*.

SE: Putting this more literally than I'm comfortable with, the Towers are gravestones of an America that's always been twinned, the America that wants to be one thing in opposition to what America really is. The America on one side of a hairline fracture that's always run down the center of the American idea, where all people are created equal, and the America on the other side, where people own other people as property. Giant stereo speakers, as Parker suggests, with all the bass on one and all the treble on the other, playing music everyone not only hears differently now but always did.

BB: As previously mentioned, in the way that *Our Ecstatic Days* was a continuation of *The Sea Came in at Midnight* [1999] with the same main character, *Shadowbahn* is tied closely to *These Dreams of You*. But despite the darkness of Parker and Zema's family losing their house and being broke, and while acknowledging how much has gone wrong with America, *These Dreams* still feels hopeful in its final passage and generally lighter, "floatier" than *Shadowbahn*, which, even when it's darkly funny or tender, is ominous from the first sightings of the Towers. The new book feels like an elegy.

SE: Well, what has become clear to me over the last few years, even before the latest presidential campaign, is that notwithstanding the collective intent to unify the country, which Obama's election represented, the country doesn't want to be unified. Tell me the last time a congressman yelled "You lie!" at a president from the well of the chamber during an address to Congress, and I'll tell you the last time we had a Black president. I don't remember anyone yelling "You lie" at Obama's predecessor when it turned out there weren't weapons in Iraq. It's no coincidence that the self-identified billionaire tycoon who began his political career questioning whether the first African American president was a real American or a real president is now president.

BB: You've expressed to me that we're at a crossroads in America's history.

SE: We're America 3.0 now. Abraham Lincoln invented 2.0 at Gettysburg in November 1863. The second American Civil War has begun, and like the first, it's about the meaning of America, only with no shooting yet. For thirty years the Right has been treating the rest of us not like opponents or adversaries but as the Enemy, and it's probably high time we started acting like it. I say this as someone who was raised a right-wing Republican and can still pathologically muster a modicum of respect for an honest intellectual conservatism despite how often its tenets are disputed by history or morality. While neither you nor I dismissed the possibility Trump could win, too many did, and the first draft of *Shadowbahn*—finished a month after Trump announced his candidacy in the summer of 2015—was a view of an America where something like a Trump presidency is possible. Trump isn't something that happened to America. America happened to America. The country took this great leap of possibility in 2008 and then betrayed it. I'd love to tell you I think it will all be okay, but I don't know how any rational person who's paying attention believes that. I do prefer the term *elegy* to, say, *dirge.*

BB: American music, or American-influenced music, threads through *These Dreams of You* and *Shadowbahn.* Music is important in your novels.

SE: Though I understand and fully respect opposing arguments advanced by smart people I admire, I was okay with Bob Dylan winning the Nobel Prize. This is because the afternoon when I was seventeen, when I first heard both *Highway 61 Revisited* and *Blonde on Blonde,* back to back—one six-sided epic from "Like a Rolling Stone" to "Sad Eyed Lady of the Lowlands"—changed me as a writer and a creative person as much as *Wuthering Heights* or *Tropic of Cancer* or *One Hundred Years of Solitude.* Dylan meant more to me than Updike or, for that matter, Mailer, which I say with no disrespect to Mailer—you can read the worst page of Mailer's worst book and there will be at least one sentence that floors you. But "Madame George," "Strawberry Fields Forever," "A Change Is Gonna Come," the late sixties music of Miles Davis . . . Ray Davies does in three minutes of "Waterloo Sunset" what it takes Proust three thousand pages to do. Okay, maybe not [*laughter*]. Novelist and essayist Michael Ventura once wrote that he would sacrifice the ceiling of the Sistine Chapel in a heartbeat to save the master tape of Ray Charles's "The Night Time Is the Right Time," which caused no small controversy, as you might imagine [*laughs*]. Having said all that, I didn't conceive of *Shadowbahn* as a novel about music in the way that *Zeroville* was meant to be a novel about movies. Music just started coming out of those Towers like it did out of the ground in *Rubicon Beach* [1986] or out of the lake in *Our Ecstatic Days.*

BB: Movies are a constant in your novels as well.

SE: Around the same time I was discovering Dylan, it also became clear to me that cinema was the art form of the twentieth century. Which was sad [*laughs*], because I had no reason to believe, then or now, that I had the talent or temperament to be a filmmaker.

BB: Any films in particular that made an impact?

SE: *The Third Man. The Passion of Joan of Arc. Black Narcissus.* Buñuel. Noir. If the third act of my novels, to the extent that they have "acts," usually upends the first two or turns the book's first half inside out in order to plunge the reader down a vortex, we can probably attribute at least some of that to *2001: A Space Odyssey*. I can guarantee that for those readers who like *Shadowbahn*, the last hundred pages raise the book to another level, while for those who don't, that's where the book falls apart.

BB: I wouldn't say "falls apart." Perhaps what makes your novels unconventional is that two-thirds of the way in, they can defy expectations, and that viscerally unsettles certain readers.

SE: Every now and then I get called an "experimental" writer, which I sort of detest. The late Alan Cheuse gave *These Dreams of You* a very kind, lovely review on *All Things Considered*, presenting it as an example of how "experimental" fiction can work, though if anything *These Dreams* is—

BB:—one of your more straightforward novels.

SE: To me "experimental" fiction is about the experiment, in which case I'm the most old-fashioned novelist in America. A novel tells a story about people, and if I decide to have a character go down a hole at the bottom of a lake that's covered Los Angeles and "swim" through the rest of the novel in a single sentence [*Our Ecstatic Days*], it's only because I believe it serves the story, and in that particular scene it was something I didn't think of until I got there. The secret to reading my novels is to take everything at face value—I wouldn't know a metaphor if it came up and kicked me, or deconstructed me, or whatever metaphors do these days. When it comes to literary theory, I'm a semifunctional half-wit. Foucault is an herb of some kind, right, like arugula? Wasn't Baudrillard a Confederate general killed in a duel?

BB: In the same way that *Shadowbahn* feels politically prescient, you were writing about changing climate and about nature in revolt against civilization more than thirty years ago in *Days Between Stations*. There are elements of this ecological prescience as well in *Rubicon Beach, Amnesiascope, Our Ecstatic Days*.

SE: I don't consider myself the least bit prescient. If I'm a prophet of anything, it's chaos, which is pretty fucking easy to be prophetic about. *Days Between Stations* began as a love story, and about a quarter of the way through the book a sandstorm blew in and buried Los Angeles, and I remember looking at what I'd just written and thinking, "Really? Can that happen in this story?" The lake that floods Los Angeles in *Our Ecstatic Days* is just existence's chaos rendered topographically, because when you become a parent, that chaos is what you're most desperate to protect your kids from, and of course it's the single thing you can't protect them from. Being entirely beyond your control is what makes it chaos. If you're a writer, parenthood opens new doors of inspiration, but not all of them take you into bright light. Most open into the dark.

BB: Especially when the characters are a son and daughter who resemble your own, readers always want to know how much of the work is autobiographical.

SE: In a way that every writer understands, fiction is a conspiracy between the experienced and the imagined, not a contest. There's more autobiography in the most far-flung moments of Philip K. Dick than we know, while those moments that seem most personal have been transformed by imagination more than anyone grasps. If there's a white brother and Black sister crossing America in *Shadowbahn*, obviously the models for those characters are my own biological son and adopted daughter, but by the time the novel is half-written, if the novel is any good, they've become their own characters. Readers tend not to believe this.

BB: I agree with both points. Why do you suppose readers react that way?

SE: They think it's an alibi. They're not familiar with the psychosis by which a novelist lives in both his experienced and imagined lives at the same time, with one constantly informing the other. In the case of *Shadowbahn*, the siblings are a few years older than my actual kids, so they're my projection more than anything, and it's in the nature of storytelling to steal from your models the larger-than-life qualities while overlooking the quieter ones. My son is wiser and less volatile than Parker. My daughter is more ebullient than Zema—if anything, I had to make her smaller than life in the novel because otherwise she overwhelms the thing. When my last editor first read *These Dreams of You*, his one objection was that no reader would accept a three-year-old saying the things she said, and I had to take some of those things out because if they don't work on the page, it doesn't matter whether she really said them—as a novelist you can't delude yourself that real life necessarily verifies your artistic interpretation of it. This is a confounding lesson to learn. In the meantime, who knows what she'll really be like at fifteen? I don't, and if she does, I'd appreciate it if she'd clue me in [*laughs*]. I can start making plans for faking my death somewhere off the coast of Tahiti.

BB: Reviews often don't talk about how funny your books are, but they're filled with humor. Is the humor in the books in spite of their intensity or because of it?

SE: Because the books are varying degrees of weird and dark, I think it took about five novels before readers started catching on. Even *Tours* *of the Black Clock*, probably the darkest book I've written, has several passages that are, well, funny *to me*, anyway. *Amnesiascope* was the one where the humor became overt enough that people got it—I was in Tokyo twenty years ago when that book came out in America, and my Japanese translator, concerned he might offend me, very carefully and tactfully asked, "It's supposed to be *humorous*, right?" I don't think the cat was fully out of the bag until *Zeroville*. "Oh, he's funny—now he tells us." Americans in particular tend to like books and movies and music to be one thing or another. They like to adhere to a single dramatic logic or sustain a single emotional tone.

BB: Yeah, tell me about it. I wonder if editing *Black Clock* affected your writing in any way.

SE: Editing other writers affects my writing, and my writing affects how I edit others. At some point I edit like a writer and write like an editor, which is to say I cut from my own work what I would cut from another's, and I edit others' work in a way I would want my own edited. In *Black Clock* I didn't edit to interfere with a writer's style but to clarify it, and if something was unclear I ran it past another editor, usually you. Actually, always you [*laughs*]. And in the end, if a writer objected to changes, we ran the story as he or she wanted because that was the policy of a magazine where we honored the voices of writers we esteemed. Usually writers appreciated the edit, as I appreciate the effort when it's on my behalf, however cranky may be my reaction in the first five seconds [*laughs*]. One of the things you spend a lifetime learning is the difference between instinct and ego.

BB: Although we both have graduate degrees in other specialties, neither of us has an MFA from a writing program, but we've both taught in programs. You've done it in different settings—colleges and residencies for nearly twenty years. What do you think about the rise of the MFA as an almost necessary step in becoming a published novelist?

SE: [*Long pause*] Obviously I believe that, constructed a certain way, a writing program is a valuable thing. I also have ideas about the enterprise that occasionally are at odds with the . . . prevailing consensus.

BB: Such as?

SE: When students workshop so much that they become addicted to it, when they get to a point where they can't change a comma without the workshop validating it, then the work becomes grist for a writing program where "program" is the operative word rather than "writing." At its essence, writing is antisocial behavior. You're locking yourself up in a room and exiling yourself to a world that exists only in your head, ranting at your self and sealing yourself off from a reality everyone else shares. One term for this is "being a writer" and another is "unhinged"—if it weren't mediated by a piece of paper or a laptop screen, it would be certifiable. And to a certain extent, a writing program can't help socializing the antisocial, and sometimes, as a result, not as much writing gets done. Rather, what gets done is the acquisition of a master's degree, which I don't knock because you have to make a living in this world and a degree will help do that. But invariably, getting that degree is going to wind up at odds with writing in the same way that everything else in life winds up at odds with writing, and if these days you can't have a writing career without that degree, then at least we ought to be clear in our own heads about what that means and acknowledge that it's a bad thing for the creation of enduring literature. One shouldn't have to argue this; it's self-evident. Faulkner never workshopped *The Sound and the Fury*. Before Carson McCullers, it's hard to think of a major American writer who came out of a writing program. So a lot of my focus is on teaching not just how to write but how to be a writer, which isn't necessarily the same thing. It's entirely possible I'm wrong about all of this, of course, since almost anybody knows more about running a writing program than I do. But I don't believe a lot of people know more than I do about being a writer.

An Interview with Steve Erickson

Jim Knipfel / 2018

Section 6 of this interview, "This Binary Moment," originally appeared in slightly different form on BelieverMag.com on September 10, 2018. Sections 1 through 5 and 7 originally appeared in slightly different form in *The Believer*, issue 123 (February/March 2019), and on BelieverMag. com on February 1, 2019. Reprinted by permission of Jim Knipfel.

Steve Erickson completed the first draft of his latest novel, *Shadowbahn*, the same month Donald Trump officially announced his presidential candidacy. Immediately after its publication, in 2017, critics hailed it as the first true novel of the new era. It's a portrait of an America shattered along ideological lines when, quite unexpectedly, the Twin Towers rematerialize in the Badlands. At its heart, though, as he does in all of his novels, Erickson offers a whisper of possible redemption for a nation gone horribly wrong.

Born in Los Angeles in 1950 and raised in a conservative household, Erickson has gone on to be hailed by the likes of Thomas Pynchon, David Foster Wallace, Dana Spiotta, Rick Moody, and many other writers as one of America's finest living novelists. He's an unparalleled visionary, blessed with a wholly unpredictable imagination, as well as a prose style that is graceful, audacious, and humane.

Over the past thirty-five years he has published ten novels, including *Days Between Stations, Amnesiascope,* and *Zeroville.* He's also authored two nonfiction works and countless magazine articles. He's received an American Academy of Arts and Letters Award for Literature, a Lannan Literary Award for Lifetime Achievement, and a Guggenheim fellowship. He was the cofounder and editor of the acclaimed literary journal *Black Clock*, and today, in addition to being *Los Angeles* magazine's film and television critic, Erickson is a distinguished professor at the University of California–Riverside.

What most readers seem to take away from Erickson's novels are what he calls the weirdnesses, from unexpected environmental disasters like

JIM KNIPFEL / 2018 **239**

sandstorms and lakes engulfing Los Angeles, to characters traveling back and forth through time, to a single incongruous frame that seems to appear in every film ever made. It's easy to latch onto those things, but there's much more going on. He writes elegantly about human relationships, desires, and conflicts, albeit often set against a background of bizarre and calamitous events. He's also been consumed with the promise of America—a promise that was betrayed, he notes, the moment the country was founded. His work, both fiction and nonfiction, has furthermore been marked by a certain prescience, as he has written knowingly for decades about environmental and social collapse, both unexpected and inevitable.

Shortly before the premiere broadcast of an hour-long BBC radio adaptation of *Shadowbahn*, I spoke with Erickson about his work, movies, Elvis, the current ugliness, and the future of fiction in a seemingly fictional world.

I. "The Fish-Nor-Fowl Syndrome"

The Believer: Over the course of your ten novels, the Twin Towers rematerialize in the South Dakota Badlands [*Shadowbahn*], Sally Hemings hopscotches through time [*Arc d'X*], a lake appears in the middle of LA through a vortex at the bottom [*Our Ecstatic Days*], Hitler's private pornographer turns the Second World War into a psychodrama [*Tours of the Black Clock*], an apocalyptic calendar is charted in the Hollywood Hills [*The Sea Came in at Midnight*], and God hides a secret movie in every movie ever made [*Zeroville*]. If there's a single thing all your books are about, a single theme they have in common, what would you say it is?

Steve Erickson: Um . . . [*laughs, pauses*] chaos.

BLVR: Do you mean chaos in general, an all-encompassing chaos, or a more specific variety?

SE: The chaos of the world, the chaos of place and time. The chaos of sex and the self, of nature and the quadrants. Of memory, and what it means to remember.

BLVR: Well, despite all the chaos, or maybe on account of it, since the publication of your first novel, critics have scrambled to come up with some kind of label to slap on you—surrealist, postmodernist, even mythologist, which I kind of like. But they all seem to fall short.

SE: I think "postmodern" has been the most prevalent, and least accurate.

BLVR: Inaccurate—how so?

SE: Well, to the extent I've ever understood it, postmodernism seems to be about a consciousness of its own artifice. It seems to be about the author's fetishizing of that artifice that then becomes part of the work. I've never been interested in that at all. I've always hoped that the stories become immersive enough that the artifice is forgotten.

BLVR: As with Mr. Pynchon's novels, I think yours elude simple classification, so I prefer to leave them as a genre unto themselves. You hear "Steve Erickson novel," and you know what you're getting into, right?

SE: I'm glad *someone* knows what they're getting into.

BLVR: But you know what I'm saying. How—if you bother with such things—would you classify them for yourself?

SE: I doubt it will surprise you that I've tried to resist genres even when I can figure out what they are. By the time I was four or five novels in, other novelists like David Mitchell came along [who were] doing something similar, and we sort of became our own genre.

BLVR: How do you think these assorted labels crop up? I mean, what's the impulse?

SE: I just think publishers in particular, and maybe readers, want to stick a writer somewhere. Obviously, I never wanted to be stuck anywhere. I spent a long time in the desert, so to speak, before I was published, the only upside of which was that what I was doing had time to gestate into its own thing, even if I resisted the gestation.

BLVR: What were you resisting?

SE: You know, burying Los Angeles in a sandstorm in *Days Between Stations* wasn't something I planned to do until I did it. Then I had to persuade myself it was okay to do a science fiction kind of thing in a novel that wasn't science fiction. Of course, as a result it took four years to get the book published. Eluding classification, as you put it, can be a slog, career-wise.

BLVR: Yeah, some supposedly "science-fictional" elements slipped into my first novel too. Publishers and other "serious lit" types decided the whole thing was science fiction and wanted nothing to do with it. And science fiction people knew immediately it wasn't science fiction—and wanted nothing to do with it.

SE: The fish-nor-fowl syndrome rubs one elite or another the wrong way.

BLVR: Speaking of classifications, there's a standard catalog of writers to whom you're regularly compared—Pynchon, DeLillo, Rushdie, García Márquez. Do you think these are valid comparisons?

SE: Maybe [Pynchon's] *V.* more than *Gravity's Rainbow*, because I came to it first, and right away I knew it was a nuclear way of narrative, an

Einsteinian way. I can't imagine ever being smart enough to write DeLillo's *The Names*. Reading *One Hundred Years of Solitude* in my midtwenties, I heard a bell go off in my head that I recognized, however far-flung the novel was from my own experience and however far out of my league it was. Like Faulkner, Márquez redefined chronology for me. It had a force of revelation that I never got over.

BLVR: At the same time, the literary influences you cited earlier in your career are sometimes wildly different and, in some ways, counterintuitive. I think that's true for a lot of writers. Faulkner and Philip K. Dick I can see, but how do you get from Henry Miller, Raymond Chandler, and the Brontës to what you do now?

SE: I suppose our erratic pathways leave footprints that only we know are there. Maybe there's some Chandler in the first third of *Rubicon Beach*, some Miller in *Amnesiascope*? Emily Brontë in *Arc d'X*? [*laughs*] But I wasn't especially aware of that when I wrote those books.

II. An Ericksonian Multiverse

BLVR: Although all your novels are radically different, there are a number of recurring motifs. One that always fascinates me is characters who are introduced in earlier books reappearing in later books. Is this something you're conscious of when you start a novel, or does it just work out that way?

SE: I'd love to tell you I'm such a mastermind that I've had a huge, tattered chart on my wall mapping out the last forty years. But not much is planned until it happens. Then I go back and rethink whatever vague coordinates I was following and whether it's where I really want to go.

BLVR: That's part of the strange magic of writing fiction. Sometimes it's a frustrating, maddening magic, but it's magic nevertheless. Things happen that you never would have expected to happen; characters do or say things that you had no idea they were going to do or say. It can throw the story you had in mind off at a sixty-degree angle, and there's not a damn thing you can do but go with it. Is this something you run into a lot?

SE: At least once in every book. You have to listen to it. You have to listen to characters taking on lives of their own. If they *don't* take on lives of their own, it's a zombie book, by which I don't mean a book about zombies . . . Or maybe I do.

BLVR: As for your recurring characters, sometimes they're older, like Parker and Zema from *These Dreams of You* showing up twelve years later in *Shadowbahn*. Sometimes they take on different guises; sometimes they appear in a photo.

SE: My stories tend to be not altogether . . . tethered. People drift from one book to the next of their own volition. The prevailing wind of one narrative blows them into another.

BLVR: It's led me to think all your fiction is a single story that takes place in what theoretical physicists began calling the multiverse a few decades back.

SE: The multiverse!

BLVR: Isn't that the fucking best? An infinite number of parallel worlds that are almost identical but not quite, with a few details missing or switched around.

SE: I like this multiverse theory a lot. It explains some things.

BLVR: An Ericksonian multiverse seems to have expressed itself over the years in several books, maybe most directly in *Our Ecstatic Days*. A mother, searching for her missing son, dives into a lake that's appeared in the middle of LA and swims down through a hole at the bottom, hoping to reemerge in a parallel lake in a parallel LA, where the boy is safe.

SE: I wrote a big part of that novel at the MacDowell Colony two weeks before 9/11, in one of those little cabins they give you out in the woods. I remember jumping up from the desk and pacing the cabin like a crazy person, thunderstruck by this brainstorm of Kristin "swimming" through the rest of the novel to a happier ending. Like LA in the sandstorm six novels earlier, it wasn't something I planned. That was another book that took a long time to find a publisher, more than a year.

BLVR: That surprises the hell out of me. By that point you were well established, respected. Esteemed, even, if I may.

SE: All that esteem and three bucks will buy you a tall cappuccino at Starbucks, Jim.

BLVR: I'm just saying that by then people knew what kinds of turns your novels can take. So what was the problem?

SE: I'm not the one to ask. My agent got the book back from one publisher after four months with a note that read, "We're sorry to pass on Mr. Erickson's haunting and extraordinary novel." I said to my wife, "What, they filled their quota on haunting and extraordinary this week?" *Oh God* [groan], *another haunting, extraordinary one.*

BLVR: [*laughs*] Y'know, I suspect it wasn't you or the book so much as a matter of timing. In those early years after 9/11, the whole publishing industry was in steep decline, and suddenly editors were scared to death to pick up anything that might in the least be considered "weird" or, God help us all, "quirky."

SE: There's a story from the mideighties about Columbia rejecting one of Leonard Cohen's albums—which happened to include what would become Cohen's most famous song ["Hallelujah"]—[by] saying, "Leonard, we know you're great; we just don't know if you're any good" [*laughs*]. *Our Ecstatic Days* was rejected by eight publishers, *Zeroville* by nine. *Shadowbahn* was rejected by six, including the publisher of the previous two, who told me it would ruin my career, such as it is. Publishers always have faux-literary rationalizations for saying no. They look for reasons to say no, because no is safer. Then after the novel is published they call my agent to say they want to see the next one, and next time we go through the same thing all over again.

III. "Sex, Westerns, and the Moon"

BLVR: Let me go back a ways here. Like I did, you got your start in the alternative weeklies. What were you writing about back then, and how old were you?

SE: Late twenties, early thirties. I wrote mostly about music, sometimes politics. I covered a couple of the national conventions. I was also living in Europe, where I thought about America a lot—it was the Reagan years. There was a sense of upheaval everywhere, a lot of social entropy. I read *To the Lighthouse* in Hyde Park the day before the IRA bombed it. A couple nights before that, I heard the Clash live in Brixton after seeing the rerelease of *Once Upon a Time in the West* in Leicester Square that afternoon. It was that kind of time, an overload of the sensory and fragmentary. From Paris I wrote a cover story for *Los Angeles Reader* called "The Center Cannot Hold" that got some attention, though I didn't know it till I was back in the States.

BLVR: You were raised in LA, but in the "serious lit" world there's certainly a stigma attached to that. Early in your career did you consider leaving?

SE: Sure.

BLVR: Going to New York?

SE: Sure.

BLVR: But you stayed put.

SE: It wasn't the savviest career move on my part. I wanted to be my own idea of a writer rather than someone else's.

BLVR: There are a lot of great novelists in LA now.

SE: They're *in* LA but not *from* LA. When they come to LA, they bring from other places other contexts in which to be seen.

BLVR: From your perspective, what does it mean to be *from* LA?

SE: Well, it's not to be confused with being from Hollywood, for starters. The LA I'm from was the outskirts, lurching from rural to mega-suburban, where as a kid I played on old Western sets in the Chatsworth Hills under the vapor trails of rockets being tested in the Santa Susana Mountains because Kennedy had decided we were going to the moon. Hollywood *pretends* to go to the moon. LA actually goes. Ten years later that part of the Valley was the porn capital of the world, and for better or worse, that's LA too. Sex, Westerns, and the moon all occupy the same psychic real estate.

BLVR: To a greater or lesser degree, autobiography has worked its way into most of your novels, most notably *Amnesiascope.*

SE: As a novelist yourself, you'll understand that these things involve navigating an extraordinarily exquisite perspective. You try forging as precise an emotional or psychological relationship to the material as you can manage, to the extent that such a relationship can be managed. One vantage point is too close, another is too far away. One is so distant you can't find yourself anymore—or at least you can't find the reason for writing the book in the first place—and another vanishes right up your own nether regions. Finding a way to be as objective as possible about the intensely personal, to be as coolly appraising as possible about your relationship to where you've come from—as juxtaposed against your relationship to how far you still have to go—it all gets harder the deeper into the work you get, until you don't know anymore whether any of the book makes sense. At that point you have to trust that your instincts were right to begin with. You have to trust that the compass has been showing you true north all along, and you need to follow through with it no matter how alienating the landscape has become.

BLVR: Wow, that's probably the most truthful and elegant description of the process I've heard. If you write fiction, it doesn't matter if you're writing about another century or another planet; you can't get away from yourself and your own experience.

SE: You can't and you don't really want to.

BLVR: The trick is that balance, keeping it disguised when it needs to be disguised. You've also made a number of guest appearances in your books, in a fashion. At least there are characters with your name.

SE: Years ago I gave an interview to . . . I forget who, but the interviewer asked me about killing myself off in one of my novels, and I had no idea what he was talking about: "What do you mean, kill myself off?" and he says,

"I mean the character based on you," and I said, "What character based on me?" And he looks me dead in the eye and, after a pause, says, "The character *named Erickson*" [*laughs*]. Oh, *that* character based on me. Sometimes writing feels like an out-of-body experience. I think for a moment he suspected I didn't write the book at all, and in a way, of course, he was right.

BLVR: Ain't it the truth. Your prose has such a direct and elegant poetry that as a reader I find myself time and again simply accepting the more surreal elements as givens. Beyond canals vanishing from Venice or music emerging from unexpected sources, there are real characters with believable emotional lives.

SE: I'm gratified if you've gotten that from the books. That's the response I get most particularly from other novelists—[Mark Z.] Danielewski, Lewis Shiner, Susan Straight.

BLVR: I by no means intend to insult anyone, but it's that deep humanity that distinguishes your work from so many of the authors with whom you're compared. A mother looking for a lost son, a brother and sister reconciling with their mother—it's around these characters that odd and unexplained things happen almost in the background.

SE: Odd and unexplained backgrounds aside, I'm old-school enough to believe that characters do drive stories, and while I would never make an argument for a sentimental literature, I also believe that if you consider emotionality the most overwrought of aesthetic sins, nothing gets risked that matters.

BLVR: Precisely, though I think that avoidance of emotion in modern lit may say something about the culture as a whole. Separation anxiety, usually through death or abandonment, is another recurring theme. It generally involves parents and children. Does a lot of that arise from your own experience?

SE: For any novelist whose work is hardwired into the nexus of experience and imagination, for any writer whose mind has any dark corners at all, parenthood isn't remotely a portal to bliss. It's the new, more terrifying door to something fearsome you didn't know existed, when everything in life was about you. I'm sure it will come as a complete shock to everyone reading this that novelists are a bit . . . self-involved [*laughs*]. They're in the business of self-involvement. Becoming a parent challenges that in a profound way.

IV. The Projectionist

BLVR: If you could go back, is there anything you'd handle differently with any of your books?

SE: I would publish *The Sea Came in at Midnight* and *Our Ecstatic Days* as a single novel. Other than that, left to my devices, I'm sure I would rewrite them all to disastrous effect.

BLVR: I can think of a few writers who should be reminded of that. So within this increasingly insular world of books, you've been called a writer's writer—

SE: *Cursed* to be a writer's writer was the way Jonathan Lethem gently put it to me over dinner a few years back [*laughs*].

BLVR: He called it a curse?

SE: He meant it in the nicest way [*laughs*]. Jonathan has been extraordinarily generous to me over the years.

BLVR: So many notable types cite you as the living writer they most admire, or wish they were. I'll confess that the moment I finished *Zeroville*, my immediate gut reaction was, Damn it! Why the hell didn't I write that?

SE: I'll confess that I'm glad I beat you to it.

BLVR: It's probably for the best. There was no rancor or jealousy about my reaction—okay, maybe a little jealousy—but the book really struck home. As I read, I found myself unconsciously ticking off every film reference and noting that I had all of them on my shelves.

SE: I wrote *Zeroville* one summer when the rest of the family was away and I had the house to myself. Worked in the mornings and early afternoons, watched movies in the evenings to fill unforgivable gaps in my cinematic education. *Tokyo Story. Rules of the Game.*

BLVR: My God, *Tokyo Story* is an astonishing piece of work. But so is everything Ozu touched.

SE: His masterstroke was understanding how most of us will personally live his movie twice, both as the grown children with parents and then later as the parents.

BLVR: At the other end of the scale, *Nightdreams*, the porn weirdie written by Jerry Stahl, plays a major role in *Zeroville*. I'm almost ashamed to admit, along with everything else you reference in the novel, I have that one too. I don't have much porn but I'm a sucker for any hard-core film with Stan Ridgway on the soundtrack.

SE: Having a lot of porn would just be peculiar, Jim. It speaks well of you that you're judicious about it.

BLVR: I'll take that as a compliment. In fact I may remind people you said as much [*laughs*].

SE: I'm sure that'll make a difference [*laughs*].

BLVR: The film adaptation of *Zeroville* has been in postproduction a long time. Did you have any involvement with the script?

SE: The filmmakers were shrewd enough not to involve me, except for a cameo in the movie.

BLVR: You have a cameo?

SE: I play a projectionist who catches James Franco stealing a canister of film [*laughs*].

BLVR: Are you happy with what Franco has done on the picture? I know it's a dicey question to ask the author.

SE: The last cut I saw was a while back. It was pretty faithful to the novel except for what had to be left out. If anything, I found most thrilling the stuff that was more purely Franco's, while stuff more directly from the novel was harder to judge—characters saying dialogue I wrote, but not always the way I heard it in my head. But that's my problem, not Franco's.

BLVR: Translating that novel in particular to the screen seems like a tricky bit of business.

SE: I suspect one of the challenges is tonal. When the novel is funny, it's funny in a way that may work on the page but not the screen.

BLVR: Do you have any idea when it might be released?

SE: I understand why no one believes this, but on the lives of my children I swear I'm as much in the dark as anyone. I'm not sure it's a project that studios or distributors understand. There also have been the recent [sexual misconduct] allegations [against Franco] that may have some bearing, regardless of what's true.

BLVR: Hitchcock noted that it's almost impossible to make a good film out of a great book and much easier to make a great film out of a bad book.

SE: That's the Hollywood maxim proved exponentially by *The Godfather* and disproved only in occasional decimals. I don't know if Kundera's *The Unbearable Lightness of Being* is a great novel, but it certainly was a serious literary effort, branded as "unfilmable" almost the moment anyone read it, when it first came out here in the eighties. I certainly didn't see a movie in it. But Philip Kaufman made a film as good as the novel, and maybe better, by breaking down the material and building his own version, which is the only way to do it—though I understand Kundera was cranky about it. *The English Patient* is more problematic, but I don't think anyone would deny it's an intelligent effort at adapting [Michael] Ondaatje's novel and was successful commercially and critically. And except for a few other like-minded crackpots, I'm a relatively lonely admirer of Baz Luhrmann's *The Great Gatsby*, which somehow managed to be faithful to both Luhrmann and Fitzgerald.

BLVR: I like that *Gatsby* too.

SE: By the time the movie got to Eckleburg's eyes and the valley of ashes, I was convinced Fitzgerald would have loved it. I was less sure about DiCaprio as Gatsby, but every woman I know, including the one I'm married to, assures me Leo is just fine and I should shut up.

BLVR: Kaufman taking on Kundera was a bit like Cronenberg taking on Burroughs.

SE: Or Cronenberg taking on DeLillo, for that matter.

BLVR: In each of these cases the adaptation is its own unique animal. Your point about casting Gatsby reminds me of Hal Ashby's adaptation of *Being There*—Jerzy Kosiński's novel was one of his best, but Ashby's film is amazing, thanks in no small part to [Peter] Sellers's performance. I went back to it again not long ago and noted a certain kinship with *Zeroville*. Does that make sense?

SE: Maybe because I haven't read *Being There*, the kinship didn't occur to me till later. After *The Disaster Artist* came out, Franco dropped me a note that said, "I guess we both love our Chauncey Gardner-in-Hollywood stories."

BLVR: Knowing the history, art, and business of film as you do, are you anxious to see any of your other novels given the Hollywood treatment?

SE: I've never written a novel that I expected to become a movie. I could certainly see in my head a movie of *Days Between Stations* when I wrote it, and as a family drama in our contemporary moment, *These Dreams of You* always seemed a possibility. Even *Our Ecstatic Days* has at its core the most basic story in movies going back to Griffith: a mother trying to protect her child.

BLVR: Does the BBC radio adaptation rule out another version of *Shadowbahn*?

SE: No. One or two of the prime cable networks have inquired. I shouldn't say more about it except that that would be the way to go with that novel, as a miniseries.

BLVR: I hope that pans out. I'd love to see it.

SE: I'll get back to you when I'm walking down the red carpet with the check in my hand.

BLVR: Particularly in these last few decades, a lot of younger novelists seem to write specifically with a film deal in mind. There's a lot more money in Hollywood than in publishing, but the result is usually a lot of hairpulling and disappointment.

SE: If you're a novelist waiting for Hollywood to do right by you, you're a fool. I'm happy if these things happen, but I try not to lose my bearings about it. The novels are the novels and the adaptations are their own animal, like you said.

V. Elvis and Jesse

BLVR: Film and music references are peppered throughout your novels. *Zeroville* is about movies, while music is front and center in *Shadowbahn.*

SE: *Zeroville* is about being obsessed with movies. *Shadowbahn* is about being obsessed with a country that has a soundtrack. The truth is that music started taking over *Shadowbahn* enough that my last major revision was to cut a lot of it.

BLVR: You mean references or lyrics? Or something else?

SE: About a quarter of the track entries from the father's music almanac were excised altogether. Then I cut those that remained in half.

BLVR: As in *Rubicon Beach*, in *Shadowbahn* you present an America torn in two. But music seems to be the single overarching redemptive force. I love the scene in the gas station. However much people may disagree about the virtues of this or that song or artist or style, music is something they all need; it's the one thing that brings them together. When the music begins to vanish, its absence overwhelms all the other differences that people have with one another.

SE: In the course of writing the book, I came to better understand the paradox of American music. How music is America's one contribution to the world that virtually everyone loves, however they otherwise feel about America, and how it's also born of an American evil that even the music can't redeem. One way or another, even when it's several degrees removed, virtually all great American music is a by-product of the blues, which is a by-product of American slavery.

BLVR: Our history with slavery and the ongoing racial divide is something else that's snaked its way through much of your work. In that way, Elvis is *Shadowbahn*'s perfect, if absent, redemptive metaphor. I can see any number of reasons why he haunts so much of the novel—beyond Sinatra or Woody Guthrie or George M. Cohan, he's the ultimate American musical icon. He's a twin, of course, and twins have played a major role in your work. His music begins emanating from the rematerialized World Trade Center, another set of twins. More important, [Sun Records producer] Sam Phillips touted Elvis as the figure in whom Black and white music came together.

SE: I think you're smarter about this novel than I am.

BLVR: [*laughs*] Or maybe you just like Elvis, is all.

SE: No, you're right. Elvis is a calculated factor in *Shadowbahn* the same way the character's obsession with the movie *A Place in the Sun* is calculated in *Zeroville*. If you're writing fiction about music or movies, they still have to serve the story's larger designs. I like *A Place in the Sun*, but it's not my favorite movie or one of my fifty favorites—I chose it because it reflected something about the main character [who has an image from the movie tattooed on his bald head]. As you say, in *Shadowbahn* Presley is the obvious musical metaphor, and though I've always thought it's a little reductive to argue that he "ripped off" Black music—I think as a nineteen-year-old truck driver he was more naïve and instinctual than that—there's no doubt he channeled a Black sensibility to a white, racist America that was marginally more accepting of it only because the medium was white himself. The metaphor aside, I had no interest in writing an Elvis novel per se. He's not in the novel except as a preoccupation of characters who nonetheless have never heard of him because, in the novel, he never existed—a preoccupation embodied by a twin who's him but not him. Elvis made music I love but, as singers go, I'll take Sinatra's late-fifties torch albums, or Ray Charles or Billie Holiday, or, for that matter, Van Morrison or James Brown or Dusty Springfield.

BLVR: Oh, I'm with you there. I like Elvis, I have a mountain of Elvis, but for my money Roy Orbison and Blind Willie McTell have it all over him. Buddy Holly, Bo Diddley, and the Ramones too. I'm more fascinated by the idea of Elvis—especially as he got older—as a simulacrum, kind of like the whole country.

SE: Another novel I'm glad I wrote before you.

BLVR: Next time we'll flip for it [*laughs*]. Now, music's clearly played a central role in your life.

SE: I'm not trying to dis anyone when I say that hearing Ray Charles the first time had more impact on me than most of the fiction of the time. Listening to Dylan's *Highway 61 Revisited* and *Blonde on Blonde* back to back for the first time on the same afternoon, as a single great American novel—from "Like a Rolling Stone" to "Sad Eyed Lady of the Lowlands"—upended the furniture in my seventeen-year-old head more than reading Updike or . . . well, I'll get in trouble if I start naming names. Suffice it to say that, notwithstanding *V.* or Borges's *Labyrinths* or Dick's novels of the period, a lot of the contemporary fiction [that came out] as I was coming of age didn't mean much to me. Then I saw *2001* and had the sort of revelation no novelist should have at eighteen, which was that whether the preeminent popular art form of the late twentieth century was film or music, it wasn't the novel anymore, and I was obsolete before I had begun. I would love to have been wrong.

BLVR: Sadly, I don't think you were, but as the man said, this is the business we've chosen, right?

SE: I think it chose us.

BLVR: Exactly. *2001* is a film you've referenced before.

SE: I saw it the summer it came out. I was a kid, obviously. I have very smart friends who make perfectly persuasive arguments that it's claptrap, but I can watch it endlessly and be mesmerized. To put it in Greil Marcus's terms, it divided film history in half as much as any American movie of the sound era did, including *Citizen Kane.*

BLVR: As despised and—as much as possible—ignored as they were when they were standing, the minute they fell the Twin Towers became a symbol of every damn thing you can think of. This may just be me making my own connections, but did you intend for their reappearance in *Shadowbahn* to echo Kubrick's monolith?

SE: I wasn't conscious of it but wouldn't deny it for a moment.

BLVR: There's a distinctly American multiverse in *Our Ecstatic Days, Rubicon Beach, These Dreams of You.* The America of *Shadowbahn* resembles the America of your other novels, except that Jesse's the Presley twin who survived and Kennedy loses the Democratic nomination for president.

SE: To paraphrase the Ginsberg epigraph at the novel's beginning, my American obsession refuses to give me up. It's particularly exhausting these days when a pall hangs over everything that I think and feel about this country that's become . . . some black, cracked mirror, barely surviving its own sharp edges.

VI. This Binary Moment

BLVR: I would never call you a political novelist, though as with Mr. Pynchon it always seems to be lurking about the subtext. But you've also written a good deal of overtly political nonfiction over the years—1997's *American Nomad,* and *Leap Year,* about the 1988 presidential campaign. Like me, you were raised a political conservative until events in the country and the world—in your case the civil rights movement—prompted you to reevaluate things. And now, well, take a look around. Do you think the lessons of history have any meaning anymore, if they ever did?

SE: That's a more precise way of asking whether truth itself has meaning anymore.

BLVR: Looking at some of your political writing two decades back, you clearly had a deep understanding of the trajectories of history and politics, of where we were headed if we weren't careful.

SE: This current president is only an end result of something that's been going on thirty years, or maybe 230. He's *Forbidden Planet's* id monster, born of our collective unconsciousness and rampaging the country at night killing democracy. It's always been part of America's mission statement to cut itself loose from history, but that means a century and a half after the fact, millions of white Americans still won't admit the Civil War was about slavery.

BLVR: You've called that "the American version of Holocaust denial."

SE: It's the most profound sort of treason.

BLVR: Almost twenty-five years ago, you published an essay in the *Los Angeles Times Sunday Magazine* ["American Weimar," January 8, 1995] about the real and tangible threats facing democracy down the line.

SE: "America wearies of democracy."

BLVR: You cited an increasing and seemingly insurmountable chasm between the Right and Left, and a general atmosphere of rage.

SE: This latest authoritarian impulse has been around forever—its authors have just gotten more brazen. One of Reagan's cabinet officers [secretary of the interior James Watt] famously said, "I never use the words Democrat and Republicans—it's liberals and Americans," so the Right drew a line long ago and has regarded the rest of us as the enemy ever since, and we're only now realizing they were correct all along. We are the enemy, and it's probably time we stop doing that old progressive thing of, you know, trying to get everyone to get along. It's a cold civil war, not over differences of opinion or even differences of values but differences of truth. There's no bringing a country together when only one side cares about bringing the country together. There's no reconciling an America that elected the first African American president with an America that never accepted he was either American or president and replaced him with a successor endorsed by the Ku Klux Klan. Better to accept that we're the enemies the Right always claimed, the enemies of their mean and constricted and oppressive America that I never believed in even when I was fourteen and that I'm guessing you never did either.

BLVR: There's a line in *Shadowbahn* where a jazz musician instructs Zema to "embrace the confusion." I realize the context is different, but I think that's what a lot of people are doing nowadays, feeling impotent to do anything else in response to a nation gone mad.

SE: Acknowledging that novelists are given to melodrama, I honestly believe this November is one last chance to repudiate not a president or a party but a version of Ourselves.

BLVR: In a piece you wrote for *McSweeney's* this past spring ["Not Him but Us," May 25], you argued that, at its most fundamental, the obvious answer is voting not for protest candidates but "every Democrat in sight."

SE: It's not the glamorous option; I'll give you that. But practically speaking, no investigation or impeachment is going to save us. The only ones who can save us are us, and the only candidate who can effectively displace a Republican in November is a Democrat. The only way to obliterate Trumpism is to vote for every single Democrat of any stripe, and if someone asks what's the difference between a conservative Democrat and a Republican, my answer is math. The more members of Congress with little Ds after their names, the better chance Adam Schiff is head of the House Intelligence Committee instead of Devin Nunes.

BLVR: But do you think a legislature full of Democrats can remedy a tidal shift in what constitutes business as usual in America? Put a slightly different way, can a political party reign in a monster embodied not only by the president but half of the country that feels he's given them the all-clear?

SE: It's a great question. It's the big-picture question. For the moment, however, we have to focus on the small picture. I'm not a registered Democrat and I hold no brief for the Democratic Party, and if you tell me the Democratic Party is corporate and compromised, I answer, What the hell else is new? But in this binary moment the choice is extremely clear, if as imperfect as it's always been. Democracy is at the wall. We don't have the luxury of protest votes, third parties, vanity gestures, quixotic pursuits, Bernie-snits, pyromaniacal Sarandonism, or the self-flattering of one's political purity. If you're still miffed about how unfairly Debbie Wasserman Schultz treated Bernie two years ago, you seriously need to get the fuck over it. It's time to grow up and get focused. It's time to stop abdicating the word *patriot* like we have for the last half century because we've been too cool for school and slightly embarrassed by it. We need to take back Americanism while there's still time to define it on our terms. Embracing confusion is one thing; succumbing to a bankruptcy of vision is another. There are ways in which this actually is the least confusing historical moment of our lives. Like the last Civil War, this civil war won't be done until one America politically annihilates the other. Repel the forces of darkness now and sort out utopia later.

BLVR: I think another problem is that the other side has a lot more guns and doesn't seem hesitant to use them.

SE: That's when the country starts coming apart not just philosophically but geographically. Someone should write a novel.

VII. "No One Aspires to Be Ahead of Their Time."

BLVR: Now that we're living in the post-satirical age, what can a novelist do? My agent has told me to stop writing fiction for a while, as there's no longer any point, the nation having become what it's become. But writing's a tough habit to break.

SE: So there are two reasons to write, one of which isn't very good but inescapable nonetheless, and the other of which is the only good reason but almost too altruistic for this culture or what passes for it. The not very good reason is to promote a career. I'm beyond that at this point, not for altruistic reasons and certainly not because I'm above sordid self-promotion, but because my career isn't promotable anymore. After you've written ten books, the concrete of collective perception sets in around you. If you haven't broken free by then from the cement that was freshly laid in the premillennial-postmillennial, weird-ass West Coast cult novelist cul-de-sac where your reputation got stuck back around novel three, you never will. Not in this lifetime.

BLVR: Has it been such a bad cul-de-sac?

SE: [*laughs*] No one aspires to be ahead of their time. Artists aspire to make an impact on the right-now.

BLVR: And what's the good, if too-altruistic, reason to keep writing?

SE: You know what it is. The good reason is you have a story that you just have to tell regardless of what you have to go through to tell it, because it isn't going to let you alone otherwise. It's eight o'clock one night, everyone else in the house is gone, you're there alone, and out of the nocturnal ether you get this crazy idea of the Twin Towers suddenly reappearing in the Badlands, and a year's worth of nights later you're still thinking about it and then you know you've just got to write it. If I get one of those ideas again on one of those nights that grow ever fewer, I'll write it. But contriving a book for its own sake is less motivating than it ever was, and less rational, and while it's up to others to decide whether my novels are any good, I can sincerely say they all meant something to me at the time when I felt driven to write them. Meanwhile, the current American reality leaves my imagination in the dust.

JIM KNIPFEL / 2018 **255**

I can't keep up with it. And anything I write that doesn't come to grips in some way with what I firmly believe is the murder of American democracy would be one more failure on top of a sense of failure that's already nearly unbearable, except it would be an ignoble failure as well, a corrupt failure. I'm speaking for myself, understand, not anyone else. I admire enormously any writer who can function in this moment and glean meaning from his or her work in whatever way and in whatever form. For me, however, frolicking on the playground of the make-believe doesn't cut it anymore.

Index

About the Editors

Matthew Luter is on the English faculty at St. Andrew's Episcopal School in Jackson, Mississippi. He is author of *Understanding Jonathan Lethem*. His work has appeared in journals including *Critique*, the *Southern Literary Journal, Genre*, and *Orbit*.

Mike Miley teaches literature at Metairie Park Country Day School and film studies at Loyola University New Orleans. He is author of *Truth and Consequences: Game Shows in Fiction and Film*. His work has appeared in *TheAtlantic.com, Critique, Literature-Film Quarterly, Music and the Moving Image, The Smart Set*, and elsewhere.

Printed in the United States
by Baker & Taylor Publisher Services